Complete Guitar Repair.

by Hideo Kamimoto.

Music Sales America

DISTRIBUTED BY

HAL•LEONARD®
CORPORATION

7777 W. BLUEMOUND RD. P.O. BOX 13819 MILWAUKEE, WI 53213

Interior photography by Ted Kurihara
Illustrations by David Gunnell
Cover designed by Pearce Marchbank
Book designed by Jean Hammons and Chris Czarny

Order No. OK 62810
International Standard Book Number: 0.8256.0156.8
Library of Congress Catalog Card Number: 74-76821

Contents

(Cont'd)

Acknowledgements

About eight years ago when I first started writing this book, my thoughts were along the lines of a simple how-to-do-it book for beginning repairmen. Over the years, by adding chapters and revising earlier ones, I have increased the size of the book to cover the complete range of guitar repairs, with special attention given to particular problems associated with each type of guitar.

The number of contributors who helped with their time and talents has also grown. I would like to express my special thanks to the following:

Stu Goldberg, guitar importer and retailer, who first suggested writing a book on guitar repairs and who contributed the last chapter on buying a guitar.

Ted Kurihara, photographer, whose excellent photographs play a key role throughout the book. With the exception of a number of photographs taken (by the author) in the Gibson service department in Kalamazoo, Mich., all photos were taken by Ted and myself and were shot either in Ted's studio in San Francisco or in my repair shop.

Dave Gunnell, an artist who has illustrated a number of other books in the past, who contributed the fine sketches and drawings.

Expert guitar repairmen (in alphabetical order): Tom Clark, Larry Higgins, Brandt Larsen, Mike McCarthy, Pat McCarthy, Rich Parker, Glen Quan, and Harry Yaglijian, who contributed their valuable comments and suggestions.

Marina Music of San Francisco and Leo's Music of Oakland for providing the guitars photographed in Chapter One.

Kent Schwab for the computer computations of fret intervals.

Ken Killman of Gibson, Inc., for providing assistance regarding Gibson's service facilities.

H. Anne Nagashima who edited and typed the manuscript.

The repair procedures and techniques described herein are strictly those of the author, and have been developed independently from the guitar factories. While the various guitar manufacturers mentioned herein have cooperated with the author and have consented to the use of their trademarks and to the use of pictures of their products and facilities, the author is in no way affiliated with any of them.

Introduction

A guitar, if it is to respond to its fullest capabilities, must be adjusted and set up to suit the style and playing preferences of the performer. Though on the surface this requirement would appear to be easily met, in actual practice, instruments which are improperly adjusted, improperly repaired, or (in the case of new guitars) not adjusted at all seemingly outnumber the satisfactory ones. When properly adjusted, repaired, and set up for the player's style, a guitar can often show a dramatic improvement in tone and playing ease. One must experience the change, before and after, in order to appreciate the benefits which can be derived from the hands of a capable repairman.

Over the years it has become quite apparent that many guitar players struggle along with instruments so badly out of adjustment and repair it is a wonder they haven't given up entirely. I'm sure many others have given up the instrument, blaming themselves for their inability to master it, when in actuality the instrument itself was at fault.

Far too many players buy new guitars with the naive assumption that their instrument is correctly set up since it has been "factory adjusted." It is so unusual, however, to find a new instrument—in any price range—which is well adjusted even for average playing, it can be safely assumed that every new instrument will require some additional adjustment and setup. Unfortunately, most music stores have either limited or no repair facilities at all and the number of people who have the ability to set up an instrument, let alone ascertain what is required, is pitifully small.

As a guitar player, you must have reliable guidelines on which to judge whether or not your instrument is in proper playing condition. Though you, as a player, may not be especially interested in the technical details behind repair and adjustment, a knowledge of the underlying principles will enable you to maintain your instrument in good playing condition. At the very least, you will know what can or can't be done and can be more articulate when expressing your wishes to the repairman. If you are also handy with tools, and are willing to pay attention to detail, you can perform many of the simpler repairs and adjustments, gaining the added satisfaction of having the guitar perfectly set up for your playing style.

Guitar making and guitar repairing are related but by no means similar, and each requires specialized skills. Happily, these skills are complementary and the experienced repairman can transfer most of his repairing techniques and abilities to guitar making. The guitar maker who is already highly skilled will find that taking an instrument apart is totally unlike the original assembly procedure and will find much of interest in the following pages.

Similarly, if you are involved with the sale and

purchase of fretted instruments, the information presented here should be very helpful. Whether it is for the purpose of setting up a repair department or for examining and adjusting new and used instruments, the guitar salesman and collector should have a working knowledge of both construction and repair.

Those who wish to repair and restore guitars and related instruments, whether as a hobby or as a full-time vocation, will find that the work is both rewarding and interesting. It is certainly an area where appreciation for the guitar's musical and artistic qualities will grow along with one's ability as a repairman and craftsman.

Perhaps a word of caution together with a few hints would be appropriate before continuing on to the actual repairs. Because of the comprehensive nature of this repair manual, many of the repairs described in these pages are best reserved for experienced repairmen. Particularly for the beginner, I would recommend a thorough reading of the entire manual before trying your hand at the beginning repairs and adjustments. In order to avoid costly mistakes it would be best to attempt only those repairs and adjustments which you *know* you can carry through to completion in a professional manner.

Of course, the big question is, how do you know whether or not you are capable of attempting a particular repair? Well, there is no easy answer, though a few suggestions should prove helpful. In the absence of past experience, which is the most important single factor, advice from professional repairmen would be very valuable. In this connection, you should note that, when asking advice, you should seek out those whose reputation is based on their abilities as repairmen rather than as builders.

It would be very helpful to examine examples of the type of repair you would like to do. Again, your source would be the professional shop, for here you will see at first hand the level of workmanship required. This is a point which is difficult to convey by words and photographs alone.

A person can spend years specializing in the repair of, say, classical guitars and still not know enough to handle *every* repair situation. You can easily appreciate, then, that the experience required to repair all types of guitars is not acquired overnight but is, rather, the result of an accumulation of experience based on exposure to a variety of increasingly difficult jobs.

By all means specialize in those areas which interest you personally, whether it's for the purpose of building up the skills necessary for a full-scale repair shop, or for the purpose of maintaining your own instrument. Proceed with care and take the time to enjoy your work.

Guitar Construction

The subject of the guitar and its construction is a fascinating area for research and study. The following discussion is aimed at promoting an understanding of the musical and technical features of the basic types of guitars available today. For the neophyte guitar maker, a working knowledge of the construction of all types of guitars is to his advantage since he will have acquired the foundations for determining the relationship between construction and tone. Even if the guitar maker chooses to limit himself to constructing one style of guitar, the knowledge of the musical and technical limitations and advantages of other types as well as his own will permit him to modify and experiment with a better chance of perfecting an instrument which is musically and technically correct.

For the guitar repairman, the need for diversified knowledge of guitars is obvious. Repairs should be carried out in an artistic manner and the result must always be musically correct. Differences between a classical and an electric guitar are obvious of course; in between are many variations —many of them quite subtle—and the repairman must be aware of this if quality work is to be achieved. Because the playing requirements between, for example, a classical guitar and a solid body rock and roll electric guitar are quite different, the repairman must adjust to the technical requirements of the player and of the music rather than adhering to preconceived ideas of a "universal standard" for all guitars.

Classical Guitar

Though all guitars with nylon strings (or, as in the past, gut strings) are sometimes classified as classical guitars, other musical and technical considerations clearly define the modern classical guitar and its variant, the flamenco guitar. Materials and method of construction do vary, depending upon the country of origin and intended price range, but as quality and craftsmanship increase, differences diminish and the best classical guitars from makers all over the world are quite similar in choice of materials and, to a lesser extent, in overall dimensions.

The dimensions of the modern-day classical guitar will generally fall within the range given below:

1) Scale length 25 1/2 to 26 1/4 inches;
2) Body length 19 1/4 to 19 1/2 inches (approximate);
3) Width of fingerboard at nut, 2 to 2 3/16 inches; at nineteenth fret, 2 1/2 to 2 9/16 inches.
4) Width of body at upper bout, 11 1/2 inches; waist, 9 3/4 inches; lower bout, 14 1/2 inches (approximate);
5) Depth of body 3 5/8 to 3 7/8 inches (approximate).

The present-day classical guitar has evolved, compared to the history of the violin, relatively recently. Though the modern dimensions date from the instruments of Antonio Torres, circa 1850, most of the instruments in use today date from well after the turn of the century. Because of improvements in materials and in methods of construction, the best guitars undoubtedly are of modern origin. Here I refer to guitars made after 1900 but with particular emphasis on those made within the last twenty or so years.

Generally, the trend has been toward larger guitars with longer scale lengths, reflecting the changing requirements for power and volume to fill the needs of the performer in the large concert hall. Even the flamenco guitar, which has traditionally been constructed with relatively shallow sides, has, over the years, reached dimensions closely approximating those of the classical guitar. Assuming that the musical requirements remain the same, the dimensions of the classical guitar should, in the future, remain fairly stable.

With the amount of energy which can be transferred to the top limited by the strings and the strength of the player's fingers, any substantial increase in overall dimensions would be just a waste of wood. These factors are dictated, to a large extent, by the technical compromises necessary to make the instrument suitable to the demands of the music—one reason why steel strings are not used. A simple increase in size does not

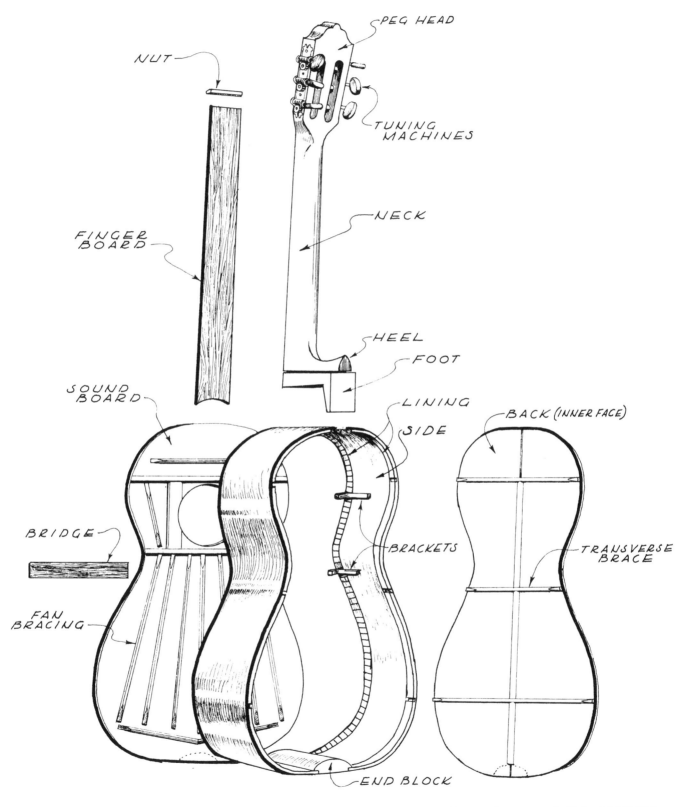

NUT

PEG HEAD

TUNING MACHINES

NECK

FINGER BOARD

HEEL

FOOT

SOUND BOARD

LINING

SIDE

BACK (INNER FACE)

BRIDGE

BRACKETS

TRANSVERSE BRACE

FAN BRACING

END BLOCK

CLASSICAL GUITAR COMPONENTS-EXPLODED VIEW

necessarily result in an increase in volume and may very well lead to poorer tone quality.

Materials used in the construction of the classical guitar vary quite widely in the lower-priced instruments, less so in the better handmade examples.

The woods used in quality classical guitars are Honduras mahogany for necks, rosewood (Brazilian usually preferred over Indian) for sides and backs, ebony for fingerboards, and spruce for tops—though pine, fir, and cedar have recently found favor with some makers. The best guitar makers invariably use the above-mentioned materials. There are, of course, fine quality guitars made of other woods, such as maple, walnut, and Honduras mahogany (for sides and backs), though none of these woods offers any serious challenge to the domination of the classical guitar with rosewood body.

Classical guitar. Kohno 8.

It should be noted that the geographical area or school of guitar making often influences the method of construction and choice of woods. Construction features (dovetail joint) and materials (maple) favored in the countries of northern Europe exert a significant influence on instruments produced in the United States. Guitars from Spanish-speaking countries, such as Spain, Mexico, and Brazil, differ significantly in method of construction. The Spanish method, while well suited for hand construction, adapts poorly to factory production and is, therefore, an important clue toward identifying a particular maker or factory.

Guitars built in the Spanish style have a foot extending out from the endblock area.

The Spanish method embodies a neck construction in which neck and endblock are all in one piece and is used principally on classical and flamenco guitars. The violin maker's method, on the other hand, which is used on all other types of guitars as well as on classical and flamenco guitars, makes use of a dovetail joint to join the neck to the endblock. Both methods of construction when well done are satisfactory. However, a number of repairs are applicable only to one or the other method of construction, and it is for this reason that the method of construction should be of more than academic interest to the repairman.

The peghead of the classical guitar is of the slotted or classical style. Its shape is a very individual thing and is one of the key identifying features of a particular maker. The overlay is usually of rosewood and is never bound, though inlay strips through the center and/or constrasting veneers beneath the rosewood are occasionally seen. It is very common for the peghead to be spliced to the neck; this method, which requires an additional step, embodies the virtues of increased strength and economical use of wood. It is the usual practice to splice the heel of the neck whenever the peghead is spliced since the maker generally starts out with wood about one inch in thickness. Instruments in which the entire neck is machine-cut from one piece of wood, while occasionally handmade, are more often the product of a factory.

Fingerboards, usually of ebony, are devoid of inlays and, in addition, are never bound. It is permissible to employ one or two position dots on the side of the fingerboard—usually at the fifth and/or seventh fret. Nineteen frets are standard on all classical instruments; usually the nineteenth fret is cut in two by the soundhole so that it is usable only on the outside strings.

Bindings are generally of wood—rosewood the usual material—as well as the purfling itself. Plastic purfling and binding are never used on quality, handmade classical guitars. Soundhole rosettes are also of wood and vary from simple alternating black and white lines, such as are found on early flamenco guitars, to the intricate mosaic patterns typically found on the modern instruments. The soundhole pattern is another identifying feature of the guitar maker, though the intricacy of the pattern really has no importance in determining quality. Inexpensive factory-produced instruments often have surprisingly high quality inlays.

Bridges of the Spanish type are usually rosewood and often employ an inlay of bone or ivory around the string bar to protect the wood from the pressure of the string as well as for decoration. Occasionally the top of the string bar is overlaid with a thin piece of ivory or mother-of-pearl. On most instruments, the saddle (and nut) is removable, allowing adjustment of the string height by means of shims.

Linings can be kerfed or solid—either method is satisfactory. The continuous kerfed lining on top and back is the usual rule for factory-produced instruments. For instruments built in the Spanish style, the lining blocks on the top edge, for reasons of convenience, are all individual. In this case, for additional strength, the blocks beneath each of the top and back braces are made longer than their neighbors.

Back braces usually are three in number and vary little from maker to maker since most makers feel that the top plays the major role in tone production.

Below Left

The classical or Spanish-style bridge is used on classical and flamenco guitars (nylon strings). The string bar where the strings are tied on is frequently edged with ivory to prevent wear and to provide a decorative touch. Traditionally, the saddle is straight, providing equal compensation to both bass and treble strings.

Below Right

The lower lining in a guitar built in the Spanish style is usually solid. The upper lining consists of individual blocks or (occasionally) is a continuous kerfed strip.

 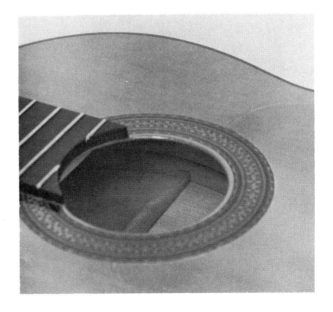

Most guitar makers employ one variation or another of the fan bracing system on their guitar tops. Though the standard system by Torres is the basis for most systems used today, the possibilities for experimentation are almost unlimited since the number, size, and placement of the braces as well as the graduations of the top all have a significant effect on tone. Some variations have involved extending the fans almost the entire length of the top in order to place more of the top into vibration. It appears, however, that for clarity of tone the conventional system is preferred. A variation which is quite popular today is to place an additional transverse brace below the lower sound-hole brace in order to stiffen the top on the treble side. The Fleta and Ramirez both make use of this variation.

The rest of the top bracing consists of transverse braces above and below the soundhole and stiffeners to the left and right of the soundhole and below the fingerboard. Occasionally the stiffener below the fingerboard, which is there to reduce the possibility of the top cracking beside the fingerboard, takes the form of another transverse brace. The soundhole stiffeners, particularly in some Spanish makes, sometimes take the form of a complete circle around the soundhole.

FAN BRACING

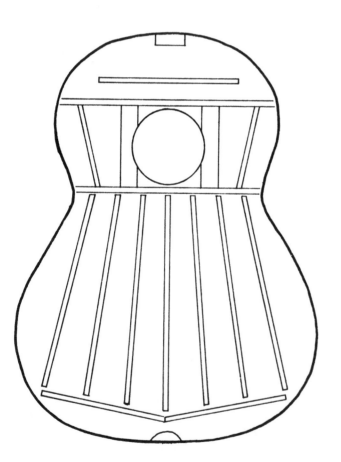

FAN BRACING - VARIATION

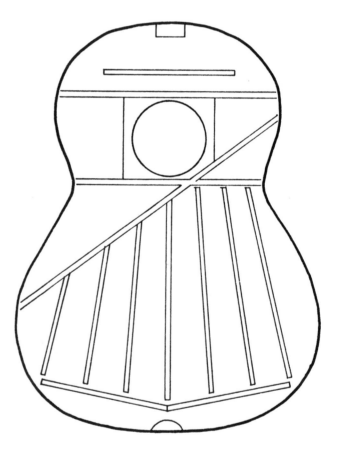

Flamenco Guitar

A variation based on the classical guitar, the flamenco guitar is quite similar to its classical counterpart in construction and dimensions. The characteristic flamenco tone, however, is quite distinctive and is achieved through a different combination of woods and construction. Originally conceived of in Spain as an inexpensive guitar, using local woods and lacking the elaborate inlays associated with classical instruments, the flamenco guitar has, over the years, evolved to the point where it is fully the equal of the classical guitar with regard to detailing and quality of construction. In general, however, the best flamenco instruments from a particular maker are less expensive than his best classicals.

The most obvious difference between the flamenco and the classical guitar is the use of Spanish cypress for the sides and back of the flamenco. Though other woods, such as cedar and maple, are occasionally used, cypress remains the standard. The sides are somewhat shallower than on the classical guitar and overall construction is lighter.

Pegheads on flamenco guitars are traditionally solid, with ebony or rosewood pegs used for tuning rather than machines. Though wood pegs have been favored for the better balance they give when playing in the flamenco position (and, according to some authorities, for better tone), the trend has been toward machine heads as well as toward the classical playing position.

String height is low, both over the fingerboard and at the bridge saddle itself. The former facilitates fast fingering at the expense of a small amount of string rattle—tolerated by most players. The low height of the saddle makes it easier to tap the guitar top while playing and, in addition, is a factor in developing the flamenco tone.

Tap plates, or *golpeadores*, traditionally white, are now almost universally of clear plastic. Three variations are commonly used. The most common type consists of one plate below the treble strings. A double tap plate consisting of two separate plates on either side of the bass and treble strings affords further protection. A last version is the full width tap plate which extends beneath the strings as well as on either side of the first and sixth strings.

Flamenco guitar. Jose Ramirez.

Flattop Guitar

The steel string flattop guitar, though outwardly similar in appearance to the classical guitar, differs substantially in construction. A relatively recently developed instrument compared to the classical guitar, the modern flattop is an American development, designed particularly for folk, country, and blues styles of music. The flattop was used briefly in the early days of jazz before being replaced by the then developing archtop or plectrum guitar. Today, the best flattop guitars are unquestionably of American make, though—unlike the classical guitar of which the best ones are handmade—the best examples, for the most part, come from a small handful of factories.

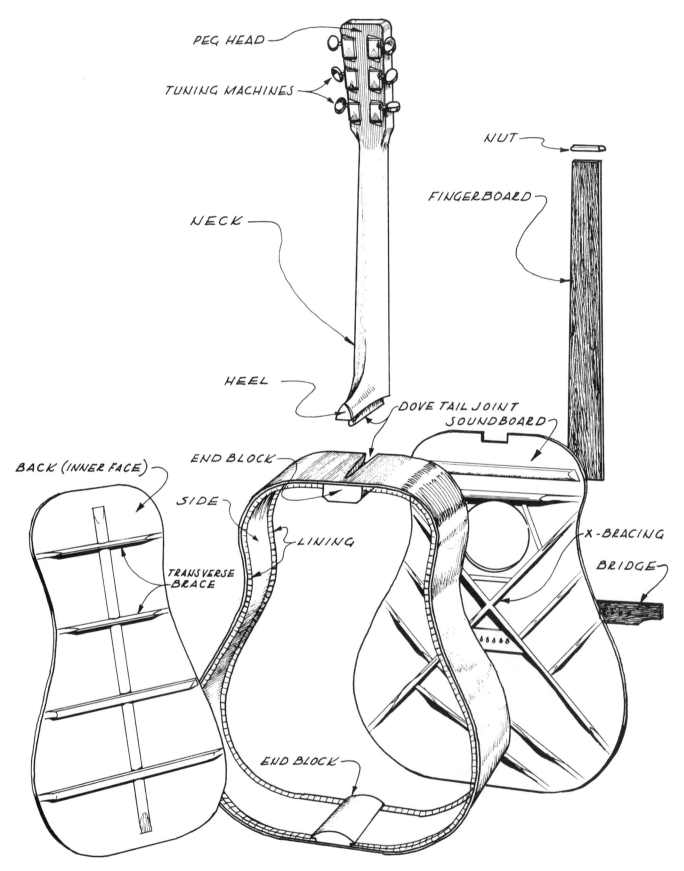

PEG HEAD

TUNING MACHINES

NUT

FINGERBOARD

NECK

HEEL

DOVE TAIL JOINT
SOUNDBOARD

END BLOCK

BACK (INNER FACE)

SIDE

LINING

X-BRACING

BRIDGE

TRANSVERSE
BRACE

END BLOCK

FLAT TOP GUITAR COMPONENTS – EXPLODED VIEW

Built in a number of sizes (unlike the classical guitar) ranging from three-quarter and ladies' size guitars up through concert, grand concert, auditorium, and jumbo or dreadnaught, the basic features, nevertheless, remain the same. The peghead of the flattop is usually solid rather than slotted, as on the classical guitar. The solid peghead is strong and the style also simplifies removal and replacement of steel strings.

Many of the older flattops were built with slotted pegheads. Today, some makers utilize the slotted peghead together with several other variations to distinguish the folk guitar from the flattop. In addition to the occasional use of binding and inlays, the peghead differs from the usual classical model in that the shape is quite simple. Though there is less variation, each maker nevertheless has his own shape and the experienced eye can readily identify the make from this point alone.

Machine heads are, more often than not, mounted singly rather than "three on a plate." The better quality machine heads are available only as singles, are of heavier construction than those for nylon strings, and often employ covers over the gears together with a sealed-in lubricant.

Necks are much narrower than on classical guitars, averaging approximately 1 3/4 inches at the nut. The narrow neck is ideally suited for the styles of music customarily played on this instrument. The techniques for playing country, jazz, and folk music differ greatly from those employed for classical and flamenco music. The thumb, for example, which is never used in a conventional classical technique, is often employed for fretting the sixth (and occasionally the fifth) string. In many of the better instruments the fingerboard is bound along the edges, partly for added smoothness and partly for appearance.

Most flattop guitar necks are joined to the body at the fourteenth fret. A few have twelfth-fret necks which are slightly wider (about 1 7/8 inches at the nut). These instruments, patterned after the early steel string guitars, are generally called folk guitars.

Tops are almost invariably of Sitka spruce though a European spruce top may be seen from time to time. Though not in the same class as those instruments with spruce tops, some of the inexpensive instruments have tops of Honduras mahogany (usually with mahogany back, sides, and neck) and these are capable of producing a surprisingly good tone when properly constructed.

Flattop guitar, dreadnaught style. Martin D-28.

Particularly with flattops, the appearance of the top is a very poor indication of tone quality. An instrument with a top of irregular wide grain can have every bit the tone of an instrument with straight narrow grain. Though my choice is for the narrow straight grain, as in classical guitar tops, this particular feature is not as critical as in the classical guitar; when judging the merits of a flattop, you should be aware of this fact and choose accordingly.

X - BRACING

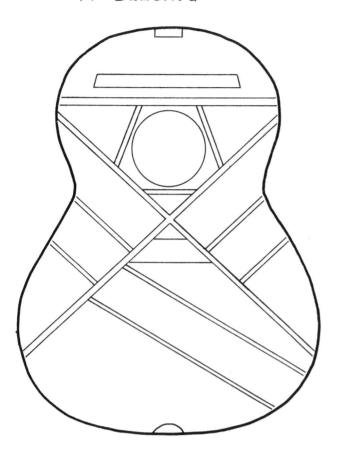

SIMPLE TRANSVERSE BRACING

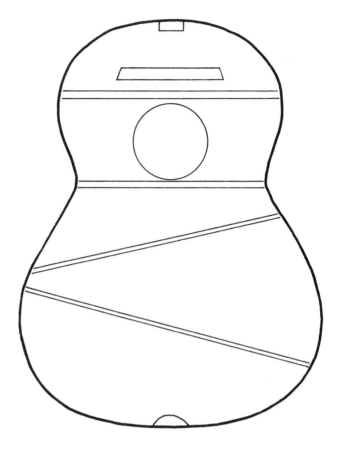

Below Left

A pin bridge is customary on a flattop steel string guitar. Notice the slanted saddle, giving additional compensation to the bass strings.

Below Right

A kerfed lining is common on steel string and factory-made guitars. Both the upper and lower linings are identical.

X bracing is usually used since it overcomes two shortcomings of the fan bracing system when applied to steel string guitars. The X brace is better able to take the stresses of steel strings; in addition, since most flattop guitars use pin bridges (for strength and for ease in changing strings), it would be all but impossible to accommodate fan braces in the area of the pins. The X bracing system doesn't require braces beneath the bridge and so is ideally suited for guitars with pin bridges. The flattop steel string guitar usually has a top arch of an eighth inch or so, and for this reason the neck can usually be set completely straight. In addition, the pull of the steel strings against the top will increase the arching even more. An action which appears "low" when the strings are not up to tension will often change to "medium" when tuned up to playing pitch.

In the top line instruments, the back and sides are usually rosewood, though maple is used by some makers. Other woods are seldom used. However, Honduras mahogany and maple are used extensively in instruments in all price ranges below the premium line. It is fairly common practice to laminate backs and sides of the lower- and medium-priced instruments (particularly in imported makes) leaving the tops of solid spruce. In the lowest price range, particularly with respect to imported instruments, all laminated construction is generally used, though when proper attention is given to design and materials, results can be surprisingly good.

Binding, purfling, and rosette designs are usually quite simple, consisting generally of black and white plastic or wood strips. Binding can be either white or black, with preference given the white binding in the better instruments. Mother-of-pearl and other more complex purfling patterns such as herringbone are, except for a few expensive guitars, seldom seen on modern instruments. These styles are more commonly seen on older high quality instruments.

Flattop Variations

Twelve-String Guitar

Twelve-string guitar. Guild 512-XL.

The twelve-string guitar is a variant based on the six-string flattop. The strings are grouped in pairs, six pairs in all, and are tuned in the following manner:

1	2	3	4	5	6	7	8	9	10	11	12
E	E	B	B	G	G higher	D	D higher	A	A higher	E	E higher
Unison		Unison		Octave		Octave		Octave		Octave	(occasionally two octaves higher)

There are no significant differences beyond the changes necessary in the peghead, bridge, and nut to accommodate the twelve strings. The neck is usually a bit wider, averaging 1 7/8 inches at the nut, and the overall construction is usually a little heavier in order to withstand the additional string tension.

A twelve-string guitar rarely sounds well unless built in the dreadnaught or auditorium (jumbo) size. It is occasionally tuned down a half step or full step for additional bass effect as well as for reduced tension on the instrument itself. Under these conditions the jumbo size guitars more readily retain their tone and volume compared to the concert and grand concert sizes.

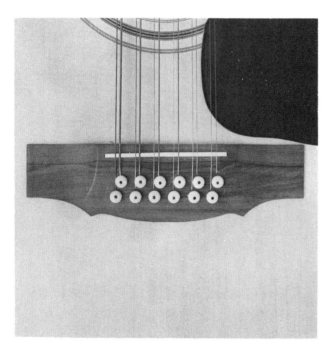

A twelve-string bridge for a flattop guitar is similar to a six-string bridge with the addition of six extra pins. String spacing depends on the accuracy of the pin spacing. Notches in the saddle are not normally necessary.

Folk Guitar

The features of this variant include a slightly wider fingerboard (1 7/8 inches at the nut) and the neck joint at the twelfth fret rather than the fourteenth. Pickguards are often left off. Pegheads are usually of the slotted type. Of course these specifications duplicate the measurements of the early steel string guitars and it is this image which the present instruments are re-creating.

Flattop guitar, folk style. Martin 0-16 NY.

A folk-style steel string guitar features a slotted peghead rather than the usual solid peghead. The narrow rollers are necessary for steel strings.

Resonator guitar. Dobro.

Plectrum Guitar

The plectrum guitar, also known as the archtop or f hole guitar, is today only occasionally played in its unamplified form. With the advent of the magnetic pickup and the quality sound systems available today, the capabilities of the plectrum

Plectrum guitar with cutaway. Epiphone Triumph (with Johnny Smith double pickup system).

guitar as an acoustical instrument are simply not in demand. Nevertheless, where sheer volume is not important, the instrument still performs capably, particularly in small groups. Since the early days of

19

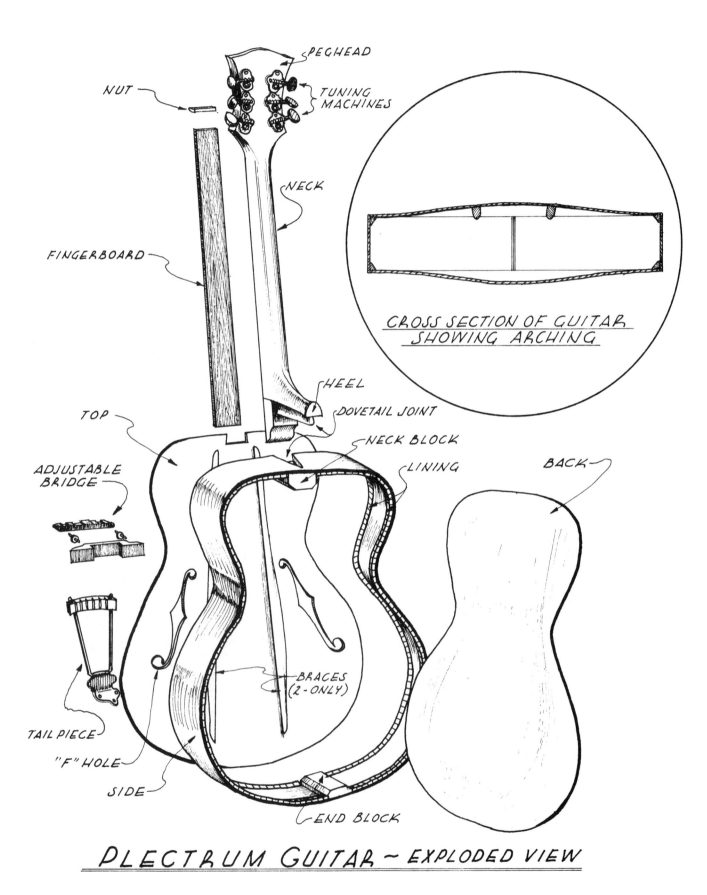

PEGHEAD

NUT

TUNING MACHINES

NECK

FINGERBOARD

CROSS SECTION OF GUITAR SHOWING ARCHING

HEEL

TOP

DOVETAIL JOINT

NECK BLOCK

ADJUSTABLE BRIDGE

LINING

BACK

BRACES (2 - ONLY)

TAIL PIECE

"F" HOLE

SIDE

END BLOCK

PLECTRUM GUITAR ~ EXPLODED VIEW

jazz the plectrum guitar has been a regular standby, having taken over from the banjo and flattop guitar because of its increased volume and "cutting power." Usually grouped with the rhythm instruments within a band, this guitar was slow to develop as a solo instrument. Today, however, the plectrum guitar, with pickups mounted, is the standard instrument of most jazz guitarists.

The body of the plectrum guitar, in basic appearance and construction, resembles more closely the violin than the Spanish-style guitar with round soundhole. Both top and back are carved and highly arched and the soundhole takes the form of two f holes, one on either side of the bridge. A tailpiece is employed to relieve the top of the forward strain of the strings; the pressure from the strings is essentially directed downward, and within the instrument, running longitudinally across the top, are a pair of bass bars to help the top take the tension of the strings. The bridge is not glued to the top, being held in position by string tension, and is usually adjustable for height, which, compared to the flattop and classical guitar, is considerable. String heights average three quarters to one inch from the face.

PLECTRUM GUITAR BRACING

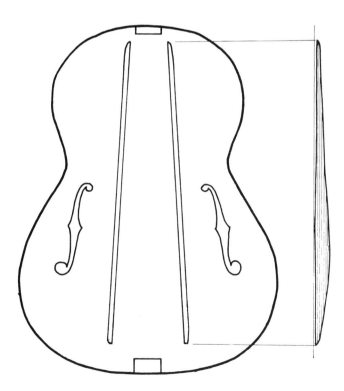

Body sizes usually are quite large, surpassing even the jumbo or dreadnaught size of the flattop. The auditorium and grand auditorium sizes are exclusively the domain of the plectrum guitar. Of course, such large body sizes would be mostly wasted without the use of a pick (plectrum) and without the use of heavy or at least medium gauge steel or bronze strings.

A cutaway on the treble side of the upper bout (more frequently found on newer guitars) facilitates fingering in the upper positions past the fourteenth fret. In the best instruments, maple is used for the sides and back and spruce for the top. Both top and back are fully carved, though cheaper instruments may have only the top carved, or employ laminated tops, backs, and sides.

The neck follows the general construction features found in steel string flattop guitars. It is angled in order to let the strings clear the top arch and to allow for the high string height above the top.

It would be a mistake to try to compare the plectrum guitar with the flattop or classical guitar in an attempt to show that one type of instrument is superior to the others, for each guitar has been designed for a special purpose. In this respect the plectrum guitar is highly specialized and, in versatility of musical styles, adapts poorly compared to other types of guitars. One can best appreciate the attributes of an instrument when playing the music for which it is intended and comparing it with other instruments of the same type.

The plectrum guitar, in its acoustical form, has been largely supplanted by a variation in which electromagnetic pickups are mounted permanently in the top. Typically, the pickups are recessed in holes cut in the top, and the tone and volume controls are mounted in the top below the pickguard. Such mounting practices can have only a detrimental effect on the acoustical tone, but in this particular application the tone is determined largely by the pickup and by the strings.

An excellent solution to the problem of mounting pickups and retaining acoustical tone is to mount the pickups on a pickguard which floats clear of the top. All controls are then mounted on the pickguard, resulting in a neat installation which avoids the necessity of cutting holes in the top. Many of the older acoustical plectrum guitars which are superior to most modern instruments in regard to tone and workmanship can be adapted in this fashion to the requirements of the modern guitarist.

Archtop electric guitar. Gibson ES-175.

Thin body (semi-acoustic) archtop electric guitar. Gibson ES-335TDC.

The sharp-eyed reader will have noted that, earlier, mention was made to the effect that amplified tone is determined *largely* by the pickup and by the strings. The body of the guitar also has a significant role in determining tone quality. Two extremes would be the solid body guitar where the pickups are mounted, quite literally, on a solid piece of wood, and the conventional plectrum guitar with the pickups mounted on the top. The vibration of the strings is influenced by the amount of flexibility of the top, and this vibration of the top causes the mounted pickups to vibrate also. With the solid body electric, secondary vibrations of the top and pickups are nil and the result is a very clean, pure sound. The conventional hollow body guitar contributes the vibration of the top as well as of the pickups to the vibration of the strings, and the result is a very full tone, rich in harmonics.

The vibration of the top can result in feedback problems, particularly when the pickups are mounted clear of the top. As a matter of fact, some of the thinline hollow body guitars which outwardly appear to be conventional plectrum guitars with pickups mounted have a block of wood glued between the top and back, beneath the bridge area, reducing top vibrations and feedback and reinforcing the arching of the top against string tension. Solid body guitars can generally be played free of feedback unless the performer wants to produce it intentionally.

Solid Body Electric Guitar

The solid body guitar is a development of the electric guitar in which the instrument's output is almost entirely dependent upon the built-in electromagnetic pickups. An amplifier is always used since very little volume and resonance is possible with the solid wood body. Pickup and control circuit design take on increased importance in the solid body and, since body design is relatively simple, increased attention is placed on fingerboard design and action. Because of its distinctive tone together with its inherent sustaining qualities, many blues and rock and roll guitarists favor the solid body.

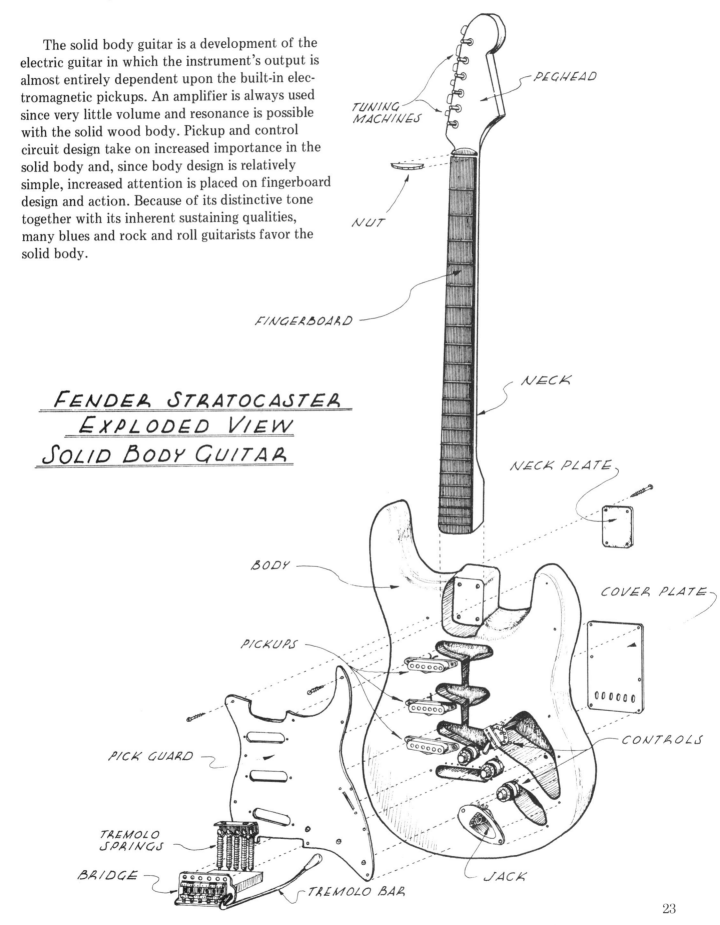

FENDER STRATOCASTER
EXPLODED VIEW
SOLID BODY GUITAR

TUNING MACHINES

PEGHEAD

NUT

FINGERBOARD

NECK

NECK PLATE

BODY

COVER PLATE

PICKUPS

CONTROLS

PICK GUARD

TREMOLO SPRINGS

BRIDGE

TREMOLO BAR

JACK

Solid body guitar with three pickups. Fender Stratocaster.

Solid body electric guitar with two pickups. Gibson Les Paul Custom.

Though minimal compared to an acoustical instrument, the body does have a definite role in tone production and is responsible for many of the differences in tone between models which may share identical pickups and wiring. All body materials are, in varying degress, resonant. In general, as the bodies become more and more resonant, the tone qualities approach those of the hollow body electric. As the body becomes less and less resonant, the tone loses the overtones generated by the body and, relying mainly on the tone qualities of the pickup, becomes more and more "pure."

At the more resonant end of the spectrum are certain thin hollow body electrics, such as the Gibson ES-335, which have a solid center section,

qualifying them as (essentially) solid body guitars. At the other end of the spectrum are guitars with plastic bodies such as the Dan Armstrong model Ampegs. In between are Fenders with maple bodies and most Gibsons with mahogany bodies. The Gibson Les Paul, with its maple top and mahogany body, shares, in some models, the same electrical components as some models of the Gibson SG. The SG has a plain mahogany body of different shape and for this reason there is a difference in tone quality. Some Les Pauls, in recent years, have been built with a laminated mahogany body and Les Paul freaks can hear the tone difference between this and the nonlaminated body.

The amount of sustain, or how long the tone lasts after picking the string, is also related to the resonant properties of the body and, to a lesser extent, of the neck, machines, bridge, and tailpiece. The less energy the body absorbs from the string, the longer it will vibrate or sustain. Since the solid body absorbs far less energy from the string than a hollow body electric, the solid body will always sustain longer.

All of the above discussion simply shows that there is more to making a solid body guitar than bandsawing an interesting shape out of a hunk of wood that happens to be lying around. When applied to electric basses, the problems of resonance and sustain become more critical. Hollow body electric basses really haven't found favor because they tend to have pronounced resonant spots. Though this is not too apparent acoustically, when amplified such instruments tend to be extremely uneven in response, with some notes sustaining and other notes dying quickly. Even conventional solid body basses sometimes have problems. Early examples of the Gibson EB-3 were made with a slotted peghead. This feature, together with its thin neck and relatively light mahogany body, produced undesirable resonance and dead spots which were quite noticeable on some notes. By contrast, the Fender basses have always used the heavier and less resonant maple for both bodies and necks.

Electric bass. Fender Precision.

Since the body is not the *main* producer of tone, more variation in style and construction is seen in the solid body than in any other style. The detachable neck, for example, popularized by the Fender line, is normally associated with solid bodies because of the detrimental effect on tone it would have in acoustical instruments. Though the solid body neck and peghead are essentially the same as on hollow body electrics, many manufacturers employ extreme cutaways on one or both sides of the neck, leaving the entire fingerboard clear of the body.

The pickups and controls are mounted directly in the body with all channels for wiring covered by a heavy plastic pickguard. Repair is actually easier on many solid bodies since, as on the Fender Stratocaster, all the electronics are mounted on the pickguard and it is possible to work on the complete pickup system by simply removing the pickguard mounting screws. The Gibson Les Paul is another instrument which is relatively easy to work on because access to the pickup switch and the control assembly is gained through cover plates fastened to the back of the guitar.

Tailpieces are fastened directly to the body and sometimes incorporate a vibrato within the assembly. Though some vibrato tailpieces, such as the Bigsby, are self-contained and fasten on the surface of the instrument, others, such as on the Fender Jazzmaster, are built into the body itself and require extensive routing to allow room for the internal parts.

Bridges are usually quite elaborate affairs and often make provision for height adjustment as well as string length adjustment. Fully adjustable bridges, with height and string length adjustment for each individual string as well as overall treble and bass height adjustment, are commonplace among solid bodies while rarely seen on acoustical instruments.

All of the above features are rarely found on acoustical guitars since tone production in most cases would be severely handicapped. In solid body guitars, however, these features are commonplace and make it possible to fully adjust the instrument with precision even with the guitar fully assembled and tuned. This easy adjustability is something of a mixed blessing for the repairman because of the playing requirements of most solid body guitar players. These players, for the most part blues and rock and roll musicians, are very demanding in matters of action and tuning, and, because they know that adjustability in these areas is built into the instrument, ask for and expect far more critical adjustments.

Perhaps the saying "*un*familiarity breeds contempt" best describes the situation surrounding the solid body guitar when approached by many acoustical and classical guitar oriented musicians and repairmen. The repairman must avoid the pitfall of lumping all solid body guitars together because, while the principles of construction are simple, there are many complex variations which govern tone production and playing action.

And while there is no need for precautionary words to preface the repair of acoustical instruments, repairmen whose experiences are based on acoustical instruments are advised to approach solid body guitars with an open mind. Many of the problems and repairs associated with the solid body are unique and must be approached from this viewpoint.

Below Left

The bridge on the Stratocaster is adjustable for individual string height and length, facilitating action and intonation adjustments. The tremolo is built into the bridge.

Below Right

String compensation is normally much greater on electric basses than on guitars. It is sometimes necessary to vary compensation by as much as one inch.

General Repair Information

The Workshop

For most people, setting up a shop for the first time is largely a matter of adapting to the existing facilities. The workbench layout, of course, is the most important item, followed by a storage area for parts and instruments, a work area for power tools, and a touchup and refinish area. All of this can be done on one bench and in one room and, if efficient use is made of the available space, the arrangement can be quite satisfactory. If there is sufficient room available, though, efficiency can be gained by setting up specialized work areas. A large factory service type of repair shop could very well have separate benches for each type of repair with special tools for working on specific models of instruments. For our purposes, though, versatility is very important since you may be required to repair a wide variety of instruments both in size and in style.

A sturdy workbench at a height which is comfortable for both standing and sitting should be constructed first and, while size is not especially critical, it should be large enough to comfortably accept the largest repair/construction job. Planing and scraping operations put a lot of stress on a workbench, so a heavy bench, possibly fastened to a wall, will pay off in better work.

The guitar repairman's workbench layout will vary widely depending on the type of guitars and the type of repairs, as well as on personal preference.

Repair workbench. Repairman: Larry Higgins.

Repair workbenches. (Gibson Repair Dept.)

The workbench surface should project at least three or four inches past the bench supports so that clamps may be used at various times to hold the work down. It would also be a good idea to keep the left front corner clear (if you are right-handed) to facilitate planing and scraping operations. The other front corner can be used to mount a vise such as a Versa-Vise.

The area behind the bench, as well as shelves above and behind, can be used to store the tools most commonly used. Tool placement is a matter of personal preference; what may be convenient for you might be completely unworkable for the next person. I would suggest keeping your tools out in the open where they can be easily seen and reached from your central work area. The most efficient layout doesn't necessarily look the neatest so keep this in mind when setting up your shop.

Various padded blocks for supporting the guitar while you are working on it can be made up. A padded support block for the neck, for example,

is frequently used to support the guitar while various neck and fret work is done. You may want to consider, for certain operations, supporting the guitar between the bench and the back of your chair. The chair back could be notched to accept the neck and the height adjusted to hold the guitar level. In this position (with the guitar body on the bench and the neck supported on the chair back) you have access to all sides of the guitar without moving the instrument, improving both efficiency and quality of work.

In general, power tools should be kept physically separate from the general work area. Tools such as a belt sander and a table saw can create a lot of dust and your cleanup chores will be much reduced if you can locate them in a separate area. Keep in mind that many power tools take up a lot of work space, so if space is limited, safety considerations will dictate what you can or cannot use.

If you have the room, a separate area for touchup and refinishing can be set up. Of course, this should be in as dust-free an area as possible. If you have spray equipment, adequate ventilation must be provided, and in most cases this means a spray booth with forced ventilation.

Try not to crowd too much into your work area. Leave plenty of room for yourself to work in and don't crowd the instruments; this goes for instruments in the process of repair as well as for completed and unrepaired ones. Three or four disassembled guitars with clamps on various parts can take up a surprising amount of space.

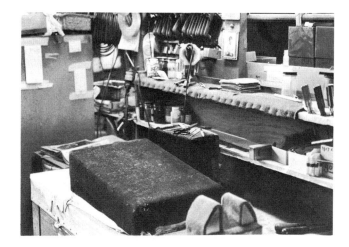 

Repair workbenches. (Gibson Repair Dept.) Left: The neck of the guitar is held in the padded vise jaws while the body rests on the slanted platform.

Tools

Hand Tools

Guitar construction and repair are really forms of specialized woodworking as far as the tools of the trade are concerned, and a well-equipped woodworking shop provides the basic foundation. Books on woodworking will give the prospective repairman a detailed account of the use and care of basic hand tools so no special mention need be given to them at this point. Beginners who are not familiar with the use of hand tools are strongly advised to study the basics thoroughly and to practice on various simple woodworking projects before tackling their first guitar repair. It takes a little while to get the "feel" of using tools, and to know when they are working properly and when they need adjustment or sharpening.

If you are at all serious about fretted instrument repair and guitar construction, it will be well worth the effort and money to get the best tools available. Particular emphasis should be placed on the basic cutting tools such as chisels, planes, and knives. The exacting nature of the work requires sharp edges, properly maintained, and the maintenance of good tools will do much toward increasing the prospects of a job well done.

Progression beyond the simplest repairs does, however, require a number of specialized tools. Some are found on the bench of the violin repairman and others are designed specifically for guitars and other fretted instruments. A few may have to be designed for one particular type of repair and, in addition, some ingenuity may be required to design a special tool to be used only once—for the particular job at hand.

Basic Hand Tool List

1) *Knife:* violin maker's, X-acto, table, palette. The violin maker's knife is the basic knife of the repairman. The blade runs the length of the handle, which is of wood and glued over the blade, and as the blade shortens through successive sharpenings the handle is cut away to expose more blade. These knives come in a variety of sizes. Your basic one should have a blade width of about half an inch.

Below Left

The violin maker's knife is available in several different sizes. The blade runs the length of the handle; it can be sharpened many times since the handle can be cut back as the blade wears.

Below Right

This bending iron is electrically heated and is built specifically for bending guitar sides. A round copper pipe with a heating element inside will also work well and, in addition, is easier to construct.

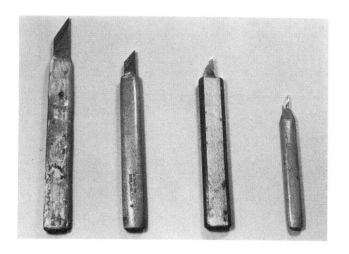

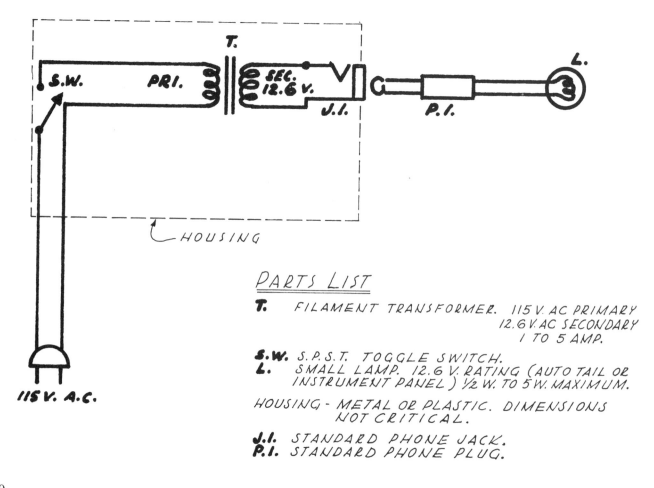

INSPECTION LIGHT

PARTS LIST

T. FILAMENT TRANSFORMER. 115 V. AC PRIMARY
12.6 V. AC SECONDARY
1 TO 5 AMP.

S.W. S.P.S.T. TOGGLE SWITCH.
L. SMALL LAMP. 12.6 V. RATING (AUTO TAIL OR INSTRUMENT PANEL) ½ W. TO 5 W. MAXIMUM.

HOUSING - METAL OR PLASTIC. DIMENSIONS NOT CRITICAL.

J.I. STANDARD PHONE JACK.
P.I. STANDARD PHONE PLUG.

2) *Plane:* block, jack, miniature or model maker's, violin maker's (available with curved bottom), rabbeting.

3) *Saw:* handsaw, coping, hacksaw, dovetail, violin or guitar maker's (looks like a miniature dovetail saw).

4) *Chisel:* straight blade wood, gouge, carving.

5) *File:* mill, wood rasp, bastard (half-round and round), slim taper, needle, surform.

6) *Plier family:* slip-joint, needle nose, diagonal cutter, metal cutting snips, scissors, end nipper (with outside surface ground flat for removing frets).

7) *Wrench:* crescent, open end, box socket, allen head, nut driver.

8) *Measuring Tools:* straight edge, ruler micrometer, caliper, divider, compass, thickness gauge, combination square, tape measure.

9) *Hand drill, brace.*

10) *Screwdriver:* straight slot, phillips, jeweler's.

11) *Soldering gun or iron.*

12) *Inspection mirror, lamp.*

13) *Alcohol lamp, propane torch.*

14) *Bending iron.*

15) *Scrapers.*

16) *Vise:* woodworker's, bench. A vise called the Versa-Vise is very popular with repairmen; it combines the features of both woodworker's and bench types.

17) *Tap and die.*

18) *Miscellaneous:* purfling cutter, peg shaper and reamer, mechanical finger, soundpost setter and various probes, circle cutter, various accessories for maintaining tools (sharpening stone, burnisher, etc.).

19) *Clamps:* C, bar, bridge, spool, cross, lever, violin maker's edge crack, woodworker's.

For most gluings, and for many other operations as well, clamps are required, and the more clamps on hand in the shop the better. There is literally no limit as to how many clamps are enough; there will always be a situation where an extra clamp or two can make the difference between just doing a job and doing it right.

Apart from the usual C clamps (in all sizes), woodworker's clamps, and bar or pipe clamps, a number of other clamps which are specifically designed for string instrument repair and construction are required. Some can be bought and others will have to be made. Edge clamps (sometimes called spool clamps) are an essential part of the shop tool inventory, since they are required for gluing edges of guitars in both repair and construction. Available in many sizes and listed in catalogs for violin making tools, the usual design consists of a threaded steel or wood shaft with two cylindrical end pieces or spools. The spools are internally threaded when used with wood shafts and are adjusted by wing nuts on the ends when the shafts are threaded steel rods. The shop should carry

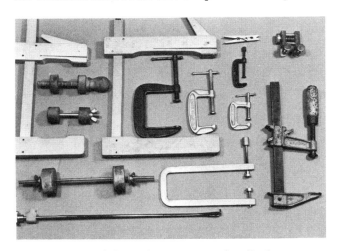

A wide variety of clamps is necessary to handle the range of gluing operations encountered in guitar repair.

EDGE CLAMP

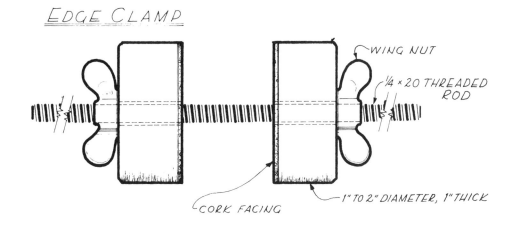

WING NUT

¼ × 20 THREADED ROD

CORK FACING

1" TO 2" DIAMETER, 1" THICK

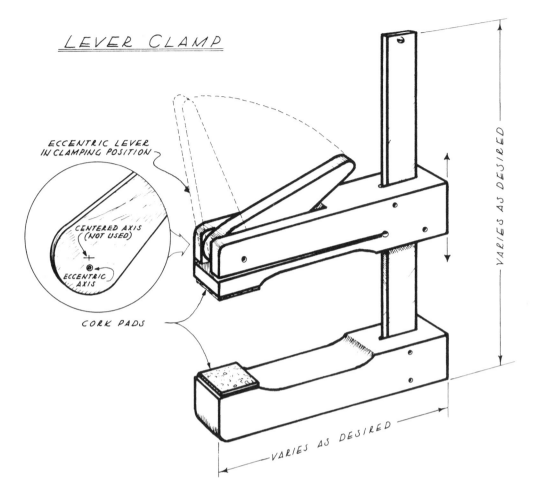

LEVER CLAMP

ECCENTRIC LEVER
IN CLAMPING POSITION

CENTERED AXIS
(NOT USED)

ECCENTRIC
AXIS

CORK PADS

VARIES AS DESIRED

VARIES AS DESIRED

these clamps in a range of sizes; end pieces of about two inches in diameter and a range of openings extending to a little over five inches will be adequate for gluing the edges and sides of most guitars.

Cross clamps, though made normally for violin repairmen, are quite useful for guitar repairs as well. Consisting of two jaws (one jaw is adjustable) on a long rod which can reach across the width of the instrument, they are useful for clamping top or back cracks. Since the jaws are curved to fit the edges of instruments belonging to the violin family, pads suitable for the guitar edge must be made.

Lever clamps are available in a wide range of sizes and are very useful where the clamping depth or reach is beyond the range of the usual C clamp. Once the movable jaw is set on the bar, the actual clamping pressure is applied by moving an eccentric lever on the end of the jaw. The range of travel, from the lever alone, is limited to about a quarter of an inch but the pressure is sufficient for our purposes.

Elongated C clamps are required for gluing bridges on guitars and can be made of wood or metal since the amount of pressure required, in a properly fitted bridge, is quite moderate. Apart from the length, the two points which should be observed are the depth of adjustment, which must be sufficient to allow insertion through the sound-hole, and a raised lower jaw which will get the lower arm of the jaw away from potentially interfering braces.

Do not try to do major gluings unless you have enough clamps on hand. This autoharp required thirty-one. Most guitars, when the top or back is being glued, require more.

Power Tools

There is no denying the fact that power tools do require a considerable amount of skill if anything near maximum performance is to be derived. I believe accuracy is the main benefit to be obtained from the use of power tools; decreased physical effort is only a secondary (though welcome) benefit. And though operations are normally faster, this is not always the case, since setup time often is far longer than the time for the actual operation with the tool.

As far as quality of work is concerned, the notion that handmade means hand tools only is outdated. Quality work requires skill and experience whether done with hand tools alone or with the assistance of power tools. Since many of the initial operations in preparing parts for repair and construction require, with hand tools, manual labor in the true sense of the word, the correct use of power tools allows more time and concentration for those finishing operations where the skill of the repairman can be more readily exercised.

The first power tool of the shop would have to be the electric hand drill, though in modern-day practice the electric drill is so commonplace and inexpensive that it is tempting to classify it as a hand tool. However, where the facilities allow the use of larger bench-mounted tools, the first tool in the shop should be the table saw. Though the radial arm saw is popular for home workshop use, the particular requirements of the guitar shop, which place a premium on accuracy, favor the conventional table saw. Particularly for the task of cutting veneers for purfling, inlays, and binding, a rugged and accurately made saw is highly desirable.

A drill press, preferably a floor model, should come after the table saw. This tool is quite versatile and with a little practice it may soon be found that a major portion of the drill press's use will be in operations other than drilling. Sanding and routing operations are two important uses in the guitar shop. Incidentally, the accuracy and smoothness of the hand electric drill leaves much to be desired for anything but the simplest drilling operations, regardless of how fancy the available attachments are. If the accuracy required calls for a drill press and one is not available, then an electric hand drill may be used, though one should be aware that its stability and capacity do not begin to approach that of the drill press.

The band saw should probably be the next power tool in the shop, though here we are getting into the "nice to have but not absolutely neces-

Below Left

In a factory repair department, more exotic tools such as this air-driven drum sander can be used to save time. Note the funnel (behind the guitar) which is part of the shop vacuum system. (Gibson Repair Dept.)

Below Right

A belt sander like this is only practical in a large factory repair department. It sure is a great time saver, though! (Gibson Repair Dept.)

sary" category. Apart from various resawing operations up to and including the resawing of guitar tops, backs, sides, and necks, the main use of the band saw, I've found, has been to saw the unbelievable number of little bits and pieces of wood required for repair and construction. A large jigsaw can perform many of the lighter operations which the band saw is capable of, though its main application would be for fine, intricate cuts for inlays.

The router is an excellent investment for both repairman and builder. Cutting the channels for the purfling and binding in a guitar takes only a few minutes' time. Another use is to cut the tops of solid body and accoustical guitars to accept pick-ups. A third use is to cut and recut saddle slots in bridges. I suggest getting one with a rating of one horsepower or more as these run cooler when cutting hard woods such as maple and rosewood and are, at the same time, smoother in operation.

The well-equipped shop will probably acquire a jointer, polisher, grinder, belt sander, portable hand sander, and possibly wood and metal lathes, and it is assumed that by this time the repairman is truly serious about repairing and construction. If the tools and the skills necessary for their operation have been acquired by way of a past woodworking hobby, the reader is one giant step ahead of everyone else!

Glues

There are a great many glues and adhesives available to the maker and repairman, but our choice of adhesive is simplified because, for all practical purposes, the glue best suited for repair work is the hot animal glue known variously as cabinet maker's glue, hide (hot) glue, and violin maker's glue. Though this glue, which will be referred to from this point on as hide glue, is the glue traditionally used by both makers and repairmen, my recommendation is based not on tradition but on the characteristics which make it well-suited for both construction and repair.

One should note that extreme strength is not the controlling factor in choosing a glue. As a matter of fact, extreme strength is not particularly desirable because such a characteristic makes it difficult to disassemble parts of an instrument which may need repair or replacement. Hide glue, while it is very strong—certainly strong enough for any operation involved in guitar construction or repair—is particularly desirable because its strength and consistency can be easily controlled. When gluing a joint or crack, the heat and moisture from the glue draws it into the opening and into the pores of the wood. Because of this characteristic, one can work glue completely through minute cracks; with other adhesives such penetrating powers are either poor or nonexistent.

Considering all the parts of an instrument which are under continuous tension or compression, a glue must be extremely rigid when dry or set. Here again hide glue possesses the desired characteristics. A number of otherwise good adhesives must be rejected because of their tendency to stretch or "creep" under continuous tension. From time to time an instrument comes into the shop with a neck or bridge pulled loose after having undergone "do it yourself" repairs. Invariably the glue used has been white glue, epoxy, or some form of household or contact cement. Since the old glue must be completely cleaned from the joint—the more exotic adhesives are very difficult to remove—the end result is extra time and trouble for the repairman and extra cost for the customer.

Other properties desirable in a good glue for repair work are quick setting time and ease in cleaning off the surplus. Hide glue dries quickly on smaller repairs (in some cases in as little as ten or fifteen minutes) though larger gluings, particularly those involving a neck or bridge, require at least twenty-four hours. For a busy shop, however, this is of no particular concern, since there are always other repair jobs to work on while the glue dries. Most of the excess glue can be wiped off while the glue is still soft; the remaining surplus which dries can be removed with a damp rag.

Since so many repair operations require gluings of one sort or another, the choice of a proper glue cannot be overemphasized. To be sure, the preparation and use of hide glue involves a considerable amount of time and trouble when only one or two gluings are involved, but in a shop where many repairs are made during the day it is customary to keep the glue pot hot all day, occasionally adding water and/or glue depending upon the requirements of the particular job at hand.

Hide glue is not without its disadvantages, however. It is susceptible to prolonged conditions of dampness—a characteristic in common with most other water-soluble glues—and is softened when exposed to extremely high temperatures. Since such conditions will damage an instrument's finish and wood anyway, extremes in temperature and humidity are to be avoided even when an instrument has been entirely constructed with a "modern adhesive."

Hide glue is available from dealers specializing in violin and guitar maker's supplies, in the form of sheets, pellets, or powder. The powdered form is to be avoided generally, as it is difficult to be certain of its purity. In general, the lighter, more highly refined glue (color varies from a light clear amber to varying shades of brown) is preferable, since it contributes toward a neater, less conspicuous glue joint.

To prepare hot hide glue, heat one part glue together with two parts water in a double boiler or old-fashioned glue pot. You can use an electric glue pot, but the hot water in a double boiler also serves conveniently to remove glue squeezed out from a joint. The glue should be the consistency of warm engine oil though this should be taken only as a general guide. Only experience can tell the repairman how thick the glue must be for a particular job; water or glue must be added until the consistency looks and "feels" right for the job at hand.

No one glue is best for all situations and hide glue is no exception. The well-equipped shop should, therefore, carry other adhesives. White glue, such as Elmer's Glue-All, is versatile and easy to use for a wide variety of miscellaneous gluings. Modern white glues *can* be used successfully for many repairs where, at one time, only hide glue was practical. It is a fact that most guitar factories use white glues for assembly, and when proper choice of glue is teamed with good gluing technique the results are excellent—a statement I wouldn't have made a few years ago.

A number of repairmen and builders report good results with Franklin Tite-Bond, a synthetic glue, and this would be worth investigating if hide glue doesn't appeal to you.

A plastic adhesive such as Duco cement can be used for gluing plastic binding. Where extreme strength is required and where a good amount of heat can be applied for curing, epoxy, of course, is the best glue for the job. Mixed with ebony or rosewood dust, epoxy is ideal for gluing mother-of-pearl inlays into fingerboards. However, for most instrument work the heat necessary for curing would be injurious to the wood and finish. In addition, epoxies and household cements cannot be removed without again damaging the finish.

Though I don't personally use it, I know of a number of repairmen who use a cold-set liquid hide glue such as Sears with success. The slower setup time, compared to the hot hide glue, is a convenience when lining up broken parts. Liquid hide glue is certainly more convenient to use and would be worth consideration in situations where only an occasional gluing is required.

A fairly recent adhesive is a quick setting compound called alpha cyanoacrylate or by the trade names Aron Alpha and Permabond. This adhesive, in certain situations, sets up within a few seconds and at the same time penetrates into the crack or joint. It works best on nonporous surfaces that are fairly tight fitting. While its uses in repair are limited (the stuff is expensive, too!), it is worth having on hand for those situations where the more conventional glues don't seem quite right for the job.

You should experiment with the various glues before you try them on an instrument. If you are not completely familiar with a glue, don't use it. In gluing operations, the work must be done right the first time!

Woods

Guitar Tops

Spruce

Spruce is the wood traditionally used for guitar tops. Most imported guitars use spruce from Europe (principally through wood suppliers in Germany) while most American-made guitars use Sitka spruce from the northern Pacific Coast. As a general rule, the European spruce is preferred for its tonal characteristics; for a given weight it is stiffer and consequently produces a brighter tone. Sitka spruce can, however, produce a fine tone, especially on steel string guitars, and at the same time is much less expensive.

When repairing and inlaying missing sections in tops, it is important to match the wood. Sitka has a reddish-brown tone while the European spruce is more golden-brown. The wood should be quarter-sawn of course and when an entire new top is made the general rule is to use the closest grain possible.

The use of close grain is flexible, though, since other factors may affect the resonance of the top wood. Traditionally, if the grain width varies, the close grain is placed in the middle and the wide grain on the outside. However, there are some notable exceptions among steel string guitars. Many Martins, for example, have tops with the wide grain in the center and the narrow grain on the outside.

Cedar, Fir, Other Woods

In recent years, the use of other woods for tops has become popular. Cedar, fir, and redwood have been used with success by various makers. In repairing, you will come across these woods in addition to spruce and it will be helpful to keep them in stock.

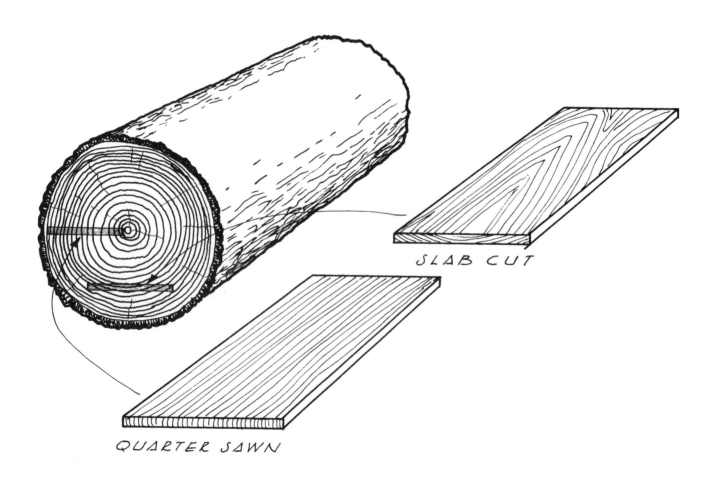

SLAB CUT

QUARTER SAWN

Back and Sides

Rosewood

Brazilian or Indian rosewood is the preferred wood for the back and sides of all classical and most flattop guitars. This wood is very hard, dense, and resonant. Brazilian is more highly figured than Indian; choice sets with straight grain bring a premium price. Indian rosewood tends to be straighter-grained. Though colors vary widely, light to dark, Brazilian is typically orange-brown while Indian is more purple-brown, especially when freshly cut.

As with tops, use the appropriate wood when repairing to match the existing back or side. Because of the wide range of grains and colors, it will be difficult to match without a fairly extensive assortment of wood.

Mahogany

Honduras mahogany is the only mahogany used in guitar sides and backs. It is fairly light in weight and resonant, making it the second choice next to rosewood. As with rosewood, Honduras mahogany is open-grained and requires a filler beneath the finish. Usually a gold-brown stain is used with mahogany, making it difficult at times to match both the wood *and* the stain. A useful tip is not to use too much red in the stain. Use mostly brown, as the reddish-brown color of the wood will show through even dark stains. Too much red in the stain will then throw your color match off.

Philippine mahogany is a lighter more open-grained wood and its visual and tonal qualities make it less desirable as a tone wood.

Maple

Maple is used on all plectrum, some flattop, and some flamenco and classical guitars. Bird's-eye maple is usually found only on American plectrum guitars while flamed maple from Europe is widely used on all types of guitars.

Other Woods

Woods such as walnut, oak, and birch are used occasionally, while Spanish cypress is used extensively in flamenco guitars. In a repair shop you will have to stock many more different kinds of wood than if you specialized in building one type of instrument.

Neck

Honduras mahogany and cedar are commonly used for the neck on a wide variety of guitars. Maple is used mainly on plectrum and electric guitars as well as on the occasional flattop. Other woods such as walnut and rosewood are rarely used. Laminated necks may be found occasionally on certain lines of steel string and electric guitars.

Fingerboard

Ebony and rosewood are always used with no finish at all on the playing surface. Maple fingerboards always employ a finish over the wood to protect it from wear and dirt. Ebony is the preferred wood for most guitars, though in one respect it is inferior to rosewood: it will shrink and expand more than rosewood, under the same conditions, and cracks in the top beside the fingerboard are more common. Maple fingerboards are found mostly on electric guitars of which certain models of the Fender line are well-known examples.

Linings

Mahogany, basswood, poplar, maple, spruce.

Braces

Top—spruce, or same as top wood. Back—Honduras mahogany, spruce.

Bridge

The bridge material in steel string guitars usually matches the fingerboard. Classical and flamenco guitars usually use rosewood in all price ranges.

Purfling, Rosette

Dyed maple is usually used in the rosette and purfling of nylon string instruments while plastic is usually used in steel string guitars. However, in American-made classical guitars plastic is commonly used and many handmade steel string guitars have wood purfling and binding as well, so there are many exceptions to this generalization.

Abalone inlays, such as used on the Martin 000-45, are difficult to work with and require extra care.

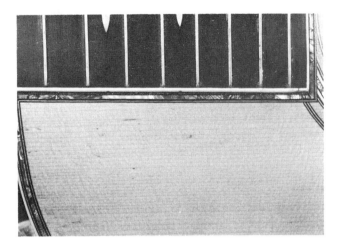

Binding

Rosewood or maple (sometimes dyed black) is usually used for binding on nylon string guitars, plastic on the steel string instruments. However, as with purfling, there are exceptions. Some old guitars such as the Martin used ivory for binding. Ivory-grained celluloid or ivoroid is occasionally seen. Mother-of-pearl and abalone are occasionally incorporated into binding and purfling designs.

End Blocks

Mahogany, spruce.

Strings

Classical

Strings for the modern classical and flamenco guitar are always made of nylon, replacing completely the gut strings used previously. The three treble strings are made of nylon monofilament and the three bass strings have a nylon core with a metal winding.

Many manufacturers produce strings in a range of gauges from low to medium to high and extrahigh tension. The materials, as well as the processing they undergo, have a substantial effect on the tone quality. In order to find the best string for your instrument and playing style, it will be necessary to experiment a bit with various brands. A few guidelines may be helpful in narrowing the selection for your guitar.

As a general rule, the larger, more heavily braced instruments require the higher tension strings. Usually the extrahigh tension strings produce the most volume, though for the average guitar high tension strings are the best all-around choice. A medium or low tension string is a bit easier to finger and should be considered if maximum volume is not a criterion.

In terms of tone quality, the processing of the nylon, and of the metal alloys used on the wound strings has much to do with the outcome. Appearance can be deceiving, and it is best to try the string on your guitar to see if the combination is satisfactory. Harder, unpolished wire alloys for the wound strings tend to produce more brilliance. A polished string will be more mellow. Sometimes the nylon monofilament for the first three strings will have a satin finish and sometimes it will be polished and this, too, will affect the tone.

Strings with pure silver wrapping tend to be full and rich (perhaps lacking a little "edge") and the tone remains relatively constant for the life of the string.

Some other strings are extremely brilliant initially but tend to die and lose their edge quickly. A variation on the monofilament treble strings is the use of a plastic winding over a nylon core for the second and third strings. These strings are more brilliant than the plain monofilament and are a help in improving the tone of cheap instruments. Some flamenco players also use the wound second and third, though the extra noise created by the finger sliding over the winding discourages use for classical guitar music.

Steel Acoustic

Steel strings for acoustical guitars are almost always roundwound over a steel core on the bass strings and plain steel on the first, second, and (occasionally) third. Since the tonal properties of the plain steel strings are pretty much the same for all brands, the main difference between various brands of strings lies in the wound strings.

Compound or silk and steel strings have a steel core, a wrapping of silk, and a metal winding. These strings are classed as light gauge, with a fairly mellow tone. They are widely used on folk guitars or on guitars which sound best with light gauge strings. Compound strings are also popular on twelve-string guitars.

Roundwound strings with a steel or nickel-steel alloy winding are a bit more brilliant than compound strings and are available in a wide range of gauges as well. These strings last a long time though they generally lack the edge of a bronze string. In acoustical guitars, the trend has been away from this type of string and toward the bronze string.

For maximum projection, volume, and brilliance, most players prefer the bronze string. This string has a bronze wrapping over a steel core and is available in a wide range of gauges. It is very brilliant initially but tends to lose its edge fairly quickly. All bronze strings do not sound alike, however, depending on the alloy used and the winding and polishing methods. As with other types of strings, it is best to experiment to see which fits your requirements for tone quality.

Electric

To a large extent, the tone produced by a magnetic pickup is determined by the magnetic properties of the strings. Though there are only two main categories of electric guitar strings—flatwound and roundwound—there are so many variations within these two categories that some explanation in detail is in order.

Roundwound strings consist of a steel core with a winding (of round cross section) possessing various magnetic properties. Depending on the magnetic properties of the steel or nickel alloy winding and on the ratio of winding to core, the tonal characteristics can vary over a wide range Roundwound strings are used whenever a tone with clarity, brilliance, and liveliness is desired.

In certain applications, the noise produced by the fingers sliding over the wound strings may be objectionable. The semipolished string is quiet under the fingers and possesses most of the tonal qualities of the unpolished roundwound string. A certain amount of brilliance is exchanged for a somewhat more full and mellow tone.

The smoothest and quietest string is the flatwound type. This string, which has a steel core and an internal round wire wrapping, is constructed with an outer flat ribbon winding of stainless steel. Flatwound strings are very quiet and contribute substantially toward a fast action. They are very mellow and lack a certain amount of brilliance, though this may be partially compensated for by pickup and tone adjustment.

Closely allied to the flatwound string in general properties are the flatground string and the nylon tapewound string. A flatground string is simply a roundwound string with the outer portion of the winding ground flat. Its characteristics lie between semipolished and flatwound strings. Tapewound strings have a final winding of nylon tape over a conventional roundwound base and possess a very smooth feel. The tone is very mellow and to some the difference in tone between the wound strings and the plain first and second may be objectionable.

A few strings which are designed for acoustical steel string guitars find application in special instances. All flattop guitars, when amplified by a magnetic pickup placed in the soundhole, produce too much bass for good balance when the normal electric-style steel string is used. Bronze strings and silk and steel strings work very well in this application because only the steel core on the wound strings affects the pickups. The decreased sensitivity of the wound bass strings, in particular, produces a more balanced sound when amplified, and at the same time the acoustical sound of the guitar is maintained.

General Repair Procedure

Inspection

A thorough inspection should be undertaken before any repairs or adjustments are made. Such an inspection not only will save time by ensuring all repairs are made in an orderly manner but will also ensure against a repair being either inadvertently left out or made in error because of a hasty diagnosis. Two simple examples will help illustrate the need for thoroughness.

A guitar with a high action is brought into the shop with the instructions to "cut the saddle down a bit" in order to lower the action. Although the adjustment may indeed be as simple as cutting the saddle height, other more extensive repairs may actually be required. Further inspection may show a warped neck or a neck that has pulled up or become unglued at the body. A bridge which is starting to pull loose from the top can also be responsible for a high action. No amount of adjustment at the bridge is going to make up for a warped and incorrectly aligned neck!

If, with this same guitar, the complaint is made that it will not play in tune, you must again consider all the parts which could conceivably cause the problem. A high action can cause problems with tuning but again the problem may be a warped or loose neck rather than a high saddle. A string may be false, mismatched, or simply the wrong kind. The correct placement of the bridge, including the proper amount of compensation, must also be checked. One should measure twice (at least!) and check everything else as well before drawing the conclusion that the bridge is in the wrong position. Even in this case, though, there are ways in which string length may be adjusted without removing and resetting the bridge.

One adjustment may cure several related problems on one guitar while on another instrument

several major repairs may be needed to cure a problem such as the high action mentioned previously. Experience must be the guide in deciding which repairs are the most important and in which order they are to be made. If the instrument isn't worth repairing, now is the time to make that decision.

Preparation of Materials

Before any actual adjustment or repair is undertaken, be sure that all tools and materials required for the operation are on hand. For most repairs, a misplaced tool or part simply means wasted time. The exceptions are those repairs involving gluings. Since hot glue must be applied and set while *hot*, the time to look for clamps is definitely *before* the glue has been applied to the parts.

Repair

The actual repairs will be explained in detail in later chapters. Beginners (and experts for that matter) should proceed carefully and not be too concerned with speed. Repairs which are both artistic and creative are, in large measure, a product of experience, but one must also recognize that a sensitive nature and creative spirit are the mark of the master craftsman.

Testing and Adjustment

All that is left after the actual repairs have been made is to test the instrument to ensure that the original problems have been solved. In many instances the cheaper instruments cannot be repaired or adjusted to as high a degree as the more expensive ones because production shortcuts at the factory make it impossible for the repairman to use his best techniques in repair and adjustment. Assuming that the cost of repair must generally be in line with the value of the instrument, one can ask no more of the repairman than to bring each instrument up to its own maximum potential, though this may occasionally require more time to be spent on the cheaper factory instruments than on the expensive handmade ones.

Guitar Adjustments

A correctly adjusted guitar is an important key to successful guitar playing. More often than not, however, one comes across instruments which have never been matched to the gauge or type of string let alone the playing style of the owner. It would be safe to assume that many players really don't know what they're missing, though one can hardly blame them entirely since a good portion of the blame must fall upon the retail store and (occasionally) the repair shop. Considering today's diversified styles of music requiring all types of guitars, the guitar repairman, in order to provide adequate service, must possess the knowledge and facilities to service all guitars rather than, for example, just classical or just electric.

Though strict attention to detail is a must, the actual tools required are minimal and every shop (including retail stores) should be able to take care of most adjustments once the basic principles and procedures have been learned. One of the very best ways in which to get started in guitar repairs is to begin with guitar setups and adjustments, for here you will get valuable experience and a "feel" for the instrument without risking serious damage to it when a mistake has been made. Excluding the pickups and controls of electric guitars, which are covered separately, the areas of adjustment include: the strings, the neck and fingerboard, the nut, and the bridge (position and height of saddle) (see p. 70). In adjusting the guitar, the two main areas of concern are correct action and correct scale accuracy. Since the required adjustments interact to some extent, especially when taken in the wrong order, the sequence shown in the following pages is suggested.

The playing style of the guitarist is the deciding factor regarding all other adjustments to the guitar. The player who plays very hard will have to content himself with a high action in order to play clearly without the strings buzzing on the frets. In addition, the use of flatpicks (in acoustical guitars) usually requires a higher action than fingerpicks or fingers alone. Fingerpicking, on the other hand, and flamenco playing require low action. Most electric guitarists, for obvious reasons, can get away with very low action. A guitarist who plays several styles must compromise on his action or use several instruments. The player, in any event, must be realistic in his demands upon his instrument and should accept the fact that duplicating another player's action, even when the guitar and strings are identical, is apt to be disappointing unless the playing styles are alike.

Classical and Flamenco Guitar

Neck and Fingerboard

A correctly adjusted fingerboard (including the frets) is the key to a successful action adjustment. Unless the fingerboard is reasonably close to satisfying several key criteria, the effort spent in adjusting the nut and saddle represents wasted time for both repairman and player. The reader is again cautioned that the cost of the guitar or reputation of the maker is no assurance that the instrument will be correctly adjusted at the time of purchase. Old guitars, in addition, present problems arising from wear of certain parts as well as more serious problems requiring repairs before adjustments can be carried out.

All guitars must have a slight relief in the neck (in varying amounts, depending upon the guitar and type of strings) and fingerboard in order to allow for a proper action over the entire fingerboard. For most classical and flamenco guitars, the relief, measured at the fifth or sixth fret and under full string tension, should be approximately 1/64 to 1/32 inch on the treble side and 1/32 to 3/64 inch on the bass side. For guitars which are always played very softly, it is permissible to allow slightly less relief. A guitar with a reverse bow or a hump in the middle of the fingerboard is defective and under no circumstances should one proceed with adjustments until this item is taken care of.

Since most classical guitars have no provision for neck adjustment, the neck relief must be built into the instrument. Any correction in this area falls under the heading of repair rather than adjustment. A certain amount of correction can be done by cutting down the fret height in the offending area, though obviously this method should be limited to minor corrections, such as adjusting the variation in relief between the treble and bass sides of the fingerboard.

All frets must be well-seated in their slots with the ends perfectly beveled and rounded and flush with the edge of the fingerboard. Loose fret ends can be a particular problem since, as with uneven fret height, the string fretted at that point will produce a poor tone. In some cases, tapping the fret down will suffice. In others, the entire fret must be removed, reshaped, and reseated.

Worn frets with grooves created by string contact will cause problems with string buzz or fret rattle. In some cases, where wear is not excessive, it will be satisfactory to level the frets with a large mill smooth file till the grooves disappear. The job must be finished by reshaping the fret contour with a file, sanding, and polishing to restore the original smoothness. In other cases, the amount of wear may dictate the partial or complete replacement of frets. Additional details on fret and fingerboard repairs will be found in Chapter Six.

Nut

Usually of ivory or bone (or plastic in some cheaper instruments), the nut dictates the height of the string above the first fret. It has very little effect upon action beyond the first fret and for this reason, after the fingerboard and neck have been adjusted, the string height at the nut should be adjusted and then left alone during all subsequent adjustments at the bridge saddle.

In most classical guitars the spacing of the strings—from the edge of the fingerboard—is customarily set so that the space between the fingerboard edge and the first string is greater than between the sixth string and the edge. The spacing, measured at the nut, runs approximately 1/8 inch on the bass side and 3/16 inch on the treble side. Some guitarists, particularly flamenco players, prefer an even greater spacing on the treble side, and it can be as much as 1/4 inch. The extra spacing on the treble side is required on classical and flamenco guitars in order to perform legato passages on the first string without danger of pulling it over the edge of the fingerboard.

The string height should be only enough to ensure a clean tone on the open strings. Our method of determining and adjusting string height at the nut is independent of the string height adjustment at the saddle. By fretting the string at the third fret (pressing the string down between the second and third frets) we can then observe the

height of the string above the first fret. The correct height is that which allows the string to just clear the first fret. The bass strings should have slightly more clearance than the treble. This slight clearance gives a bit more height above the first fret and

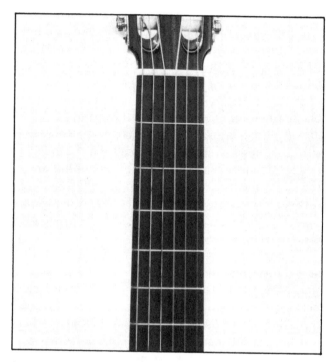

Classical and flamenco guitars require greater clearance between the first string and the edge of the fingerboard than steel string instruments do. The first string has more clearance than the sixth string.

compensates for the tendency to play harder on the open strings.

By adjusting the nut according to the rules given in the preceding paragraph, the open string height at the nut is automatically obtained. It is important to adjust the neck for relief *before* adjusting the nut because any neck adjustment, if done last, will affect the string height at the first fret. When adjusting, the notches should be cut with a fine diameter needle file, and should be matched to the diameter of the string under adjustment. The depth of the notches should be no more than half the diameter of the string and any excess height should be removed with file and sandpaper.

Some classical and flamenco instruments have removable nuts, and on these guitars fine adjustments in overall height can be made by adding or removing paper shims beneath the nut. On guitars which have a zero fret the overall string height is automatically made and you will be concerned with cutting the string notches in the nut deep enough so that the string rests firmly against the fret. With the zero fret, adjustment for individual strings is more difficult to make, and for this reason the conventional system is preferable even though the time required for the initial adjustment is longer.

If replacement of the nut is necessary, this should only be done in ivory or bone even though the original may have been plastic. The superior wearing qualities of ivory make the cost difference between the different materials a negligible factor when making a choice. If the nut is to be glued in place, white glue may be used as well hide glue. All excess material should be neatly trimmed and the ivory should be given a final finish sanding with 600 grit sandpaper. Be absolutely certain that the string notches are angled back toward the peghead and that there are no sharp edges present which may lead to premature string failure.

Saddle

Once the fingerboard and nut have been adjusted there is seldom any need for readjustment unless a radical change in playing style or in string gauge is contemplated. In effect, the main action adjustment is done on the bridge saddle. Made of ivory or bone, or plastic in some of the inexpensive instruments, the saddle determines the overall height of the strings above the fingerboard.

For classical guitars with medium action, the string height above the twelfth fret is approximately 5/32 inch on the bass side and 4/32 inch on the treble side. Flamenco guitar action generally runs on the low side and the height at the twelfth fret is approximately 1/32 inch less than the classical for both bass and treble strings.

The correct adjustment, of course, depends upon the style and preferences of the player. Most beginners tend to favor low actions because strength and control have not been fully developed, and of course this must be taken into account when setting up the guitar. Low actions do tend to inhibit playing with a wide range of dynamics because of string buzz at forte levels. On the other hand, poor technique can cause string buzz even with a high action!

If replacement of the saddle is necessary, it should always be done in ivory. The saddle is always fitted into the slot in the bridge without gluing; this feature allows for minor corrections in string height to be accomplished with the use of paper or wood shims. When shaping the saddle,

strive for a snug fit with the top surface rounded off smoothly. It is permissible to angle the saddle surface back toward the string holes in the bridge.

Steel String Flattop Guitar

Neck and Fingerboard

The neck and fingerboard of the steel string flattop guitar should be adjusted only after the strings have been selected. String tensions vary so much, depending on the gauge and type selected, that one cannot adjust for neck relief until the strings have been installed. In general, the amount of relief on the usual flattop guitar is the same as that on the classical. All steel string guitars must have some sort of reinforcement and on most guitars this takes the form of an adjustable truss rod. A notable exception is the Martin which uses a very rigid steel T bar or, in recent models, a hollow square steel bar.

With the usual adjustable rod, it is a simple matter of turning with the appropriate wrench until the tension of the strings has been compensated for and the proper amount of relief has been obtained. On many guitars it helps to loosen the strings when tightening the bar; on all guitars the strings may be left at full tension when the bar is loosened. When making a final check for relief, however, all strings must be up to full tension since the neck, particularly with heavy gauge strings, may flex considerably as the strings are brought up to pitch.

Do *not* make the mistake of trying to adjust the action with the use of the truss rod because that is not its purpose. Another common mistake is to tighten the truss rod whenever fret buzzes are heard. Probably more truss rods are broken from these two mistakes than for any other reason; in normal use, most rods require only a half turn or so of adjustment regardless of the type of string used. Finally, remember that most truss rods will not cure a reverse warp because the basic purpose of a truss rod is only to counteract the effects of a weak neck coupled with strong string tension.

Because steel strings cause frets to wear much faster than nylon ones do, particular care should be taken so see that the frets are in proper condition, well-shaped and polished. A fingerboard with binding requires an additional check to see that there is no looseness and that the binding is smooth and properly beveled.

Nut

On all steel string guitars, the nut is always glued in place. In the main, remarks in the classical section regarding the shaping of the nut, the choice of material, and the proper height adjustment apply equally to the steel string flattop. Of course, with the crowned fingerboard the nut must also be crowned and, because of the greater tension, string height is more critical and requires more care in adjustment.

The notable difference from the classical guitar is that the strings are spaced more closely to the edges of the fingerboard. The spacing runs approximately 3/32 inch at the nut and is almost always equal on both treble and bass sides since, with the added tension, the risk of pulling the string off the edge of the board isn't nearly as great as with nylon strings.

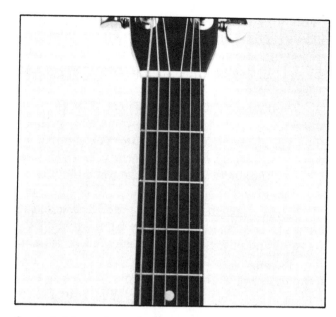

On steel string guitars, the first and sixth strings are set in from the edge of the fingerboard an equal amount.

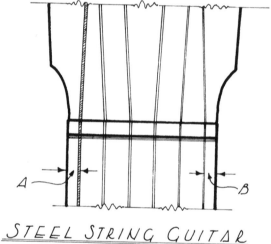

STEEL STRING GUITAR

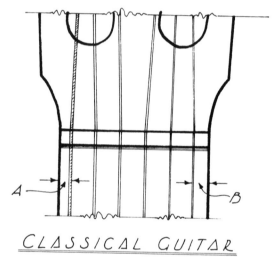

CLASSICAL GUITAR

ON THE STEEL STRING GUITAR, CLEARANCE BETWEEN FINGERBOARD EDGE AND STRING (A AND B) IS THE SAME ON BOTH SIDES.

ON THE CLASSICAL GUITAR THE CLEARANCE ON THE TREBLE SIDE, B, IS GREATER THAN ON THE BASS SIDE, A.

Saddle

The action adjustment at the saddle is much more critical with steel strings than with nylon. With a wide variety of strings available, and a number of diverse playing styles from which to draw, the "correct" action can vary considerably. In addition, the scale accuracy of most steel strings is appreciably affected by the action adjustment; adjustments for compensation must be done *after* the adjustments for action.

If one applies the same playing style to guitars strung with light, medium, and heavy gauge strings, the light gauge strings will require the highest action and the heavy gauge the lowest. This is because the light gauge string, with relatively low tension, vibrates more widely when picked and thus requires more clearance in order to avoid fret buzz. In addition, when played with thumb and fingerpicks rather than with fingers alone, all guitars require a higher action. The use of the plectrum or flatpick allows the player to play with even greater volume and force and this in turn requires another increase in action height.

The most important factor in determining the correct action adjustment, however, is the player's playing style (blues, fingerpicking, country flat-picking, etc.). In actual practice, for example, light gauge strings are usually used with low action even though the potential for fret buzz is increased. Fret buzz is not a problem, because when light gauge strings are used it is customary to play lightly since extreme volume is of secondary importance. The usual requirements of the fingerpicking style dictate a low action. In addition, blues guitarists require light gauge in order to facilitate "bending" the strings and a low action is customary even when a flatpick is used. Beginning guitarists can also make use of the light gauge/low action combination since volume is again not the main consideration; the player can develop coordination and tone quality more easily if he doesn't have to fight the stiffness of heavy strings with high action.

At the other extreme, heavy strings are usually used with a fairly high action because a primary aim is good volume and projection together with the solid tone quality that can come only from heavy gauge strings. Most rhythm guitarists, including jazz, country, and bluegrass players, require heavy or medium gauge strings together with an action high enough to allow fairly strong playing with a pick.

Obviously, it is essential for the repairman to be familiar with the string and action combinations required for the various playing styles as well as with the guitarist's personal style. For the flattop guitar as well as the plectrum (acoustical), the approximate string height above the twelfth fret for a low action is 5/64 inch treble side, 7/64 inch bass side. A medium action is approximately 6/64 inch treble, 8/64 inch bass. Heavy or high actions run around 8/64 inch treble, 10/64 inch bass.

When the string and action combinations have been decided upon, it is a relatively straightforward matter to adjust the saddle for correct height. Saddles which are removable are most easily adjusted for height and contour when placed in a vise. Many saddles, however, are glued into place and, unless an increase in height is required, it is just as well to leave the saddle in place and work on it while it is on the bridge.

If increased height is required, paper or wood shims may be used for very small changes. Greater height changes require a new ivory saddle. The replacement should be trimmed for a snug fit whether or not it is to be glued into place. Because of the greater tension of steel strings, the saddle will wear better when the upper surface is adjusted so that the string contacts the saddle along a major portion of the width. The top surface of the saddle should be perfectly smooth for six-string guitars (and tenors). The *one exception* to the rule of no notches in the saddle is for twelve-string guitars. With the twelve-string, the string pairs must be spaced very accurately and in some cases this requires notching the saddle. Pairs should be spaced 1/8 inch apart on the treble side, gradually increasing to 5/32 inch on the bass side.

Plectrum Guitar

Plectrum guitars, also known as f hole or arch-top guitars, are only occasionally seen today in their original acoustical form. Nevertheless, though the majority of these guitars are electric versions (or conversions) of one sort or another, there are enough differences between the acoustic plectrum and other types of acoustic guitars to warrant a separate action.

For good tone and projection, the plectrum guitar is invariably set up with medium or heavy gauge strings. Compared to a flattop, the plectrum guitar does not respond well to a light touch; consequently the instrument is usually played with a pick rather than finger-style. The plectrum or flatpick allows the player to "force" the guitar when it is necessary to develop maximum volume and projection. Since the basic design of the acoustical plectrum guitar is to provide maximum volume and projection, it is well to keep this in mind when setting up the instrument. A medium or heavy gauge string together with a medium action or higher is the correct combination for most applications.

All the remarks in the previous section on flattop guitars regarding the fingerboard, neck, nut, strings, and action are applicable to the plectrum.

The bridges, however, on all plectrum guitars are held in place by string tension. They are usually adjustable up or down for string height as well as forward or backward for scale accuracy. In addition, some bridges employ individually adjustable saddles for each string. Most guitars perform best, however, with a wood bridge with adjustments for height only.

The correct sequence for adjusting the bridge is to adjust first for correct action and then for correct scale accuracy. Since the bridge must first be positioned so that the guitar will play reasonably in tune, you must take a rule and determine the scale length. The correct position for the bridge will be (approximately) the scale length plus 1/16 inch for the first string and the scale length plus 3/16 inch for the sixth string. Having determined the bridge position you may now proceed to adjust the bridge height for the desired action. Care should be taken to ensure that the bridge has not tipped forward from the string tension and that the neck and nut adjustments have not changed.

The final adjustment is for scale accuracy. Since the bridge is movable this is easily accomplished. With a straight saddle, it is almost impossible to obtain equal scale accuracy for each string; a reasonable compromise can usually be accomplished, however, when the strings are matched and in good condition. A "compensated" saddle allows for more accurate adjustment by providing for increased compensation for the plain B string. With this saddle, care should be taken to see that the "set back" portion is on the B string. A plain third string must not be used with the compensated bridge since the compensation for the original wound third string is far too little for the plain third. A bridge, such as the Gibson Tune-O-Matic, with individually adjustable inserts, is the best solution when a plain third is used. If a wood saddle is preferred (with the plain third) it must be carved in the repair shop since none is available commercially.

Electric Guitar

The electric guitar, whether the archtop plectrum, thin hollow body, or solid body, requires attention in two separate areas. The first area is composed of the adjustments required of all guitars, such as the neck, frets, action, etc. The second area encompasses the pickups and controls, and requires specialized knowledge and repair techniques. Fortunately, the "electronics" of most electric guitars is relatively simple and straightforward; adjustment of the pickups and controls takes very little additional time.

The best way to adjust the electric guitar is first to go through the entire instrument as if it were an acoustical guitar. All adjustment procedures outlined for the steel string flattop and the plectrum guitar apply equally well to the electric guitar. Generally, most guitarists play with a light touch, relying on the amplifier to produce the required volume. String height and action are usually quite low and string gauges are almost never heavier than medium. As a consequence, action adjustments are more critical than usual and particular care must be taken with neck adjustment, fretwork, and action adjustment.

In addition to the usual adjustments, some electrics have peculiarities of construction which occasionally require additional attention. The detachable neck is found principally on the electric solid body (certain thin hollow body electrics also incorporate this feature as well as the occasional

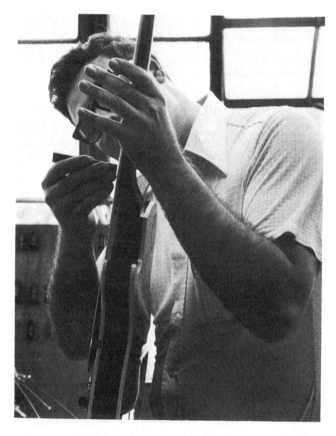

Adjusting the action requires measuring as well as playing. (Gibson Repair Dept.)

acoustical flattop), with the Fender solid body guitar perhaps the best known line of instruments incorporating this feature. The neck is held to the body with large wood screws and it is possible to adjust the neck angle (as well as remove the neck entirely).

The adjustable feature of the neck becomes important when the action adjustment at the bridge is insufficient to produce the proper string height. Many electrics have only a limited range of height adjustment at the bridge and large changes must be accomplished at the neck. Neck angle adjustments are accomplished by placing shims between the body and the neck. To adjust a neck in this manner, remove the neck by unscrewing the screws from the back of the body. The shim stock may be made of business cards or thin wood veneers; in any case, it is seldom necessary to use a thickness totaling more than 1/32 inch since small changes at the heel of the neck have a large effect on the overall action. The shim should be 3/8 inch wide and long enough to cover the width of the neck. If the action is too high, place the shim beneath the neck at the extreme end of the fingerboard. If the action is too low, place the shim beneath the neck at the outer edge of the body. After a couple of trials (bolt the neck down firmly before testing for action) you should arrive at a suitable angle where final adjustments can be taken care of by the bridge and saddle adjustment. Very low actions are used by some players and can range down to 3/64 inch treble and 5/64 inch bass (at the twelfth fret) or less. By the way, do not confuse a low fret height with low action. Very small and low frets, although increasing the "fastness" of the neck, have no effect at all on the actual action or string height above the fret.

Some guitar bridges, such as the Fender Stratocaster, have provision for adjusting the string height of each individual string, in addition to the usual adjustment for string length or compensation. This feature can compensate for inconsistencies in string gauge and tension. As an example, a small change is required when changing from a wound third string to a plain third. The plain third, for the same gauge, has less tension and has a greater tendency to buzz on the frets. A small increase in height at the third string saddle may be required to clean up the sound.

Adjusting the pickups and controls on most electrics is quite simple and can usually be done in a few minutes after the guitar has undergone the basic adjustment for correct acoustical playing. The pickup adjustment consists of adjusting for correct height, balance between pickups, and balance between all strings. The overall height of the pickups can be set by fretting the first and sixth strings at the highest fret and adjusting the two height adjustment screws on each pickup so that each one is approximately 1/16 inch below the string. If the pickup has individually adjustable pole piece screws, the tops of the screws should be about 1/16 inch below the strings when fretted at the highest fret, and the screws should project slightly from the top surface.

With this preliminary adjustment completed, the guitar should be plugged into the amplifier. With all controls on the guitar set at maximum, play the guitar and check for volume on all pickup combinations—front alone, rear alone, front and rear, etc. Minor adjustments may be made to even up the output between all pickup positions. If it is desired to increase the treble response, the bass side of each pickup should be lowered slightly. On the other hand, if increased bass response is desired, the treble side of the pickup must be lowered.

The Gibson Tune-O-Matic bridge can be used on many kinds of guitars including flattops, archtops, solid bodies, and, as in this example, thin body semiacoustics. The bridge is adjustable for overall height and for individual string intonation. The indiviudal string height can be varied by adjusting the depth of each string notch. Note the position of the pole piece screws on the humbucking pickups. In a dual pickup system such as this, they should face toward the bridge and toward the fingerboard.

On many of the early Gibson and Epiphone solid body guitars, conversion to the Tune-O-Matic style bridge, as on the current Les Paul models, required plugging and tapping the original tailpiece-bridge stud holes to take the new bridge studs. In addition, new studs had to be set behind the Tune-O-Matic bridge for the separate tailpiece. A recent development, the Leo Quan "Badass" bridge, offers a neat conversion to a compensated bridge without the need for drilling any additional holes. The two screws at the ends are for coarse adjustments while the individual saddles give fine adjustments for each string.

 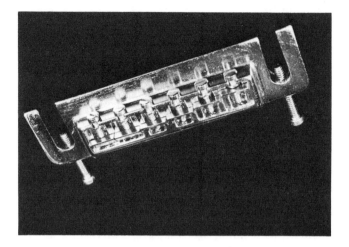

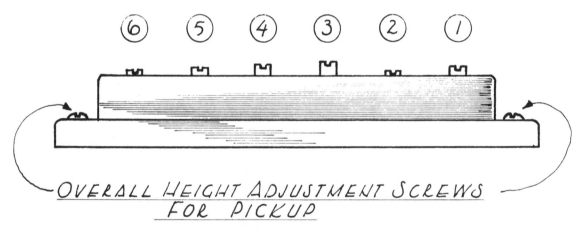

OVERALL HEIGHT ADJUSTMENT SCREWS
FOR PICKUP

PICKUP POLEPIECE SCREWS ADJUSTED FOR
GUITAR WITH WOUND G (3) STRING.

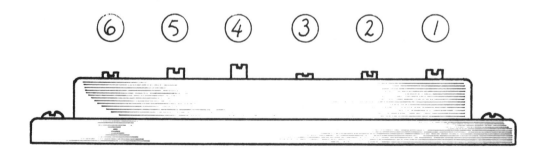

PICKUP POLEPIECE SCREWS ADJUSTED FOR
GUITAR WITH PLAIN G (3) STRING.

When adjusting the pole piece adjustment screws (this feature is usually found on the better quality pickups), you should remember two points: 1) the pickup responds better to a plain string than to a wound one; 2) the response increases as the string gauge is increased. In practical terms, this means that, for even response, the B string screw should be slightly lower than the high E string screw. If a plain third string is used, the G string screw should be lower than the B. For the wound strings, the G (if it is wound) will be highest, the low E will be lowest, and the D and A will be intermediate between the E and G. A little trial and error with the adjusting screws, as well as with overall pickup heights, should result in even response on all strings and on all pickup combinations.

If you have tried to adjust the pickups as close to the strings as possible in order to obtain the maximum volume, you may encounter a problem with tone distortion. The tone gets increasingly poorer progressing up the fingerboard, especially past the twelfth fret. With the fifth and sixth strings especially, the tone deteriorates to the point where it starts to warble and it becomes difficult to detect a single pure note. Intonation can suffer as well.

Pickups with very strong magnets are more apt to cause this problem; consequently, you are more apt to find trouble with certain models of Fenders, than, for example, with Gibsons. The Fender Stratocaster, with three pickups, is especially troublesome, while the Gibsons with humbucking pickups almost never interfere. Keep in mind that rock and roll gauge strings are more likely to warble than heavier gauge strings.

The problem is related to the fact that every time the string swings near the pickup the magnet tries to attract it. When you fret a string in the upper position, it is placed close to the pickup, increasing the attraction and warble. While the problem may seem perplexing when encountered for the first time, the solution is simple; lower the pickups just enough to clean up the sound. Usually the bass side has to be lowered more than the treble side.

The final step in adjustment is to check the switches and controls for smooth operation without noise or intermittent loss of volume. If the switch contacts or potentiometers (controls) need clearing, a small application of contact and control cleaner may be sufficient to solve the problem. These cleaners come in a small aerosol can with a thin plastic tube in the spray head so that the cleaner may be directed into hard to reach areas. In some cases, partial disassembly will be required in order to reach a switch or control.

Additional Notes on Fitting Ivory Saddles and Nuts

The usual woodworking tools can be used to cut and shape ivory though as you can imagine, the hardness of the material will dull the tools fairly quickly. Rough nuts may be made with a dovetail saw, coping saw, band saw, etc., and initial shaping can be done with wood rasps and mill files. Sandpaper of various grades should be used for the final finishing; you should finish up with 600 grit in order to get a nice polish on the surface.

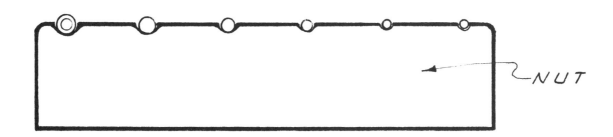

WHEN NOTCHING THE NUT FOR THE STRINGS, ADJUST THE NOTCH SO THAT THE STRING IS SEATED IN THE NOTCH APPROXIMATELY HALF ITS DIAMETER. THE EXCESS NUT MATERIAL ABOVE THE STRING SHOULD BE REMOVED.

If the nut is for a classical guitar and is not glued in place, all of your shaping and polishing may be done with the nut clamped in a vise. If the nut is to be glued in place, it should be roughly shaped before gluing into position. With the nut glued on, the final shaping and polishing can be done a little more easily.

When laying out the spacing for the notches, you may use templates (to select one with the correct spacing, you will have to have a good selection on hand) or lay it out fresh for each instrument. I prefer to start fresh with each instrument so that the spacing of the E string to the edge of the fingerboard can be adjusted precisely to the needs of the player and instrument. With the two outside notches determined, lay out the inside notches with a pair of dividers.

A double slim taper file will quickly cut the string notches down to the approximate string height. The final notching must be done with fine needle files so that the diameter of the strings will be exactly matched by the notches. As a general rule,

the string should be seated in its notch to a depth of approximately one-half its diameter. For the plain steel strings on steel string guitars, use a violin maker's saw; the notches will match the plain steel strings much better than those made with the smallest needle file.

Saddles are shaped with the same tools and methods as nuts. Most saddles are movable and can be shaped easily while held in a vise. With those which are glued in place, do your final shaping *after* the saddle is in position.

It is very important to obtain a snug fit (without forcing) for several reasons. In the first place, a loose fitting saddle will tip forward, decreasing the string height and causing the intonation to go sharp. Second, when a loose saddle tips forward it puts excessive pressure on the front edge of the bridge and can cause the bridge to break. A loose saddle will also contribute toward poor tone quality, so attention paid to proper fitting will pay dividends.

SADDLE CONTOUR

IN SHAPING THE SADDLE, THE TOP SURFACE MAY BE GENTLY ROUNDED AS IN 'A', OR ANGLED SLIGHTLY AS IN 'B'. THE ANGLED SADDLE IS A LITTLE EASIER ON THE STRING AND WILL WEAR LONGER AS WELL. BE SURE TO ALWAYS ROUND OFF ANY SHARP EDGES.

Endpin

An endpin is required whenever a guitar strap is to be used. As a general rule, only one endpin is required since the upper end of the strap is attached to the peghead. Some guitarists, however, prefer to have an additional endpin installed in the heel or upper body because they prefer the type of balance which this attachment point produces. A number of solid body and thin hollow body electrics are produced with two endpins as standard equipment, while most acoustical instruments usually have only one installed.

All steel string guitars, both acoustical and electric, come with an endpin while classical guitars never have one. Though a properly installed endpin does no harm to the tone or the physical structure of the guitar, one should be installed only when absolutely necessary.

Installation

Endpins which are made of plastic (sometimes wood) with a tapered shaft require the use of a reamer to give the proper fit. A pilot hole 1/4 inch in diameter is first drilled in the endblock—centered exactly in the middle. The hole is then opened out with a violin peg reamer so that with a push fit the endpin is seated to within 1/16 inch of the end of the shaft. With a small hammer, the endpin is tapped in the rest of the way.

Metal endpins with a wood screw require only that a small pilot hole be drilled before installation. This type of endpin is required for all solid body guitars and for all endpin installations at the heel of the neck or on the upper body of the guitar.

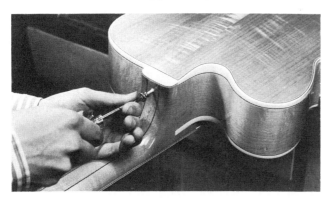

Many guitarists prefer attaching the upper guitar strap at the heel of the neck rather than at the peghead. When installing a metal endpin, drilling a pilot hole and soaping the threads is a prerequisite.

Side Dots

Position markers on the side of the fingerboard are used on most steel string guitars. The usual positions are at the third, fifth, seventh, ninth, twelfth, fifteenth, and seventeenth frets, with most variations occurring in the upper positions. As a general rule, the more expensive guitars—particularly the fancier electrics—carry the most markers.

Classical guitars, as a rule, have no position markers of any kind. It is permissible, however, to install a marker at the seventh fret or, at most, one each at the fifth, seventh, and ninth frets.

Installation

Markers are usually of black or white plastic, depending on the color of the fingerboard or binding. Ivory and mother-of-pearl are also occasionally used. They are usually no more than 1/16 inch in diameter, especially when the marker is for a classical guitar. Ivory markers cannot be purchased ready-made so you must cut and file your own. Bridge saddles are a convenient source and can be made up in easily handled lengths of two or three inches.

The installation procedure is the same for all materials. A pilot hole is first drilled, exactly centered between the frets on either side and large enough to allow a tight fit. Household cement (Duco) is used with plastic though white glue may be used with ivory and mother-of-pearl. If you do use a household cement, use sparingly and be sure to wipe away all surplus immediately before the cement has a chance to eat into the finish.

The marker is pressed firmly in place with a small amount left projecting. When the glue has dried, the marker is filed and sandpapered flush with the edge of the fingerboard. A final French polish completes the job.

Pickguard

Pickguards for flattop guitars can be purchased ready-made for a particular model or, for a custom installation, can be cut from sheet plastic. In general, black and tortoise shell colors are used and when selected, care should be taken to ensure that the material is not too thick. Thirty or forty thousandths of an inch is an acceptable range.

After cutting the plastic, bevel the edge at about a 45 degree angle and smooth with sandpaper for a more finished appearance.

You may use a plastic cement specifically designed for the type of plastic you are using or you may use a contact cement. You must be very careful to keep any cement from the surfaces surrounding the pickguard area as it will soften and damage most surfaces. If you intend to strip the finish later and refinish with the pickguard on, this is no problem.

When gluing a pickguard to a finished guitar when the finish must not be damaged, the choice of glues is limited. White glue is satisfactory since with proper preparation it will hold and at the same time allow the excess to be removed with a damp rag. Proper preparation requires the gluing surfaces of both pickguard and guitar top to be thoroughly roughed up with sandpaper (about 100 grit).

In most cases, it will help to cut templates of quarter inch plywood to spread the pressure from

A full pickguard offers extra protection compared to the original size.

the clamps evenly while the guard is being glued. Spread the glue in a thin even layer and position the pickguard carefully, making sure it doesn't move while tightening the clamps. As many clamps as can be accommodated through the soundhole should be used; in most cases, this will total nine or ten.

Tap Plate

Where protection from fingers and fingernails is required on the top of nylon string guitars, a tap plate is used. Tap plates are always installed on flamenco guitars while classical guitars normally do not have them. Many folk guitarists who play classical guitars (as well as classical guitarists who also play flamenco), however, prefer to have a tap plate installed as it does not detract noticeably from the tone.

Though tap plates were once commonly made with white plastic (and occasionally thin wood) clear plastic is preferred today. The clear plastic—usually eight to ten thousandths of an inch—is glued to the finished guitar with hide glue and, when applied properly, appears perfectly clear and flat. Though this traditional method of application is still used, particularly in Spain, and does not offer the opportunity to select from various thicknesses, the best method makes use of clear contact plastic sheets of the type used for laminating maps and documents. The gauge is correct (two thicknesses available), the plastic is easily cut to size with a pair of scissors, and, when correctly applied, it is durable and clear.

The tap plate, whether single, double, or full width, is first cut to size and checked for fit directly on the guitar. The position of the tap plate may be marked by a couple of pieces of masking tape laid next to an edge. Peel the backing paper off an edge for a distance of three quarters of an inch or so and position this edge carefully on the guitar top. This is the most critical step and care should be taken to see that alignment is perfect before continuing. Once the edge is positioned you may proceed to peel the backing paper, pressing the plastic down as you go so that air bubbles will not be trapped. The final step is to burnish (firmly press down) the entire tap plate, after which the tap plate and top may be polished and the guitar restrung.

<u>TAP PLATES</u>

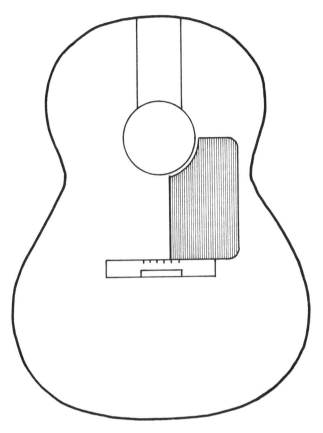

SINGLE TAP PLATE

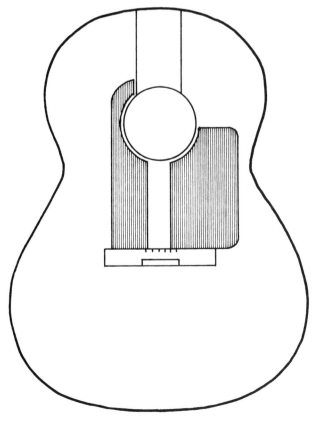

DOUBLE TAP PLATE

FULL TAP PLATE

53

Action and Scale

Equal-Tempered Tuning

A stumbling block for guitar players and guitar makers alike is the concept and application of equal-tempered tuning for the guitar. For some guitar players this takes the form of a futile search for a guitar which will play in tune and/or a repairman who can *make* it play in tune. And the guitar repairman? . . . He's caught in the middle trying to satisfy the player's quest for the perfectly tuned guitar and trying to overcome the shortcomings of the guitar—often without really knowing what to look for! Hence, the reason for this chapter, which is to explain what can or cannot be done by the player in tuning and playing the guitar, and to explain what can or cannot be done by the repairman/builder in setting up and adjusting the guitar for accurate intonation.

Guitar tuning is based on the equal-tempered scale, in which the ratio of each successive semitone to the next is based on the twelfth root of two. The octave is divided into twelve equal semitones, and to achieve this end the frets must be precisely placed. The early lute and viol makers were well aware of the concept of equal temperament and incorporated it in the construction of their instruments. But rather than using lengthy tables or wrestling with calculations for each individual semitone, it is likely that the early makers, in common with many contemporary builders, made use of simple ratios which lent themselves to geometric construction of their scales.

The twelfth root of two equals 1.0594631 (correct to seven places) and it is this ratio of 1.0594631:1 which is used as the basis for computing semitone intervals in equal-tempered tuning. Other ratios have been used in an attempt to derive a simplified means of computing semitone intervals. Among these are the ratios 84:89 (1:1.05952), 101:107 (1:1.05941), and 17:18 (1:1.05882). The first two ratios, 84:89 and 101:107, are very close approximations to equal temperament and find application, for example, in the Stroboconn electronic instrument for measuring frequencies. The last ratio, 17:18, is incorporated in the well-known "eighteen rule" used by guitar makers for laying out scales for fingerboards.

Simply stated, the ratio 17:18 indicates that if a selected string length is divided into eighteen parts, the distance from the saddle to the first fret will equal seventeen parts. The distance from the nut to the first fret will equal 1/18 of the string or scale length. If the remaining distance is again divided into eighteen parts, 1/18 of that distance will be the interval between the first and second frets. By continuing on for each fret, the fret positions for the entire fingerboard can be laid out.

Although the eighteen rule generally serves well for laying out a scale, there are shortcomings which should be noted by the guitar maker. In laying out the scale, the octave or twelfth fret must come out at exactly the midpoint of the scale length. The eighteen rule divides each semitone slightly smaller (1/100 of a semitone per semitone) than the correct amount and the cumulative result is that the octave ends up slightly flat. This amount is equal to 12 cents or 12/100 of a semitone, an amount which is noticeable to the ear.

Obviously, the first step for the guitar maker, when building for the best possible intonation, is to lay out an accurate scale. This requires going back to the original value of the twelfth root of two (1.0594631). The ratio between the scale length and the distance from the bridge to the first fret is 1.0594631:1.

The figure 17.817 is, therefore, a more accurate figure to use than 18 when maximum scale accuracy is desired.

An understanding of the relationship between those musical intervals which are pure and those which have been adjusted through equal temperament is very important. Though the subject is relatively familiar to those associated with keyboard instruments (piano and harpsichord), guitar players, builders, and repairmen have had very little exposure and therefore a short discussion is in order.

Though there are many frequency intervals used in music, the basic ones may be expressed in terms of rather simple mathematical ratios. Two tones of the same frequency are said to be in unison and therefore the frequency ratio is 1:1. An

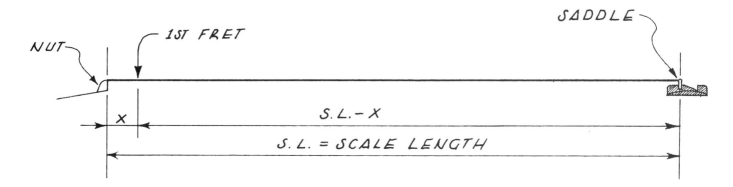

X = DISTANCE FROM NUT TO 1ST FRET.
S.L. = SCALE LENGTH
S.L.-X = DISTANCE FROM BRIDGE SADDLE TO 1ST FRET.

$$\frac{S.L. - X}{S.L.} = \frac{1}{1.0594631}$$

$$S.L. = 1.0594631 \, (S.L. - X)$$

$$S.L.(1.0594631 - 1) = X \, (1.0594631)$$

$$\frac{S.L.}{X} = \frac{1.0594631}{.0594631}$$

$$\frac{S.L.}{X} = 17.817$$

interval of an octave, where the higher frequency is twice as high as the lower, is expressed as a ratio of 1:2. An interval of a fifth is produced when the frequency of the higher tone is one and a half times greater than the lower. This ratio is expressed as 2:3. A few additional intervals are the interval of a major third with a frequency ratio of 4:5 and a fourth with a frequency ratio of 3:4. These intervals or ratios are considered pure or perfect because of the absence of beats.

The octave interval of 1:2 *must always* be pure. If, however, an octave is derived from a cycle of twelve pure fifth intervals, the octave will be wider than the pure octave by 24/100 of a semitone or 24 cents. An octave derived from a succession of fourth intervals will be narrower than a pure octave by 24 cents. Similarly, a succession of major thirds falls short of an octave by 42 cents. A succession of minor thirds is wider than an octave by 64 cents. In the case of the major and minor thirds, the discrepancies from the pure octave equal approximately a half a semitone.

An octave derived from pure intervals of a fifth, fourth, major third, etc., is not usable because it is wider or narrower than pure. Since octaves must be pure, the discrepancies from the pure octave must be absorbed within the various intervals inside the octave and so we come back to the system of equal temperament. Since the intervals must be equalized to fit within the octave, equal temperament, by equalizing the twelve semitones in the octave, gives us an acceptable compromise by allowing us to play all intervals in all keys with the same relative accuracy.

In practice, the only pure intervals normally attainable on the guitar are the unison (1:1) and the octave (1:2). Each fifth interval must be narrowed from pure by 2 cents. Each fourth interval must be widened by 2 cents. Each major third must be widened by 14 cents and each minor third must be narrowed by 16 cents.

In translating the differences between equal-tempered intervals and perfect intervals into the actual mechanics of tuning the guitar we must rely on the use of beats to determine the correctness of our intervals. Beats are produced when two notes, not quite the same in pitch, are sounded together. The alternate increase and decrease in volume is termed beats. Beats can also be produced from intervals such as fourths, thirds, and fifths as well as unison and octave intervals whenever these intervals are not "pure," or exact. Equal temperament requires narrow fifths, very narrow minor thirds, wide fourths, and very wide major thirds. The number of beats per second varies and increases as the intervals ascend. Around middle C (first fret, second string), the fifth interval C-G beats about one per second, the fourth C-F beats one and a half per second, and the major third C-E about ten per second. The beats double in each ascending octave.

Within the range of the open strings of the guitar, the range in which most people do their tuning, the number of beats between strings are as follows.

String	6		5		4		3		2		1
Note	E		A		D		G		B		E
Interval		Fourth		Fourth		Fourth		Major Third		Fourth	
Beats		0.3/sec		0.5/sec		0.6/sec		8/sec		1/sec	

You can see that in all the intervals except one the beats are very slow—so slow that most people will have difficulty counting them. The G-B interval beats at approximately eight per second which is very noticeable. The third interval is significant because the beats stand out so much more noticeably than the fourth interval; the inexperienced player may attempt to tune the third interval pure or beatless.

It is now time to put our theory into practice with regard to the various methods of tuning the guitar.

Tuning Open Strings

For those who can recognize fourth and third intervals, tuning with the open strings is convenient since both hands are free for simultaneous playing and tuning. The important point to remember is that pure intervals, except for the two octave interval E to E, cannot be used. All the fourth intervals must be tuned wide (though the difference is actually very small) and the major third interval is tuned very wide. The tendency is to tune the G-B interval to smooth (beatless) and this must be avoided. The G-B interval must be tuned wide and, though it is difficult to count the beats, nevertheless, practice will give the tuner an ear for the tempered third as opposed to the pure third.

Tuning by the 4-5 Fret Method

In applying this, the most popular method, the B string fretted at the fifth fret is matched (unison) to the high E open. The G fretted at the fourth fret is matched to the B open. The D fretted at the fifth fret is matched to the G open. The A fretted at the fifth fret is matched to the D open, the low E fretted at the fifth fret is matched to the A open. And the low E should also be exactly two octaves below the high E.

Interval	Ratio	Note Interval	Interval in Cents Perfect	Tempered	Difference from Pure (in cents)
1:2	Octave	E:E	1200	1200	Pure
2:3	Fifth	E:B	702	700	2, narrower
3:4	Fourth	E:A	498	500	2, wider
4:5	Major Third	E:G	386	400	14, wider
5:6	Minor Third	E:G	316	300	16, narrower

In principle, this method can be very accurate since we are tuning unison intervals, which are beatless. In actual practice, inaccuracies and errors in tuning often occur, depending upon other outside factors. For example, unless each string is true and has been properly compensated at the bridge, the fretted note will not be accurate. If one string is off, this will introduce errors in tuning the rest of the strings since, it will be noted, only one string is tuned independently—the high E. Each of the other strings is tuned by comparing to another, and if one is mistuned or is false, one or more others will also carry the same error. Since errors tend to be cumulative, this method, which depends upon successive comparisons with adjacent strings, will give widely varying results depending upon how well adjusted the guitar is and upon the skill of the player.

Tuning by the Harmonic Method

The harmonic method is probably the most misunderstood tuning method commonly used today. Held in high esteem by many players, particularly beginners who have difficulty producing the harmonics, the mystique surrounding this method covers the fact that it is *inherently inaccurate*. One of the reasons for going into a fairly lengthy discussion of equal-tempered tuning is to explain exactly why harmonic tuning is unsatisfactory for the guitar.

A short explanation of harmonic tuning in its most common form is in order. Harmonics are produced when a vibrating string is made to vibrate in multiples of its fundamental pitch. Harmonic intervals are always pure, or "perfect." Usually, the high E is tuned according to a reference standard, such as a tuning fork. The low E is then tuned two octaves lower so that it is beatless. Sometimes the harmonic E on the fifth fret is used rather than the fundamental. The A string is next tuned so that its harmonic on the seventh fret will be the same as the harmonic on the low E, fifth fret. The actual note produced is an E, two octaves up from the low E, and the same as the high E. The D string is next tuned so that its harmonic on the seventh fret is the same as the fifth fret harmonic on the A string. This note is an A, two octaves up from the open A. In like fashion the G string harmonic, on the seventh fret is tuned to be beatless with the A string harmonic, fifth fret. The B string harmonic on the fifth fret is tuned to coincide with the seventh fret harmonic on the high E. In addition, the fourth fret harmonic on the G is supposed to equal the fifth fret harmonic on the B string.

If you have tuned accurately—so that the harmonics of each comparison pair, such as the A-D, are beatless—you will find that the high E and low E cannot be maintained at an interval of exactly two octaves. And the proof is in the playing. A guitar tuned strictly according to the harmonic method simply will not play in tune.

The reason, though requiring some explanation, is simple: when tuning by harmonics, you are tuning by pure intervals, rather than by equal-tempered intervals. For example, when tuning the seventh fret harmonic of the A to coincide with the fifth fret harmonic of the E, what is actually produced on the A is an interval of a perfect fifth. You will recall that an equal-tempered fifth is narrower than a perfect fifth. The open string A, in other words, is lower in pitch than the desired equal-tempered A. Since the open string interval between the E and A must be an equal-tempered fourth which is *wider* than a perfect fourth, the lowered A which has been produced through harmonic is too flat and results in an E-A fourth interval which is too narrow. The D and G produced through this method will also be flat and since the G depends on the D and the D upon the A, each successive string will be progressively flatter.

With the B to high E relationship which also makes use of the perfect fifth interval, the resulting open B will be too sharp compared to the open E.

The really convincing demonstration of the differences between equal-tempered and pure intervals comes when tuning the G to the B by use of harmonics. The fourth fret harmonic of the G (which is a B) is tuned in unison with the fifth fret harmonic (a B, two octaves higher than the open B) of the B string. This puts the open G a pure major third away from the B. The interval is much too narrow and will be badly off (the G string too sharp) when the G is fretted at the fourth fret to match the B open. The equal-tempered major third is much wider than pure, especially when compared with the small differences between pure and equal-tempered fourths and fifths.

At this point, it should be clear that harmonics can't be relied on when tuning in the equal-tempered system. Harmonic tuning does have its uses, however, and is very handy for doing the rough or preliminary tuning. Since the harmonic of the string sounds freely without having to fret the string, tuning can be accomplished while the string is still vibrating, speeding up the whole process.

Tuning by Octaves

Since the octave and unison intervals are the only ones which are pure, this system lends itself to accurate tuning since we can tune for beatless intervals and at the same time be assured that the tuning will be equally tempered. Harmonic octaves which are pure in equal temperament can also be used and are not to be classed with harmonics of other intervals.

There are various combinations of octave intervals which can be used. Also, you may use an octave harmonic of a fretted string. For example, the octave harmonic of the E string fretted on the fifth fret will be in unison with the high E. I would suggest, however, that rather than tuning successive adjacent pairs of strings, you tune each new string to the original reference string. In this way, errors which may be introduced will not throw everything off.

If, for example, the reference standard is the high E, a typical tuning procedure by octaves can be as follows. B string fifth fret will be in unison with the high E. G string ninth fret will be E unison. D string fourteenth fret will be E unison. A string seventh fret will be E octave. Low E will be two octaves below high E.

An additional octave check can be made between various string pairs. This order is suggested to minimize cumulative errors.

Compare the first and sixth: tune the sixth.

Compare the first and fourth: tune the fourth.

Compare the first and third: tune the third.

Compare the fourth and second: tune the second.

Compare the third and fifth: tune the fifth.

This octave check can be used in any fret position, since all strings are fretted.

Each string can usually be compared with several others so that a quick cross-check between various strings can be made. Errors in tuning show up more clearly in the upper positions so it is recommended that octave comparisons be done in the area between the seventh and twelfth frets.

Avoid tuning with chords. If you tune, adjusting for pure or perfect intervals within that one chord, other chords will be thrown completely off. This comes back to the reason for using equal temperament in the first place—to equalize the semitone intervals so that all chords in all keys will sound equally agreeable. Do use chords to *check* on the accuracy of your tuning; no one chord should sound any worse (or better) than any other.

The important points to remember are that equal-tempered tuning is the basic system in use and that the guitar is constructed to play in equal temperament. This means that perfect intervals and chords in all keys are an *impossibility*. However, chords and intervals *can* be made to sound quite acceptable in all keys provided the guitar player tunes within the guidelines of tempered tuning and provided the guitar maker and repairman construct and adjust the instrument within those same guidelines. *(See chart at top of next page.)*

Stroboconn Tuning

A visual frequency measuring device which has proven extremely useful in the repair shop is an electronic instrument called the Stroboconn. This instrument, as well as a smaller version called the Strobotuner, manufactured by the Conn Instrument Corporation, greatly simplifies the adjusting of a compensated bridge and enables the repairman to determine the scale accuracy of a fingerboard as well as the accuracy of each individual note produced by a string. The instrument will detect frequency changes smaller than the ear is able to and gets around the problem of tone quality obscuring the actual pitch of the note.

In brief, the Stroboconn converts the incoming signal from the guitar to a flashing light of the same frequency as the note being played. Twelve stroboscope discs driven by a motor and geared to turn at speeds corresponding to all of the notes of the equal-tempered scale are illuminated by the strobe light. When the frequency of the note corresponds exactly to one of the discs, that disc will appear to have stopped and the marks on the wheel will appear stationary. When the note is sharp the marks will go to the right and when the note is flat the marks will go to the left. The speed at which the marks move left or right gives a rough indication of how flat or sharp the note is. In addition, the instrument is calibrated in one cent intervals (one hundred cents between successive semitones)

The Notes of the Guitar
(A = 440 Hz)

Name	No.	Hz	No.	Hz	No.	Hz	No.	Hz
E	1	82.407	13	164.814	25	329.628	37	659.255
F	2	87.307	14	174.614	26	349.228	38	698.456
F♯	3	92.499	15	184.997	27	369.994	39	739.989
G	4	97.999	16	195.998	28	391.995	40	783.991
G♯	5	103.826	17	207.652	29	415.305	41	830.609
A	6	110.000	18	220.000	30	440.000	42	880.000
A♯	7	116.541	19	233.082	31	466.164	43	932.328
B	8	123.471	20	246.942	32	493.883	44	987.767
C	9	130.813	21	261.626	33	523.251	45	1046.502
C♯	10	138.591	22	277.183	34	554.365	46	1108.231
D	11	146.832	23	293.665	35	587.330	47	1174.659
D♯	12	155.563	24	311.127	36	622.254	48	1244.508

E1 is sixth string open. C45 is first string twentieth fret.
E37 is first string twelfth fret. Bass guitar, divide frequency in half.

This table is based on a table in: W.B. White, *Piano Tuning and Allied Arts*, 5th ed., Boston, Mass., Tuners Supply Co.

and can determine the actual amount of error.

While the Stroboconn has been used by band directors and piano tuners for many years, its use in the guitar repair field has, to my knowledge, never been reported. Although it is a substantial monetary investment, it is worth consideration for the repair shop which has the volume of business to put it to frequent use. Besides saving the substantial time needed to tune by ear and taking the element of guesswork out of the procedure, the following applications have become "standard" procedures over a number of years.

Uses of Stroboconn and Strobotuner

Adjusting Compensated Bridges

On those guitars with individually adjustable string saddles, adjusting the compensation for each string becomes a matter of routine, is quick, and, most important of all, is very accurate. Play the harmonic at the twelfth fret, fret the note, and adjust the saddle so that both harmonic and fretted note leave the strobe disc stationary. With electric guitars, you may plug the instrument directly into the strobe without using an amplifier. With an acoustic guitar, a microphone placed near the top will feed the signal to the strobe. For many years, a "Strobe-tune" has been a standard adjustment for electric guitars and basses.

Making a Compensated Saddle

When making a compensated saddle for a guitar, you are able to measure the amount of compensation required for each string, reducing the amount of trial and error. In most cases, measuring the amount of error with the original saddle will give you a good idea how much to compensate each string. You will find that, in a saddle compensation job, a thick saddle 1/8 inch in width will provide a more effective range of compensation than the usual 1/16 inch thickness.

See photos on following page.

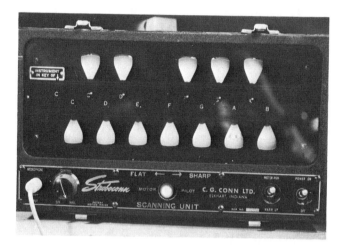

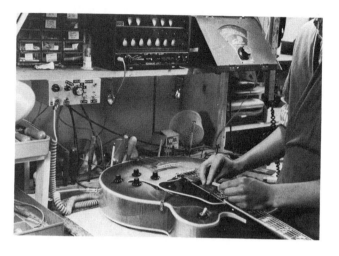

Checking Accuracy of Strings and Fingerboards

Strings, even when new, can be false and play out of tune just as easily as old ones. Fingerboards on guitars of any quality rarely cause problems related to accuracy of fret placement. With the Stroboconn you can determine whether a tuning problem is in the string, the fingerboard, or the bridge.

Checking Accuracy of Tuning

It is a simple matter to check whether or not the guitar is tuned since you can see, simultaneously, the tuning of all six guitar strings. It is possible to see, for example, the tuning of the individual notes within a chord simultaneously! Using the Stroboconn is one of the best ways in which to prove to yourself and to the customer the principles of equal-tempered tuning as applied to the guitar.

Tuning Autoharps

While not a fretted instrument, autoharps are closely allied to other folk instruments and when they need repairs they are brought to the guitar shop. In tuning the autoharp, all strings are played "open" and, except for octave comparisons, must be tuned in terms of intervals such as third, fourth, and fifth. Unless you have had training in hearing intervals (in equal temperament at that) you must

use a pitch pipe which is not always accurate. The fastest and most accurate way, of course, is with the Stroboconn.

String Compensation

No guitar will play in tune unless the strings have the proper amount of compensation. The scale length and the proper fret intervals are determined by formula. In practice, however, the actual string length of the instrument is always slightly greater than the mathematical scale length; it is this small extra length (that must be added to the scale length) that is generally referred to as compensation.

The mechanics of playing the guitar or any fretted instrument requires that the strings be raised a certain distance above the frets in order to keep them, when vibrating, from buzzing or rattling on the frets. Since the vibrating string has its widest swing in the open position and because the widest part of its arc occurs at the twelfth fret, the clearance above the frets gradually increases from a minimum at the first fret to a maximum at the nineteenth (or highest) fret. When the string is pressed down to the fret, it is stretched a certain amount; this amount increases as one goes toward the higher fret positions because the distance from the string to the fret also increases.

60

The effect of this slight stretching is to raise the frequency of the desired note higher than what would be expected from a mathematical calculation. Since the stretching increases in the higher positions, the difference between the desired and the actual note produced also increases—many readers have probably played instruments which became increasingly out of tune as they progressed up the fingerboard.

A second reason for compensation is that each string, depending on its method of construction, requires a different amount of compensation. With nylon strings, for example, the third will require slightly more compensation than the first, and the sixth will require a bit more than the fourth. For nylon strings, the wound fourth requires less than the plain third. With steel strings, the second will require more compensation than the first and the sixth will require more than the third. With steel strings, in addition, the wound third generally requires less compensation than the plain second.

The range of compensation required with nylon strings (from first to sixth) is quite small and for all practical purposes a straight saddle giving equal compensation to both bass and treble strings is satisfactory. With steel strings, however, the bass strings require much more compensation than the treble strings; a compensated bridge can vary from a simple slanted saddle (giving maximum compensation to the sixth string) to a saddle which compensates for every string. The latter type of bridge, which is found principally on plectrum and electric guitars, may even have individually adjustable saddles for each string.

The repairman can check the instrument for correct compensation by comparing the harmonic produced at the twelfth fret with the fretted note produced at the twelfth fret. If the fretted note is higher than the harmonic the string in question needs more compensation. If the fretted note is lower, the string needs less compensation. In summary, the following rules can be used as *general* guides to help the repairman determine the proper amount of compensation.

1) Classical guitars (nylon strings) with medium scale length should be compensated 1/32 to 1/16 inch. Although it is customary to give equal compensation to all strings, most guitars will benefit by slanting the saddle so that the sixth string has 1/64 to 1/32 inch more compensation than the first.

2) Guitars with steel strings require 1/8 to 3/16 inch compensation on the bass side and 1/32 to 1/16 inch on the treble. The amount of compensation required for steel strings varies considerably, depending upon the scale length, gauge of string, and string action; only *very* general guides can be given when details of a particular guitar are unspecified.

3) In general, short scale length guitars require more compensation than long scale instruments.

4) High tension strings require less compensation than low tension strings. The difference between high and low tension nylon strings is quite small and in most instances can be ignored. Steel strings, on the other hand, vary radically in their requirements and for best results the repairman should adjust the instrument together with the type of strings normally used by the player.

5) A high action requires more compensation than a low one; steel strings are more sensitive to changes in action than nylon strings. As a matter of fact, it is useless to adjust compensation until the instrument has been adjusted for a suitable string action.

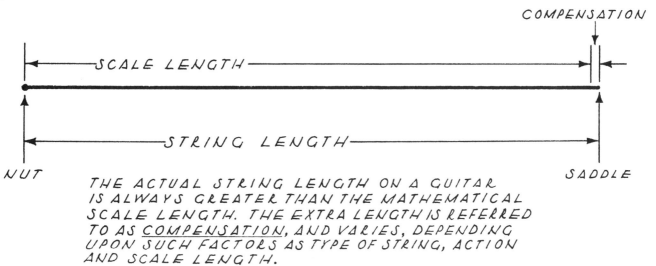

THE ACTUAL STRING LENGTH ON A GUITAR IS ALWAYS GREATER THAN THE MATHEMATICAL SCALE LENGTH. THE EXTRA LENGTH IS REFERRED TO AS <u>COMPENSATION</u>, AND VARIES, DEPENDING UPON SUCH FACTORS AS TYPE OF STRING, ACTION AND SCALE LENGTH.

String Action and Scale Accuracy

Before any work is undertaken on the bridge, neck, or fingerboard, you should be thoroughly familiar with the principles and methods involved in adjusting a guitar to scale accurately and to play with the best possible action. A correct diagnosis and repair or adjustment is particularly important in this area not only from the player's standpoint but also to prevent damage to the instrument through carelessness or lack of understanding. Unlike instruments of the violin family where the fingerboard and bridge are relatively easily replaced or adjusted, the fretted fingerboard and glued-on bridge of the classical or flattop guitar do not lend themselves to easy replacement. All adjustments must also be held to close tolerances and, because of the difficulty of replacement, must be done correctly the first time.

Neck Relief

Many people assume that an instrument must have an absolutely straight neck in order to be acceptable. If the instrument shows the slightest deviation from this standard, the instrument is discarded or sent out for repair with the remark, "warped neck."

An instrument in perfect adjustment, however, does not have a straight neck. Such an instrument will have a slight curvature or relief in the fingerboard. This relief, which may look like a warp caused by the tension of the strings, is essential for a soft action in the upper positions of the fingerboard. If carried to an extreme, of course, the neck will indeed be warped, causing buzzes which can be eliminated only by raising the strings high off the fingerboard and causing, in return, problems in scale accuracy.

Relief Chart — *Measured at* *Fifth Fret*	Guitar Type	Relief — Treble	64ths Bass	Notes
	Classical or Flamenco	1-2/64	2-3/64	One setting is suitable for most classical and flamenco guitars—the majority of scale lengthss and string tensions fall within this setting.
	Steel String Acoustic	1-2/64	2-3/64	Country flatpicking and heavy bass rhythm may require slightly more relief. This setting is fine for most fingerpicking. Lead players may require slightly less relief.
	Steel String Electric	1-2/64	2-3/64	Lead players may require less relief. Rhythm playing may require slightly more relief.
	Rock & Roll Electric	0-1/64	1-2/64	This setting is best when strings are "bent" frequently in the upper positions.
	Electric Bass	2-3/64	3-4/64	For all Fender and long scale basses. Increase slightly for short scale basses. Adjustment can vary widely for each bass.

GENERAL NOTES

1. All measurements are based on the use of medium gauge strings except as otherwise noted.
2. Long scales require less relief.
3. Short scales require more relief.
4. Emphasis on the lower positions and open strings requires more relief.
5. Emphasis on the upper positions requires less relief.
6. Light gauge strings and light playing requires less relief.
7. Heavy gauge strings and heavy playing require more relief.

FINGERBOARD RELIEF

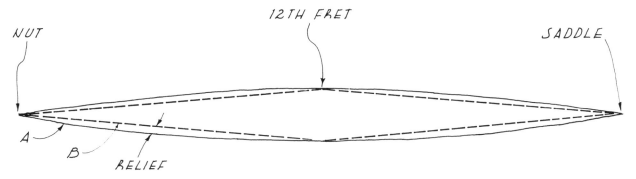

NUT

12TH FRET

SADDLE

A

B

RELIEF

(A) = OUTLINE OF VIBRATING STRING (OPEN POSITION, FUNDAMENTAL)
(B) = STRAIGHT LINE FROM NUT OR SADDLE TO 12TH FRET (MIDPOINT)
RELIEF = DIFFERENCE BETWEEN A AND B AT 5TH FRET

Our concern, for the moment, centers around the slight relief that is *intentionally* put in by the guitar maker/repairman to obtain proper action. An outline of a vibrating string in its simplest form will appear similar to A (see diagram). Note that the string is curved along its entire length. A string does not vibrate in the manner indicated by the dotted line B. Though this string behavior is most pronounced in a string bass, the player can observe this for himself on any stringed instrument.

The reason for the curvature now becomes clear. In order to keep the strings from buzzing on the frets near the nut, the fingerboard must be relieved at that point. The only other alternative is to raise the string height at the saddle. The unavoidable consequence of this alternate adjustment is that the instrument will have a hard action because the strings in the upper position will be higher than the minimum height actually required for a clean sound. A properly relieved fingerboard will follow the curvature of the vibrating string.

The relief is of greatest importance in the open position and is confined to the distance between the nut and the twelfth fret. The fingerboard past the twelfth fret should be straight. Of course the relief will become incorrect in the upper part of the fingerboard but since the strings vibrate less widely in the higher positions, the amount of relief required becomes so small that it may be disregarded.

One can make a quick check of the correct amount of relief by sighting down the neck with the strings up to playing tension. A very slight curvature along the length of the fingerboard with a rise of approximately 1/64 to 1/32 inch between the first and twelfth frets can be expected in a properly relieved neck. The amount of relief will vary a small amount, of course, with the scale length, strings, etc. A more accurate method of checking relief and action is to *deliberately* force a buzz by extra hard playing.

1) If buzzes are heard on all frets, the action and relief may be considered nearly correct; no buzzes will be heard in normal playing and only small adjustments will be required at the saddle to suit the playing style of the individual.

NECK ANGLE

LINE OF NECK

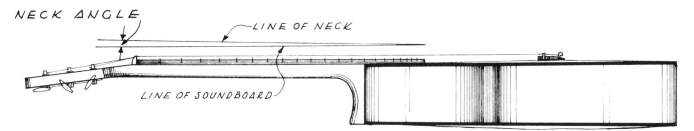

LINE OF SOUNDBOARD

THE NECK ANGLE ON CLASSICAL, FLAMENCO AND STEEL STRING FLAT TOP GUITARS WILL VARY SLIGHTLY, DEPENDING UPON GUITAR STYLE, SCALE LENGTH AND TOP ARCHING. THE ACTUAL RISE AT THE NUT VARIES BETWEEN 0" AND 1/8".

2) If the strings buzz only in the upper positions, the neck may be warped or have too much relief. In some cases, the neck may have pulled up through the tension of the strings.

3) If buzzes are encountered only in the lower positions (near the nut), the neck may have insufficient relief or may be warped backwards.

4) If no buzzes are found at all, the saddle height may be lowered if a softer action is desired.

5) The string height at the nut should be just enough to give a clean sound on the *open strings*. The height at the nut has negligible effect on the action other than on the first fret.

No one adjustment will satisfy all people; the string action must be set to suit the playing style of the individual.

Neck Angle and Bridge Saddle Height

The height of the saddle must be within certain prescribed limits in order to produce maximum tone and volume. For classical and flamenco guitars (and steel string flattops as well) this height from top of saddle to guitar face varies between 3/8 and 1/2 inch, with flamenco guitars closer to the lower figure and classical guitars the higher. Assuming that the fingerboard relief is correct, it is a simple matter to check for proper neck angle; the angle is automatically correct if, when the saddle height is within our allowable limits, the action is also correct for that particular instrument. At the nut the neck will be tipped up anywhere from 0 to 1/8 inch in relation to the plane of the top (viewed from the side), depending on the fingerboard thickness, the arching of the top, and the style.

The repairman will be concerned more with the steps necessary to correct an incorrect angle than with the actual angle used by the builder. Plectrum guitars with their high arching and fingerboard clear of the body require that the neck be set at an angle opposite to that of the usual classical guitar. The bridges which are movable and adjustable for height (around 1 inch) make it relatively easy to adjust for correct scale and action.

New guitars may come to the shop with neck angles either too high or too low and the repair-man should know how to correct both conditions. In older instruments the neck may be at too high an angle because the tension of the strings has, over the years, pulled up the neck and top of the instrument. A cracked heel or loose dovetail joint will also give the same effect. By sighting down the edge of the fingerboard from the peghead toward the bridge, a sharp angle where the neck joins the body is an almost sure indication that the angle is not correct. Such an angle will, of course, make it impossible to obtain the correct relief along the entire length of the fingerboard.

Fingerboard and Frets

The fingerboard must always be included when checking an instrument for faulty response, though for the present our discussion will omit actual checking of the fret intervals. The laying of a scale and the method for checking fret accuracy is covered in Chapter Six. An inspection should show, for the present, that the fingerboard and frets are reasonably free from wear, that the fingerboard is straight (allowing for relief), and that the string notches in the nut are properly cut. Wear or improper adjustment in any of these areas will give intonation problems which must not be confused with problems caused by improper fret placement.

It should be noted that even the cheapest factory guitars generally have accurate fingerboards. The worst examples are usually the inexpensive handmade guitars of which an example would be the cheap "border" guitar from Mexico. On particularly bad examples, errors in fret spacing are readily apparent to the eye; for instance, the space between the fifth and sixth frets may be greater than the space between the fourth and fifth. It's extremely unlikely that an expensive instrument (factory or handmade) will have a fingerboard with improperly placed frets. Here, however, the cost of replacing a fingerboard is justifiable. With a cheap instrument (discount store special), however, the owner faces the prospect of paying more for the repair than the instrument is worth. Fortunately, the cause of faulty scale and intonation generally is something other than the fingerboard, and if inspection shows that worn and uneven frets can be dressed down and leveled satisfactorily, you can then turn your attention to string compensation.

The Peghead

Repairs

Repairs to pegheads can range from fixing small splits, requiring no more than gluing and clamping, to replacement of the entire peghead. The replacement of a peghead requires much the same skills as needed for making a new neck plus the extra effort of matching and splicing the new work to the old. In most cases, however, repairs are hardly this extensive, though care must be taken to ensure that the finished repair is as strong or stronger than the part was before the break.

For a number of reasons, most of the problems associated with pegheads occur on the lower-priced instruments. Poor wood, greater overall number of instruments, and abusive treatment all contribute. Construction practices have a direct bearing on the frequency of repair; the one-piece band-sawn neck is weaker than the spliced variety. The provisions for adjusting torsion bars, when at the peghead end, can also seriously weaken a neck because a substantial amount of material must be removed from the peghead at one of its weakest points.

It would be natural to assume that classical guitars with the more delicate slotted pegheads require more frequent repair than those instruments with solid pegheads. In actual practice most peghead breaks occur on steel string guitars with solid pegheads, and of this group the largest number occur on electric guitars. A number of separate conditions are responsible, the first one being the weakening of the neck from the adjustment provisions for the truss rod. In addition, the machines used on steel string guitars are frequently large and heavy and put more stress on the peghead in an accidental fall. But probably the main reason more electric guitars break pegheads than any other group is related to the overall weight of the instrument. Electrics are much heavier than other guitars, and in an accidental fall that extra weight is

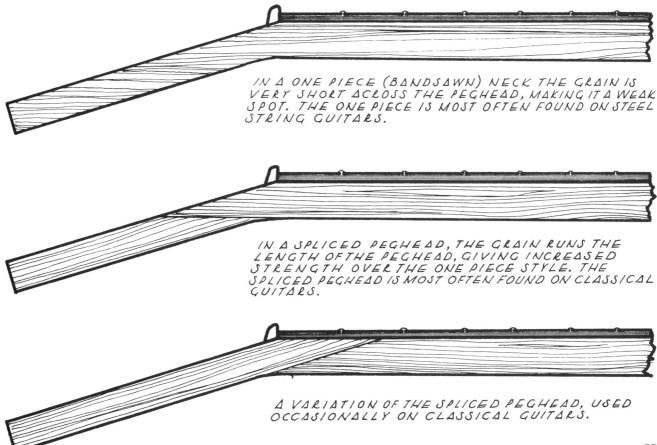

IN A ONE PIECE (BANDSAWN) NECK THE GRAIN IS VERY SHORT ACROSS THE PEGHEAD, MAKING IT A WEAK SPOT. THE ONE PIECE IS MOST OFTEN FOUND ON STEEL STRING GUITARS.

IN A SPLICED PEGHEAD, THE GRAIN RUNS THE LENGTH OF THE PEGHEAD, GIVING INCREASED STRENGTH OVER THE ONE PIECE STYLE. THE SPLICED PEGHEAD IS MOST OFTEN FOUND ON CLASSICAL GUITARS.

A VARIATION OF THE SPLICED PEGHEAD, USED OCCASIONALLY ON CLASSICAL GUITARS.

often enough to snap a peghead. When a neck is band-sawn from a single block of wood, the grain runs diagonally across from upper to lower surface; the short grain makes the peghead highly susceptible to splits or breaks caused by accidental pressure or force. The spliced peghead, on the other hand, with the grain running the entire length of the peghead, is much stronger and is less likely to break under strain.

Hot glue is best suited for mending breaks in the peghead. Such adhesives as contact cement and household cement should never be used since, under continuous tension, they tend to creep. Even epoxy cements, unless of the highest grade and exactly mixed, stand a good chance of failure, since curing at high temperatures is out of the question; in addition, there is the difficulty of working the adhesive into the break and cleaning up the excess.

Simple splits or cracks, when the peghead has not completely broken away and where the length of the break is relatively long (added gluing surface), can usually be repaired by working in hot glue and clamping. More extensive breaks, where the peghead has broken completely away, require much care in fitting and gluing. Since the break is usually on the bias, great care should be taken to ensure that the parts do not slip during clamping.

Extensive cracks with many pieces broken and missing may require replacement of the peghead overlay. The overlay veneer contributes to the strength of the peghead; a strong veneer, such as rosewood, can, in many situations, greatly enhance the strength and appearance of the repair. Wood inserts can also be used, these being inserted and glued from the underside.

If the damage is severe and the value of the instrument warrants it, a new peghead can be spliced onto the existing neck. The method of splicing will vary, depending on the nature and location of the break. If enough of the peghead remains, one of the simplest and strongest methods is to splice the new section on a long taper the same as a peghead splice on a new neck. When well done, such a splice will look like the original construction, giving no hint that it has been repaired.

One can also splice in a modified dovetail fashion, such as used on many old guitars, particularly of European origin.

For situations in which the peghead has broken away beneath the nut, a very nice solution is to splice beneath the fingerboard at about the second

Reinforcement of a broken peghead is required in some cases. This Gibson S-400 peghead has been routed to accept two inlays which extend the full depth of the neck and peghead. After the glue dries, the inlays are trimmed and the finish is touched up.

fret. With a long glue joint and the fingerboard above it for reinforcement, this type of splice is strong and quite attractive. Some handmade classical guitars are originally constructed in this fashion.

The final shaping of the new peghead is best done after the splicing operation. It should be made to look as much like the original as possible. Regardless of the repairman's artistic talents, those of the original maker should be respected and adhered to; one should not try to "improve" the shape of the peghead since it is one of the identifying marks of the maker.

Little else remains to be said about making and splicing pegheads. A router bit can be used to cut the slots for classical pegheads. The ends of the slots may be either squared off or left round, depending on the style of the original. The veneer overlay is generally glued on after the splice has been completed. Improvements in style and quality of machine heads can be made at this time since, in

many cases, the original machines have been damaged along with the peghead. When a new peghead is necessary it might in some instances be practical to change from a slotted peghead with machines to a flamenco peghead with friction pegs. The slotted peghead of a steel string folk guitar can, in similar fashion, be converted to a solid peghead.

Machine Head Installation

Solid Peghead Steel String

Individual heads are the simplest type to install; keeping a few rules in mind, you should experience no difficulties whatever. In arranging the spacing of the heads on a new guitar or new peghead, or on a peghead which has been plugged because of excessive wear of the pegholes, you should make certain that, aside from arranging the heads to suit the proportions of the peghead, the strings do not foul each other when going to their respective rollers. Holes for the rollers should be drilled absolutely perpendicular to the face of peghead—a drill press should be used if available—and eyelets should always be used, these being installed with the aid of a reamer to give a tight hand fit. The rest of the installation is perfectly straightforward and should be concluded with a drop of oil on the gears and a check to see that all heads turn smoothly. Many of the better machines are covered and contain a supply of grease; these machines, of course, require no oil. The turning pressure on some heads, such as the Grover Rotomatic can be regulated by means of a screw in the end of the button; this should be tightened only enough to prevent accidental movement of the button.

If the machine heads are of the three or six on a plate variety, one will have to exercise additional care to ensure that all holes are drilled with correct spacing and alignment. The heads should be installed so that counterclockwise rotation of the button, looking at the peghead from the side, increases string tension.

Slotted Peghead

The installation of classical machine heads with wide rollers in the slotted type of peghead requires a great deal of attention for proper fitting. Because of the construction of the peghead and because of the greatly reduced tension of the nylon strings compared to steel, any inaccuracies in spacing and alignment will result in unsatisfactory operation due to jamming or sticking of the gears and rollers. Details of installation which follow will yield the best results with the minimum amount of time.

Classical machine heads are almost universally made with three gears on a single plate, with a set consisting of left and right plates. With a few minor exceptions, the heads are usually supplied in either long (European or Spanish) spacing 1 9/16 inch between rollers, or short (American) 1 3/8 inch spacing. "Metric" spacing (1 1/4 inch) is found on many inexpensive guitars—primarily Japanese—though it should be noted that most Japanese guitars utilize the short American spacing. The spacing refers to the distance from centerline to centerline between rollers. If the work requires replacement of the existing machine heads, the job is simplified if the new heads have the same spacing as the old set, though plugging and drilling may be required anyway if the original installation was poorly done.

With a new peghead or one with the holes plugged, the choice of heads is determined by aesthetic considerations—whether they fit the proportions and style of the peghead—and by mechanical considerations—whether there is adequate clearance for the strings as they pass to their respective rollers. Given a choice and provided the peghead is long enough to accept it gracefully, the long spaced machine heads give the most pleasing appearance because a peghead designed with these machines in mind achieves the best feeling of balance against the proportions of the usual modern classical guitar.

In drilling the holes for the rollers, it should be kept in mind that occasionally the gears have been so tightly assembled that the rollers are sometimes not exactly perpendicular to the plates. The holes should be drilled so that the angle of the roller to the plate of the machines is exactly matched.

Lacking a drill press, a doweling jig is a useful tool when drilling the holes since it has provision for holding different size drills as well as for aligning the drill identically for each hole. A 3/8 inch hole serves for most roller sizes with the final sizing done with a reamer.

The use of the reamer is important because the bearing surfaces for the roller should be at the outer end and at the hole drilled in the plate for the roller shaft. The hole in the cheek of the pegbox should be large enough so that it completely clears the roller. In addition, many rollers are tapered as well so that the reaming of the peghole becomes doubly important. A cello peg reamer serves nicely for reaming the pegholes. The final step in fitting is to gouge small depressions in the cheeks to clear the rivet ends protruding from the underside of the plates. With a little oil applied to the gears and a little soap rubbed on the end of the roller, the machines can be assembled onto the peghead.

As in the case with the solid peghead, counterclockwise rotation of the buttons (viewed from the back of the peghead) should increase tension of the strings. The lyre on the plate, if it has one, is usually at the upper end of the peghead.

Types of Machine heads

The selection of machine heads is so varied in terms of price and style that a brief description of the major types together with their applications is in order. It is necessary to use the correct type of machine head for a particular guitar. Also, quality and price is a necessary consideration since a set of heads can run from less than four dollars to sixty dollars or more, though the cost of installation doesn't necessarily increase with the quality of the heads.

Machine heads designed for the classical or slotted peghead can have wide or narrow rollers, depending on the application and the type of strings used. The wide roller, usually plastic pressed over a brass or steel core, is used only with nylon strings. The large diameter of the roller quickens the winding rate and, because the nylon strings stretch much more than steel, the faster rate enables tuning to be accomplished more quickly and with less effort. Steel strings must not be used with this type of machine head because the greatly increased tension plus the wide roller place an excessive strain on all parts of the machine. With few exceptions, such as the folk guitar designed for either steel or nylon strings and some twelve-string

Guitar machine heads. Classical: upper and lower right (wide rollers); steel string: upper and lower left (narrow rollers).

guitars, machine heads for the slotted peghead with narrow rollers are found only on the lower quality classical guitars; they are never used on the better quality ones. Items to look for in quality classical machine heads, apart from clean workmanship and good materials, are buttons that are riveted rather than pressed onto their shafts, engraving on the plates rather than stampings, substantial construction throughout, and a smooth functioning of the gears. Machine heads with mechanical features equal to the best available can be bought for less than twenty-five dollars. Above that, one pays for extra ornamentation such as silver or gold plating, mother-of-pearl buttons, and fancy engravings.

Machine heads for the solid peghead—found, for example, on flattop and plectrum guitars—are made for use almost exclusively with steel strings. These heads feature narrow rollers (with the string hole at the end), are frequently available as individual heads rather than the usual three on a plate, and generally are constructed much more sturdily throughout compared with the usual classical head. The price range is similar, though the higher-priced heads are available only as individuals, reflecting the style and requirements of the guitars they are most often fitted to. Eyelets for the rollers should always be used since without them the tension of the strings would quickly wear the peghole, allowing the roller and gears to lose alignment and bind.

Occasionally one encounters guitars fitted with banjo-type machine heads, either 1:1 ratio or geared. The geared types are much more satisfactory for use with steel strings than the simple 1:1 friction type; if it is desired to retain this style of peg, the geared type should be used if possible. Though the peghead can be converted to the conventional machine, requiring, at most, plugging and redrilling pegholes, one should take into consideration the style and quality of the guitar before deciding to change. Some of the older Martin guitars, for example had geared banjo-type pegs as a distinguishing feature, and it is best to preserve these instruments in their original condition.

Flamenco Peg Installation

The pegheads of flamenco guitars traditionally require the violin type of peg, held by friction only, and though this type of peg has declined in popularity, it is still to be seen occasionally on new flamenco guitars. The flamenco peghead has a feeling of grace and simplicity that is missing in the

Below Left

A violin peghole reamer is used for fitting flamenco pegs. Care should be taken to ensure that the hole is reamed accurately and perpendicular to the plane of the peghead surface. Note that the end of the peg is only 3/8 inch above the peghead and that the holes for the strings are close to the peghead. The peghead splice can be clearly seen in this photo.

Below Right

Flamenco pegs must project above the peghead about 3/8 inch to allow room for winding the string. The string should be wound from the string hole down toward the peghead.

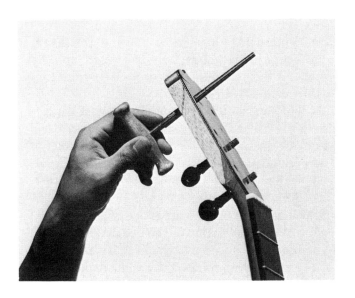
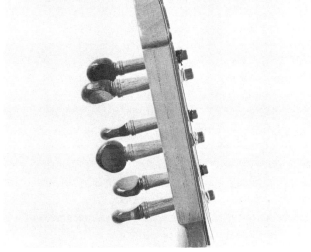

usual head with patent machines. The lightness of the peghead contributes to the balance of the guitar, enabling the guitarist to more easily hold the instrument in the flamenco position than if the peghead were fitted with machine heads. Because the use of wood pegs in flamenco guitars is functional and artistic and contributes to the whole concept of the flamenco guitar, one should keep such instruments original rather than give in to the temptation to convert to machine heads. Adhering to the original purpose or concept of the flamenco guitar (as opposed to the different requirements of, say, the classical guitar) is of particular importance with the better or older instruments, though the fitting of machine heads to a guitar not originally equipped isn't nearly as bad as the fitting of patent heads to a fine old violin!

Wood pegs can and will work quite well when properly fitted. The fitting of pegs, however, requires knowledge and tools normally associated only with violin repair shops. The requirements in the way of tools are: violin peghole reamer, peg shaper of the same taper, soap and blackboard chalk (or peg dope). If the old pegs are in good condition, they can be simply refitted. If the pegs are to be replaced, or pegs installed in a new guitar, some attention will have to be devoted to the choice of pegs.

Ebony and occasionally rosewood are the only materials used for pegs which are suitable for the purpose and character of the flamenco guitar. Boxwood pegs, though quite elegant on a violin, are not in keeping with the style of the instrument. You must use your own judgment in choosing quality, style of peg, and ornamentation. As for the size of peg, the best are those of somewhat generous proportions intended for violas. Violin pegs are too small in proportion to the peghead size. The pegs sold as flamenco pegs are sometimes of mediocre quality and are a bit undersized as well, though they do have the ornamentation expected of them (mother-of-pearl in the ends).

With a new guitar, the pilot holes must first be drilled, taking care to drill perpendicular to the peghead surface. Small discrepancies in alignment can be taken care of when reaming the hole, though the amount is usually limited when refitting pegs or when fitting new pegs in an old peghead. The holes are reamed to fit each individual peg; the peg end should project about 3/8 inch above the peghead surface.

It may happen that the pegholes in an old head have become so worn that reaming a sufficient amount to remove the wear will make the hole too large for the peg. The solution is to plug the holes and drill, shaping the plug with the peg shaper tool to fit the taper of the hole. As in violin repair, the best material for plugging pegholes is boxwood. Properly done, the boxwood bushing will provide a better and longer lasting fit than the softer, original mahogany.

When plugging and drilling any oversize hole, whether for flamenco pegs or for machine heads, you will find that it is always easier to obtain a good fit by using a tapered plug rather than one with a constant diameter. It is always best to ream the old hole slightly to true the hole and to expose a fresh wood surface for gluing the plug. By following the same steps for fitting the plug or for fitting a peg you should be able to fit a plug to very close tolerances. Boxwood has a very fine and even grain so that it is unimportant which direction the grain faces when inserting into the hole. With other woods where the grain is more prominent and where the choice is based upon appearance, or in plugging holes for machine heads, you must of course match the grain direction.

Coat the gluing surfaces of the tapered hole and the plug with hide or white glue (medium thick) and insert the plug, twisting at the same time to squeeze out the excess glue. A few taps may also be helpful. Trim the ends when dry and touch up the finish.

The key to a well-fitted peg lies in matching exactly the taper of the peg to the taper of the

pegholes, and for this reason a peg shaper must be used, even on new pegs. The peg shaper is used to eliminate out-of-roundness, to obtain a perfectly matching taper, and to trim down an oversize shank. Proper adjustment of the peg shaper takes a little experience, though there is nothing difficult in the process if a few rules are followed. The blade should be kept quite sharp and should be set to give very fine shavings. The taper can be varied a bit by adjusting the blade to cut more (or less) at one end, though. Again, only fine cuts should be made. A little soap rubbed on the peg shank for lubrication is helpful.

The final step in fitting the peg, after work with the reamer and peg shaper, is to apply peg dope to the peg shank. The application of this compound allows the peg to hold without slipping while allowing it to turn smoothly without sticking. Although a commercial peg dope such as Hill Peg Compound may be used, one will obtain better control over the fitting of the peg by applying a combination of soap and chalk. A few rubs with a piece of dry soap followed by a like application of chalk will do for a trial fit. Generally, excess soap will cause slipping and excess chalk will cause sticking. Experience will determine whether additional amounts of soap or chalk or both are required.

After drilling a small hole for the string in the

Below Left

The pegs used for the flamenco guitar must be trued up in a violin peg shaper. The size and taper of the peg must match the peghole so that it will turn without slipping or sticking.

Below Right

Strings are wound onto flamenco pegs as in this photo. The sixth and first strings are each wound from the outside. The other strings are wound from the inside. Mother-of-pearl inlays in the peg ends are customary.

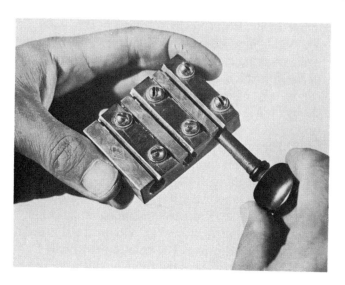
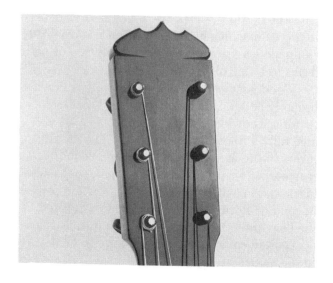

shank a quarter inch from the end, the job is completed. One should observe the correct method of winding the strings on the pegs.

Grover and Schaller Machine Head Installation

Two very popular machine heads for use with steel string guitars are the Grover Rotomatic and the Schaller M6. Both machines come as standard equipment on a wide range of guitars, including certain models of the Martin, the Guild, and the Gibson. In addition, many handmade guitars, such as the Gallagher and Gurian feature them.

The unique features of the Grover Rotomatic are: 1) an individual enclosed gear with grease sealed inside; 2) a button with a tension adjusting screw; 3) a threaded collar used to fasten the unit to the peghead with a single screw used to prevent accidental rotation of the machine; 4) a variety of finishes including nickel, chrome, and gold; 5) availability as three right and three left, or six left for Fender-style pegheads.

The Schaller, which appears to be a copy of the Rotomatic, shares the same features though it is available in chrome and gold only. Some years ago, when the Schaller first appeared, there was a considerable price differential in favor of the Schaller on the order of five or six dollars, and for this reason as well as because of its quality construction it rapidly became a popular conversion. Today, however, the Schaller's price has risen to the point where there is no price advantage. For all practical purposes, the choice is a matter of personal preference.

The unique construction of these machines requires a different kind of installation than the usual method. The internally threaded portion of the case which passes through the peghead is much larger in diameter than the usual narrow roller. The original hole should be opened out with a peghole reamer till the machine fits easily but without excessive play. A drill should not be used to open out an existing hole as there is a grave risk of breaking away wood chips where the drill enters and exits. A drill would be fine, though, for an original installation or where the original roller holes have been plugged.

The original wood screw mounting holes on the back of the peghead must be filled before the new machines are installed. For this purpose, round toothpicks, coated with white glue and pushed firmly into the hole, can be used. After the excess wood is trimmed away, the exposed plugs which will not be covered by the machines can be stained and touched up to match the surrounding peghead. If, however, the peghead is finished clear, it is preferable to cut plugs out of wood of the same type as the peghead.

When the machine is assembled on the peghead, the ear for the single locating wood screw faces down toward the body of the instrument. After tightening down the threaded collar, drill a small pilot hole for the wood screw and install the screw. The screws supplied with the Schallers are fairly soft and sometimes break if the correct size pilot hole is not first drilled.

On Fender solid body pegheads (six in a line) the clearance between each machine is limited, so extra care should be taken when reaming each hole. In some cases it may be necessary to file the ear on the housing slightly, or to countersink the wood screw in order to provide adequate clearance.

Since the machine cases overlap they must be installed in sequence, starting with the first string peg and ending with the sixth. Check for clearance and alignment as you progress with the installation; take particular care to ensure that the buttons of adjacent machines do not foul each other.

Incidentally, the Fender-style slotted rollers which are available with the Schallers have proven to be unsatisfactory for most installations. The tension of the string around the roller tends to bend the end of the roller and close the slot.

Schaller and Grover replacement. After removing the original machines, the exposed screw holes must be plugged and the roller holes opened up to accept the new machines —Schallers in this example.

Schaller has the M4, a bass equivalent to their guitar peg. This machine has all the good features of the M6 and is installed, for example, on certain models of the Gibson electric bass as original equipment. Installation or conversion on most basses is similar to that outlined for guitars and should pose no special problems.

Many conversions involve Fender basses and on these instruments the original hole for the roller is larger than the roller on the Schaller. In this case it is advisable to fit a wood bushing to ensure an accurate fit.

Below Left

The screw holes are plugged. Note that only the plugs which are exposed require touchup. The untouched plugs will be hidden beneath the machine.

Below Right

The roller holes are opened up with a cello peghole reamer. The tape on the reamer indicates the correct diameter of the hole.

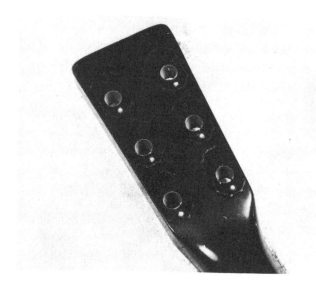 

Below Left

The finished installation. The locating screw on each machine always points in the direction of the body.

Below Right

Though the installation sequence shown is for Schallers on a Martin guitar, the sequence is exactly the same for Grover Rotomatics. This photo (of a Gibson peghead) shows the correct method for reaming the roller hole.

The Neck and Fingerboard

Warped Neck

String tension is only one of a number of reasons for neck warpage. Storage in a hot place can cause warpage as can wood which is weak or poor in quality. Poorly seasoned wood can cause a warp in either direction as well as a twist in the neck. The repairman has to be careful when refretting an instrument because, improperly done, this too can cause a warped neck.

A neck can be straightened permanently only when the causes of the warp have been removed. Such causes as poor glue joints, loose frets, and weak or excessively thin necks or fingerboards must be remedied before a neck straightening operation can be expected to be permanently successful. The neck will respond most successfully when the causes for warpage have been accidental, such as an improper choice of strings, or when the instrument has been subjected to adverse climatic conditions. A neck that has slowly bowed up over a period of many years may also be successfully straightened because it may be assumed that it will be many more years, if at all, before the neck will again need straightening or other more extensive corrective measures. A final instance where straightening measures can be carried out successfully occurs when, during the process of fretting or refretting a fingerboard, the neck straightness and relief are inadvertently altered slightly. Neck straightening will not cure the effects caused by an improper neck angle and since neck warpage and neck angle problems do occasionally occur at the same time, any repairs must be preceded by careful examination.

The process of straightening a neck of the

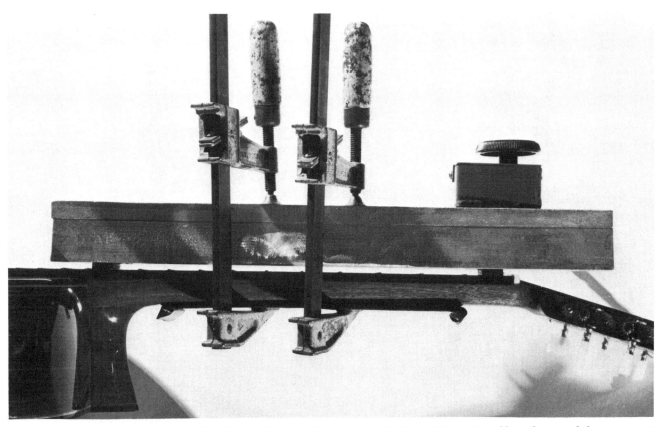

A normal warped neck is straightened by first heating and then clamping in the middle section. Note the use of the spacers at the ends of the neck. Though an electric neck straightening tool is used in the photo, equal results may be obtained by thoroughly heating the neck and clamping against a heavy board.

nonadjustable variety involves the application of heat to the neck, followed by the setting of clamps to hold the neck in the proper shape while it cools. The heat, applied most easily with a small alcohol lamp, softens the wood and the glue joint between the fingerboard and neck. When cool, the neck permanently retains its straightened form.

The tools needed consist of: a small alcohol lamp, several clamps including one long enough to clamp the neck at the heel, various pieces of shim stock, pads for cushioning the clamps, and a hardwood block roughly 2 by 2 by 14 inches.

Start the repair by turning the guitar over and heating the fingerboard slowly with the alcohol lamp. Heating should be thorough and can take as long as a half hour. The back of the neck should be very warm when adequate heating has taken place. Only the experience of the repairman can determine the amount and rate of heat each neck requires, though, as a general guidline, necks and fingergoards of harder materials as well as necks with fixed metal rods inside require a slightly longer heating time.

Now, assuming that the neck in this case has bowed upward, place a shim at the first fret and a second one on the fingerboard over the heel. Place the hardwood block over the shims and apply the clamps. Better control is gained by using two clamps rather than one, spacing them over the fourth and seventh frets. Tighten the clamps down so that the neck is bowed slightly in the opposite direction to allow for the slight amount of springing back that will occur when the clamps are removed. Most of the straightening action will occur during the first few minutes in clamps if the heating operation has been thorough, and because of this it is well to check the neck at short intervals. Occasionally, the straightening process will have to be repeated in order to obtain satisfactory results.

Straightening a neck with a reverse bow is similar to the regular procedure except that the shims are placed in the middle and the clamps at the ends, over the heel and at the first fret. In both cases, the necks should be allowed to cool before rechecking, touching up the frets, adjusting the action, and stringing up.

When correcting for a reverse warp, the neck, after heating, is clamped at the outer ends. The spacers in the middle allow the neck to be bent to the proper position.

74

All guitar necks will flex a bit when brought up under string tension so you should plan for this when straightening a neck. Most steel string guitar necks, when strung with light to heavy gauge strings, will flex a moderate amount, requiring a small amount of "reverse bow" in the neck when not under string tension. Twelve-string guitars may require considerably more reverse bow as the string tension on these instruments is sometimes very heavy.

For the most part, classical guitar necks can be adjusted absolutely flat. The string tension will, in most cases, flex the neck enough to give the correct amount of relief.

Perhaps the most critical guitars are electrics strung with light rock and roll strings, such as Ernie Ball Slinkys or Super Slinkys. It has been my experience that when these guitar necks need straightening it is almost always to correct a condition of too much reverse bow. With rock and roll strings, the neck flexes very little and you can't depend on string tension to pull the neck up for you. Since the truss rods in most guitars can't be adjusted to correct the condition of a reverse bow, straightening is the only answer.

Loose Neck or Broken Heel

The heel of the neck and the upper endblock are subjected to a continuous heavy strain from the tension of the strings. It is small wonder, then, that many of the problems associated with guitar construction and repairing fall in this area. Because of the continuous strain, the smallest bump, aggravated by poor wood, construction, and defects in design, can cause the neck to become unglued, to break at the heel, or, in more spectacular instances, to split the sides of the guitar in two, clear down to the lower endblock. In addition, the continuous tension can, over a given period of time, cause the neck angle to change due to settling of the guitar body. The neck must be reset in order to restore proper action. Small changes in fitting and repairing the heel will have much effect on neck angle and overall action; repairs must be done correctly with due regard to the requirements of the individual instrument.

Guitars built with a dovetail joint between neck and endblock rarely suffer major problems in this area, at least insofar as major breaks are con-

cerned. Loose necks, however, resulting from a variety of causes, are the most common problem, particularly with the lower-priced instruments. Necks which have been poorly fitted and glued, when accidentally bumped or abused, can come loose, necessitating resetting and regluing. For results that will remain permanent, the neck must be removed, cleaned of old glue, refitted properly, and finally glued, making sure the neck angle is correct. Instruments which have been handmade by master craftsmen, and the better factory instruments as well, possess excellently fitted joints; these instruments, due to the strength inherent in the dovetail method of construction, rarely have problems of breakage even under the most abusive conditions. A blow on the neck will usually snap off the peghead before the neck loosens or breaks at the heel. The same cannot be said for the Spanish style of construction. The strongest form of dovetail construction is produced when the grain of the endblock runs vertically across the grain of the sides. This is universal practice for instruments of the violin family but, unfortunately, not so for guitars. The more serious breaks, when they do occur, happen to instruments where the grain of the endblocks runs (with the grain of the sides) horizontally. It sometimes happens that the endblock splits rather than the heel.

A loose fitting dovetail joint can be made satisfactory with the use of wood shims. When well fitted (dry), the joint will be tight enough to allow a person to vigorously shake the guitar by the neck without loosening the body. After gluing and clamping the neck, using hot heavy glue, a final check must be made to ensure proper alignment and angle.

Measures taken to repair broken or split heels or endblocks can vary from simply working in glue and clamping, to pinning, reinforcing, and aligning the broken part. A small crack in the heel of a neck which is otherwise securely glued to the endblock may be repaired by working in thin glue and clamping. Larger breaks in the heel as well as breaks in the endblock may require, in addition to the first step of gluing and clamping, wood pins to reinforce the break. Generalizations are difficult to make as to when a neck has to be pinned and when it doesn't. If the break is extensive, old, or in a place that was broken previously, or if the wood is soft and of small proportions, it is safest to pin the heel so that the area will be stronger than the original.

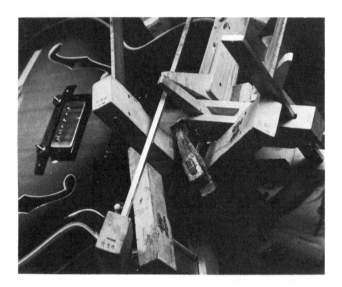 

Pins are prepared from hardwood dowels and may be inserted either from the fingerboard side or from the back, depending on the location of the crack and on considerations involved in making the repair as inconspicuous as possible. If the guitar has mother-of-pearl dots on the fingerboard over the desired area, the simplest solution is to remove a dot, drill and pin below the dot, and replace the dot. If the guitar has a truss rod, the only solution in most cases is to reinforce from the heel or from the back of the guitar. The best solution for guitars with a separate plastic or wood cap on the heel is to conceal the pin beneath the cap. Other alternatives are to simply drill through the fingerboard or back, pin, and then plug the hole with matching wood. Using a little more imagination, a chip can be pried from the fingerboard or back, the pin inserted beneath the chip, and the chip replaced. A last alternative is to remove the fingerboard completely, install the pin beneath it, and reglue. This last step is best reserved for finer instruments or where other repairs would, in any case, require removal of the board.

The guitars built in the Spanish style have the neck, heel, and endblock all in one piece. The depth may be built up by laminating—but the characteristics are the same as if sawn out of one large block. These guitars have no problem with loose necks, of course, but to offset this advantage is the fact that damage is extensive when it does occur. In the Spanish method, the proportions of the neck comprising the endblock section are quite small; though pretty to look at, this feature combined with the wood grain running horizontally across from heel to endblock is an inherent weakness in the style of construction. A crack, starting with an accidental drop or blow, will start in the heel and, following the direction of the grain, continue clear on into the endblock area. In more serious cases, the sides will be split as well.

In an instrument where the entire upper section has split away, alignment must be correct in all planes; the fit of the sides must be attended to as well as the neck angle. The more extensive repairs can be done most easily in two or three gluings, working on the heel and endblock first, the sides second, and pins and cleats, as necessary, third.

If a broken neck must be replaced, the quickest way is to first saw it off. (Gibson Repair Dept.)

With the neck sawn off, the portion remaining in the body is drilled away. (Gibson Repair Dept.)

The neck slot is finally cleaned up with a chisel and adjusted to fit the new neck. (Gibson Repair Dept.)

Resetting Neck Angle

Few areas of the guitar require more careful adjustment and regulation than the neck angle. Tolerances must be held to quite close limits in order to obtain a string height at the bridge which results in both good tone and good action. If a good action can't be obtained within the limits prescribed for that particular style of guitar, the neck angle is wrong and, by one means or another, must be corrected in order to get the most out of the instrument.

Viewing the classical guitar from the side, face up, the neck at the nut should be about an eighth of an inch above the plane of the top. Checking from the peghead end of the fingerboard, sighting down toward the bridge, an imaginary line extended from the top of the fingerboard should appear to hit the bridge an eighth of an inch above the top.

Plectrum guitars, it should be noted, have their necks tipped back in the opposite direction to make up for the high arch and the high bridge height. The exact angle is unimportant as long as saddle height and action are acceptable.

Usually, when resetting becomes necessary, it is because of too high an action. Through settling of the body, the neck occasionally pulls up at the body, putting a sharp angle and rise in the fingerboard at that point. Another reason for resetting occurs when the top arch changes (usually increases) through the effects of string tension and changes in wood dimensions, both from aging and from climatic conditions.

The height of the strings at the bridge, for an average action, runs about 1/4 to 3/8 inch for flamenco guitars, 3/8 to 1/2 inch for classical and flattop guitars, and 3/4 to 1 inch for archtop guitars. Some variations can be expected such as a string height of 1/4 inch for some classical and flattop guitars, though the reasons for the change can range from accidental to intentional depending on the quality of the instrument and on the maker.

Resetting a neck by the usual method requires the prior removal of the fingerboard. The neck must be removed from the instrument (a difficult task when working with the better quality instruments), the dovetail recut, the neck reglued, and the fingerboard replaced. The whole operation is, admittedly, time consuming and tedious.

(See photos on next page.)

Below Left

By sighting from the peghead toward the bridge, you can check for neck straightness and relief as well as for neck angle. As a general rule, the end of the fingerboard should appear to touch the bridge about an eighth of an inch above the top. This guitar checks out fine!

Below Right

Solid body guitar necks are often fitted into a slot in the body, rather than with a dovetail joint as on an acoustical guitar. (Gibson repair Dept.)

An alternative, particularly when the amount of change is minor and when the fingerboard is not heavily inlaid, is to replace the original with a fingerboard which has been tapered to give the correct angle. This method is used even on new guitars (thick at the nut, thin at the soundhole); instruments using this method, including most Mexican guitars, get the proper neck angle without angling the neck at all. Since guitars built in the Spanish method cannot have the neck reset because the neck and endblock are in one piece, the fingerboard method is one of the few alternatives left.

A third method which can be used on all types of guitars is to "slip the endblock." The binding is peeled back along the upper bouts and the back is separated from the endblock and sides—for a distance of four or five inches each side of the endblock. The neck is set to the proper angle and the back reglued. After trimming the back to restore the channel for the binding, the binding is reglued and the finish touched up. Repairs made in this fashion are practical only when the neck angle is to

be reduced or tipped back; the small amount of overhanging back material which must be trimmed off—1/32 to 1/16 inch—is insignificant and cannot be noticed by eye. This operation takes experience to master, but the repair can be effected relatively quickly and, when well done, gives no outward indication that the angle has been reset. The chief drawback is that elaborate purflings and bindings, particularly those of delicate wood patterns, make loosening of the binding and purfling from the upper bout difficult or impractical. Care must also be exercised, when loosening the back with a thin table knife, that the knife does not dig into or split the wood. In some cases, the reinforcing strip along the center seam must be cut away at the upper end in order to allow movement of the endblock.

All guitars will respond to at least one of the above methods. This is an area where, unless you have a fair amount of previous experience, it would be wise for you to consult with an established repairman who is competent in neck repairs. In time you will develop your own favorite tools and techniques.

Fingerboard Replacement

The replacement of a fingerboard with a new one, particularly when the new board must be specially made and fretted for the instrument at hand, is a major undertaking. The amateur or inexperienced repairman should thoroughly familiarize himself with the steps and processes involved before tackling a repair of this type. Fine guitars and other fretted instruments rarely require new fingerboards; in most cases, refretting is all that is required. The lower-priced instruments, which use the more inexpensive woods for fingerboards, or even wood veneers, are the ones which will most often require new fingerboards. Because of the time and labor involved, however, the value of the instrument will be an important factor in deciding whether to go ahead with the repairs.

The most important reasons for replacing the fingerboard are: excessive wear, insufficient fingerboard strength, incorrectly spaced frets, and damaged or excessively worn fret slots. Wear is unavoidable even with the best ebony fingerboard; when wear occurs to the extent that it interferes with the action and cannot be restored by dressing down the fingerboard after removing the frets (done in conjunction with refretting), the board should be replaced.

Insufficient fingerboard strength reveals itself through occurrence of a warped neck. A substantial portion of the strength of the neck is derived from the fingerboard; a brief glance will show that between the peghead and the heel, upwards of one-fourth of the wood in the neck is represented by the fingerboard. A poor quality fingerboard will cancel the benefits to be gained from the use of good neck wood. In addition, most adjustable torsion bars, on those instruments so equipped, will operate poorly or not at all with a poor fingerboard since they depend on the strength of the fingerboard for proper operation. A board of insufficient thickness will show results similar to that displayed by wood of poor quality. A poor glue joint or a fingerboard that is partially loose will also contribute toward a warped neck. Because of the many factors which must be considered, one should not be too hasty in concluding that the fingerboard must be replaced. The trouble may only lie, for example, in improper fretwire.

Fretwire with tangs which are too small for the fret slots allows the top part of the fingerboard to compress slightly. The strength to be derived from the thickness of the fingerboard—from the bottom of the fret slot to the top of the board—is lost, and in many cases this effective loss of fingerboard thickness is enough to allow the neck to warp. Refretting with the proper fretwire will, in this case, restore neck straightness. As a matter of fact, an occasional badly warped neck can be straightened by installing frets with slightly oversize tangs. The oversize tang will create a wedging action when driven into the slots and with care (and a little luck) one will end up with a straight neck.

Fingerboards with worn fret slots usually can be saved with the proper choice of fretwire. Many of the older instruments—banjo and mandolin as well as guitar—are fitted with a fretwire whose cross section is constant, top to bottom, rather than like the T of the conventional fret. Replacing this bar type of fret with the conventional fret is unsatisfactory unless the slot is first filled and then recut. A simpler solution, in terms of overall time involved, is to replace the fingerboard, particularly when it has few inlays to contend with. Since the old fretwire is difficult to obtain, it is best to try to save the frets if at all possible. A small but useful feature of this old fretwire is that life can often be extended by shimming the frets up a small amount when they have worn low.

Fingerboard Removal

A fingerboard may be removed cleanly and with no difficulty by using the following procedure. With a small alcohol lamp, warm the fingerboard slowly but thoroughly. It is easier to remove it from the soundhole end first so more heat should be applied there than at the nut end. When sufficiently warm—the warmth can be determined by touching the top beneath the fingerboard—start the opening knife at one corner of the board. As the heat-softened glue gives way, work the knife slowly in, first on one side and then on the other. By working carefully with the knife, stopping at intervals to rewarm the fingerboard ahead of the knife, the operation can be concluded with hardly a sliver out of place. After removal of the fingerboard the neck should be scraped free of old glue and inspected for any needed repairs such as resetting or straightening. After determining that all is satisfactory, attention can then be turned to the construction of the new fingerboard.

Fingerboard Construction

Ebony and rosewood are the only materials which should be considered for replacements. Ebony is the superior wood and should be used when good quality stock is available since the cost difference is only a matter of a dollar or so.

Fingerboard blanks are available rough-cut to a thickness of about three eighths of an inch and of length and width suitable for banjo and mandolin as well as guitar. Unless your shop has facilities for resawing wood, this is the only practical way to buy stock. The blank must be dressed to a thickness of a quarter inch or so depending on the strength of the neck, type of guitar, and other factors which your experience has found to be relevant. If the original fingerboard was O.K. in terms of straightness you may duplicate the original dimensions. If the old fingerboard was warped, it would be good insurance to make the new board a bit thicker.

A jointer and/or drum sander in a drill press is useful to dress the blank down to the proper thickness. Lacking power tools, a sharp and correctly set up plane and a scraper must be used. In determining length and width, the old fingerboard can be used as a model. In general, classical fingerboards will run 2 to 2 1/8 inches wide at the nut and 2 1/2 to 2 9/16 inches wide at the nineteenth fret. Fourteen-fret flattops and most electric guitars run about a quarter inch less in width. In most cases, the contour of the neck will allow adjustments slightly over and under the original width. If the fingerboard is to be bound, one must allow for the width of the binding when determining widths. Finally, in the case of the classical guitar, the end of the fingerboard over the soundhole is cut away in an arc matching the diameter of the soundhole, taking away the middle section of the nineteenth fret.

The fingerboard blank now has the proper width, length, and height. The next step, the cutting of the fret slots, is critical and must be done *right;* most of the problems encountered when driving frets, as well as some neck warpage, can be traced to incorrectly cut slots. For obvious reasons the fretwire to be used should be on hand before cutting the slots. In cutting the slots by hand, a thin, stiff-backed saw such as used for dovetail work will give excellent results once it has been adjusted for slot width. Most fret tangs have widths such that it is only necessary to remove all or part of the set on the teeth of the saw, though mando-lin or banjo fretwire may require that the teeth be hollow-ground to obtain widths less than the original thickness of the saw. The slots can be cut freehand or with a fence clamped to the board, depending on the skill and experience of the worker. The tang itself should be a moderate press fit into the slot; the serrations on the tang will hold the fret in place.

If a table saw is available, a thin circular saw blade can be hollow-ground to the correct width. This blade, together with a specially constructed miter gauge to fit the blank, will cut slots quickly and with precision. For shops which must turn out more than an occasional fingerboard, the table saw (simple or elaborate as the situation requires) will pay for itself in terms of quick and accurate work.

A final step to be taken care of before cutting the slots is to lay out a scale and mark the position for each fret. If the original fingerboard is known to be accurate, all that is required is to copy the scale onto the new board. If the old board is inaccurate or if the fingerboard is for a new guitar, the following procedure should be used.

The scale length must first be determined. For an old guitar with a fixed bridge, the scale length can be measured directly from the nut to the saddle, making an allowance for compensation. For a plectrum guitar or a new guitar there is more room for variation; a scale can be chosen which will most closely suit the requirements of the particular instrument. My recommendation in choosing a scale length for best all-around results is as follows: acoustical guitars with steel strings, 25 1/4 to 25 1/2 inches; classical and flamenco guitars with nylon strings, 25 1/2 to 26 1/4 inches. Electric guitars, student guitars, and smaller instruments often have scales up to 3/4 inch less than the above figures.

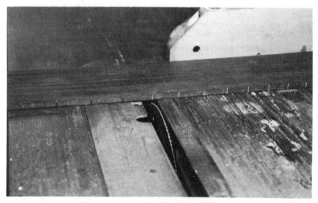

Fret slots may be cut with a table saw if a blade of the proper thickness is used. A fine-toothed blade, hollow-ground to the proper thickness, is used in this photo.

Fret Calculations for Guitars and Electric Basses

Guitar Scale Lengths: 23.5 to 26.25 inches in 1/8 increments
Electric Bass Scale Lengths: 30.5 to 34.5 inches in 1/4 increments

SCALE LENGTH = 23.5

Fret	Fret Interval	Remaining Scale Length
1	1.31897	22.181
2	1.24494	20.9361
3	1.17506	19.761
4	1.10911	18.6519
5	1.04686	17.6051
6	0.988105	16.617
7	0.932646	15.6843
8	0.8803	14.804
9	0.830892	13.9731
10	0.784258	13.1889
11	0.74024	12.4486
12	0.698693	11.7499
13	0.659478	11.0904
14	0.622464	10.468
15	0.587528	9.88046
16	0.554552	9.3259
17	0.523427	8.80248
18	0.494049	8.30843
19	0.46632	7.84211
20	0.440147	7.40196

SCALE LENGTH = 23.625

Fret	Fret Interval	Remaining Scale Length
1	1.32598	22.299
2	1.25156	21.0475
3	1.18131	19.8661
4	1.11501	18.7511
5	1.05243	17.6987
6	0.993361	16.7053
7	0.937607	15.7677
8	0.884983	14.8828
9	0.835312	14.0474
10	0.788429	13.259
11	0.744178	12.5148
12	0.70241	11.8124
13	0.662986	11.1494
14	0.625775	10.5237
15	0.590653	9.93301
16	0.557502	9.37551
17	0.526212	8.8493
18	0.496677	8.35262
19	0.468801	7.88382
20	0.442489	7.44133

SCALE LENGTH = 23.75

Fret	Fret Interval	Remaining Scale Length
1	1.333	22.417
2	1.25818	21.1588
3	1.18756	19.9713
4	1.12091	18.8503
5	1.058	17.7924
6	0.998617	16.7937
7	0.942568	15.8512
8	0.889665	14.9615
9	0.839732	14.1218
10	0.792601	13.3292
11	0.748115	12.5811
12	0.706126	11.8749
13	0.666494	11.2084
14	0.629086	10.5793
15	0.593778	9.98557
16	0.560452	9.42512
17	0.528996	8.89612
18	0.499305	8.39682
19	0.471281	7.92553
20	0.44483	7.4807

SCALE LENGTH = 23.875

Fret	Fret Interval	Remaining Scale Length
1	1.34001	22.535
2	1.2648	21.2702
3	1.19381	20.0764
4	1.12681	18.9496
5	1.06357	17.886
6	1.00387	16.8821
7	0.947529	15.9346
8	0.894348	15.0402
9	0.844151	14.1961
10	0.796772	13.3993
11	0.752053	12.6473
12	0.709843	11.9374
13	0.670002	11.2674
14	0.632397	10.635
15	0.596903	10.0381
16	0.563401	9.47472
17	0.53178	8.94294
18	0.501933	8.44101
19	0.473762	7.96725
20	0.447171	7.52008

SCALE LENGTH = 24

Fret	Fret Interval	Remaining Scale Length
1	1.34703	22.653
2	1.27142	21.3815
3	1.20006	20.1815
4	1.13271	19.0488
5	1.06913	17.9796
6	1.00913	16.9705
7	0.95249	16.018
8	0.89903	15.119
9	0.848571	14.2704
10	0.800944	13.4695
11	0.75599	12.7135
12	0.713559	11.9999
13	0.67351	11.3264
14	0.635708	10.6907
15	0.600029	10.0907
16	0.566351	9.52433
17	0.534564	8.98976
18	0.504561	8.4852
19	0.476242	8.00896
20	0.449512	7.55945

SCALE LENGTH = 24.125

Fret	Fret Interval	Remaining Scale Length
1	1.35404	22.771
2	1.27805	21.4929
3	1.20631	20.2866
4	1.13861	19.148
5	1.0747	18.0733
6	1.01438	17.0589
7	0.957451	16.1014
8	0.903713	15.1977
9	0.852991	14.3447
10	0.805116	13.5396
11	0.759928	12.7797
12	0.717276	12.0624
13	0.677018	11.3854
14	0.639019	10.7464
15	0.603154	10.1432
16	0.569301	9.57393
17	0.537348	9.03659
18	0.507189	8.5294
19	0.478722	8.05067
20	0.451854	7.59882

SCALE LENGTH = 24.25

Fret	Fret Interval	Remaining Scale Length
1	1.36106	22.8889
2	1.28467	21.6043
3	1.21257	20.3917
4	1.14451	19.2472
5	1.08027	18.1669
6	1.01964	17.1473
7	0.962412	16.1849
8	0.908395	15.2765
9	0.85741	14.4191
10	0.809287	13.6098
11	0.763865	12.8459
12	0.720992	12.1249
13	0.680526	11.4444
14	0.64233	10.8021
15	0.606279	10.1958
16	0.572251	9.62354
17	0.540132	9.08341
18	0.509817	8.57359
19	0.481203	8.09239
20	0.454195	7.63819

SCALE LENGTH = 24.375

Fret	Fret Interval	Remaining Scale Length
1	1.36808	23.0069
2	1.29129	21.7156
3	1.21882	20.4968
4	1.15041	19.3464
5	1.08584	18.2606
6	1.0249	17.2357
7	0.967372	16.2683
8	0.913078	15.3552
9	0.86183	14.4934
10	0.813459	13.6799
11	0.767802	12.9121
12	0.724709	12.1874
13	0.684034	11.5034
14	0.645641	10.8578
15	0.609404	10.2483
16	0.5752	9.67315
17	0.542917	9.13023
18	0.512445	8.61778
19	0.483683	8.1341
20	0.456536	7.67756

SCALE LENGTH = 24.5

Fret	Fret Interval	Remaining Scale Length
1	1.37509	23.1249
2	1.29791	21.827
3	1.22507	20.6019
4	1.15631	19.4456
5	1.09141	18.3542
6	1.03015	17.3241
7	0.972333	16.3517
8	0.91776	15.434
9	0.86625	14.5677
10	0.81763	13.7501
11	0.77174	12.9783
12	0.728425	12.2499
13	0.687541	11.5624
14	0.648952	10.9134
15	0.612529	10.3009
16	0.57815	9.72275
17	0.545701	9.17705
18	0.515073	8.66198
19	0.486164	8.17581
20	0.458877	7.71694

SCALE LENGTH = 24.625

Fret	Fret Interval	Remaining Scale Length
1	1.38211	23.2429
2	1.30453	21.9384
3	1.23132	20.707
4	1.16221	19.5448
5	1.09698	18.4479
6	1.03541	17.4125
7	0.977294	16.4352
8	0.922442	15.5127
9	0.870669	14.642
10	0.821802	13.8202
11	0.775677	13.0446
12	0.732142	12.3124
13	0.691049	11.6214
14	0.652263	10.9691
15	0.615654	10.3535
16	0.5811	9.77236
17	0.548485	9.22387
18	0.517701	8.70617
19	0.488644	8.21753
20	0.461218	7.75631

SCALE LENGTH = 24.75

Fret	Fret Interval	Remaining Scale Length
1	1.38912	23.3609
2	1.31116	22.0497
3	1.23757	20.8122
4	1.16811	19.644
5	1.10255	18.5415
6	1.04066	17.5008
7	0.982255	16.5186
8	0.927125	15.5915
9	0.875089	14.7164
10	0.825974	13.8904
11	0.779615	13.1108
12	0.735858	12.3749
13	0.694557	11.6804
14	0.655574	11.0248
15	0.618779	10.406
16	0.58405	9.82196
17	0.551269	9.27069
18	0.520329	8.75037
19	0.491125	8.25924
20	0.46356	7.79568

SCALE LENGTH = 24.875

Fret	Fret Interval	Remaining Scale Length
1	1.39614	23.4789
2	1.31778	22.1611
3	1.24382	20.9173
4	1.17401	19.7433
5	1.10811	18.6351
6	1.04592	17.5892
7	0.987216	16.602
8	0.931807	15.6702
9	0.879509	14.7907
10	0.830145	13.9606
11	0.783552	13.177
12	0.739574	12.4374
13	0.698065	11.7394
14	0.658885	11.0805
15	0.621905	10.4586
16	0.586999	9.87157
17	0.554053	9.31752
18	0.522957	8.79456
19	0.493605	8.30095
20	0.465901	7.83505

SCALE LENGTH = 25

Fret	Fret Interval	Remaining Scale Length
1	1.40315	23.5968
2	1.3244	22.2724
3	1.25007	21.0224
4	1.17991	19.8425
5	1.11368	18.7288
6	1.05118	17.6776
7	0.992177	16.6854
8	0.93649	15.7489
9	0.883928	14.865
10	0.834317	14.0307
11	0.78749	13.2432
12	0.743291	12.4999
13	0.701573	11.7984
14	0.662196	11.1362
15	0.62503	10.5111
16	0.589949	9.92118
17	0.556838	9.36434
18	0.525584	8.83875
19	0.496085	8.34267
20	0.468242	7.87443

SCALE LENGTH = 25.125

Fret	Fret Interval	Remaining Scale Length
1	1.41017	23.7148
2	1.33102	22.3838
3	1.25632	21.1275
4	1.18581	19.9417
5	1.11925	18.8224
6	1.05643	17.766
7	0.997138	16.7689
8	0.941172	15.8277
9	0.888348	14.9393
10	0.838488	14.1009
11	0.791427	13.3094
12	0.747007	12.5624
13	0.705081	11.8573
14	0.665507	11.1918
15	0.628155	10.5637
16	0.592899	9.97078
17	0.559622	9.41116
18	0.528212	8.88295
19	0.498566	8.38438
20	0.470583	7.9138

SCALE LENGTH = 25.25

Fret	Fret Interval	Remaining Scale Length
1	1.41719	23.8328
2	1.33764	22.4952
3	1.26257	21.2326
4	1.1917	20.0409
5	1.12482	18.9161
6	1.06169	17.8544
7	1.0021	16.8523
8	0.945855	15.9064
9	0.892767	15.0137
10	0.84266	14.171
11	0.795365	13.3756
12	0.750724	12.6249
13	0.708589	11.9163
14	0.668818	11.2475
15	0.63128	10.6162
16	0.595849	10.0204
17	0.562406	9.45798
18	0.53084	8.92714
19	0.501046	8.42609
20	0.472924	7.95317

SCALE LENGTH = 25.375

Fret	Fret Interval	Remaining Scale Length
1	1.4242	23.9508
2	1.34427	22.6065
3	1.26882	21.3377
4	1.1976	20.1401
5	1.13039	19.0097
6	1.06694	17.9428
7	1.00706	16.9357
8	0.950537	15.9852
9	0.897187	15.088
10	0.846831	14.2412
11	0.799302	13.4419
12	0.75444	12.6874
13	0.712096	11.9753
14	0.672129	11.3032
15	0.634405	10.6688
16	0.598798	10.07
17	0.56519	9.5048
18	0.533468	8.97133
19	0.503527	8.46781
20	0.475266	7.99254

SCALE LENGTH = 25.5

Fret	Fret Interval	Remaining Scale Length
1	1.43122	24.0688
2	1.35089	22.7179
3	1.27507	21.4428
4	1.2035	20.2393
5	1.13596	19.1034
6	1.0722	18.0312
7	1.01202	17.0191
8	0.95522	16.0639
9	0.901607	15.1623
10	0.851003	14.3113
11	0.803239	13.5081
12	0.758157	12.7499
13	0.715604	12.0343
14	0.67544	11.3589
15	0.63753	10.7213
16	0.601748	10.1196
17	0.567974	9.55162
18	0.536096	9.01553
19	0.506007	8.50952
20	0.477607	8.03191

SCALE LENGTH = 25.625

Fret	Fret Interval	Remaining Scale Length
1	1.43823	24.1868
2	1.35751	22.8293
3	1.28132	21.5479
4	1.2094	20.3385
5	1.14152	19.197
6	1.07745	18.1196
7	1.01698	17.1026
8	0.959902	16.1427
9	0.906026	15.2366
10	0.855175	14.3815
11	0.807177	13.5743
12	0.761873	12.8124
13	0.719112	12.0933
14	0.678751	11.4146
15	0.640655	10.7739
16	0.604698	10.1692
17	0.570759	9.59845
18	0.538724	8.05972
19	0.508488	8.55123
20	0.479948	8.07129

SCALE LENGTH = 25.75

Fret	Fret Interval	Remaining Scale Length
1	1.44525	24.3048
2	1.36413	22.9406
3	1.28757	21.653
4	1.2153	20.4377
5	1.14709	19.2907
6	1.08271	18.2079
7	1.02194	17.186
8	0.964584	16.2214
9	0.910446	15.311
10	0.859346	14.4516
11	0.811114	13.6405
12	0.76559	12.8749
13	0.72262	12.1523
14	0.682062	11.4702
15	0.643781	10.8265
16	0.607648	10.2188
17	0.573543	9.64527
18	0.541352	9.10392
19	0.510968	8.59295
20	0.482289	8.11066

SCALE LENGTH = 25.875

Fret	Fret Interval	Remaining Scale Length
1	1.45226	24.4227
2	1.37075	23.052
3	1.29382	21.7582
4	1.2212	20.537
5	1.15266	19.3843
6	1.08797	18.2963
7	1.0269	17.2694
8	0.969267	16.3002
9	0.914866	15.3853
10	0.863518	14.5218
11	0.815052	13.7067
12	0.769306	12.9374
13	0.726128	12.2113
14	0.685373	11.5259
15	0.646906	10.879
16	0.610597	10.2684
17	0.576327	9.69209
18	0.54398	9.14811
19	0.513448	8.63466
20	0.48463	8.15003

SCALE LENGTH = 26

Fret	Fret Interval	Remaining Scale Length
1	1.45928	24.5407
2	1.37738	23.1633
3	1.30007	21.8633
4	1.2271	20.6362
5	1.15823	19.4779
6	1.09322	18.3847
7	1.03186	17.3529
8	0.973949	16.3789
9	0.919285	15.4596
10	0.867689	14.5919
11	0.818989	13.7729
12	0.773023	12.9999
13	0.729636	12.2703
14	0.688684	11.5816
15	0.650031	10.9316
16	0.613547	10.318
17	0.579111	9.73891
18	0.546608	9.1923
19	0.515929	8.67637
20	0.486972	8.1894

SCALE LENGTH = 26.125

Fret	Fret Interval	Remaining Scale Length
1	1.4663	24.6587
2	1.384	23.2747
3	1.30632	21.9684
4	1.233	20.7354
5	1.1638	19.5716
6	1.09848	18.4731
7	1.03682	17.4363
8	0.978632	16.4577
9	0.923705	15.5339
10	0.871861	14.6621
11	0.822927	13.8392
12	0.776739	13.0624
13	0.733144	12.3293
14	0.691995	11.6373
15	0.653156	10.9841
16	0.616497	10.3676
17	0.581895	9.78573
18	0.549236	9.2365
19	0.518409	8.71809
20	0.489313	8.22878

Electric Bass Fret Calculations

SCALE LENGTH = 26.25

Fret	Fret Interval	Remaining Scale Length
1	1.47331	24.7767
2	1.39062	23.3861
3	1.31257	22.0735
4	1.2389	20.8346
5	1.16937	19.6652
6	1.10373	18.5615
7	1.04179	17.5197
8	0.983314	16.5364
9	0.928125	15.6083
10	0.876033	14.7322
11	0.826864	13.9054
12	0.780455	13.1249
13	0.736651	12.3883
14	0.695306	11.693
15	0.656281	11.0367
16	0.619447	10.4172
17	0.584679	9.83255
18	0.551864	9.28069
19	0.52089	8.7598
20	0.491654	8.26815

SCALE LENGTH = 30.5

Fret	Fret Interval	Remaining Scale Length
1	1.71185	28.7882
2	1.61577	27.1724
3	1.52508	25.6473
4	1.43948	24.2078
5	1.35869	22.8491
6	1.28243	21.5667
7	1.21046	20.3562
8	1.14252	19.2137
9	1.07839	18.1353
10	1.01787	17.1175
11	0.960737	16.1567
12	0.906815	15.2499
13	0.855919	14.394
14	0.807879	13.5861
15	0.762536	12.8236
16	0.719738	12.1038
17	0.679342	11.4245
18	0.641213	10.7833
19	0.605224	10.1781
20	0.571255	9.6068

SCALE LENGTH = 30.75

Fret	Fret Interval	Remaining Scale Length
1	1.72588	29.0241
2	1.62901	27.3951
3	1.53758	25.8575
4	1.45128	24.4062
5	1.36983	23.0364
6	1.29295	21.7435
7	1.22038	20.5231
8	1.15188	19.3712
9	1.08723	18.284
10	1.02621	17.2578
11	0.968612	16.2892
12	0.914248	15.3749
13	0.862935	14.512
14	0.814501	13.6975
15	0.768787	12.9287
16	0.725637	12.203
17	0.68491	11.5181
18	0.646469	10.8717
19	0.610185	10.2615
20	0.575938	9.68554

SCALE LENGTH = 31

Fret	Fret Interval	Remaining Scale Length
1	1.73991	29.2601
2	1.64226	27.6178
3	1.55008	26.0677
4	1.46308	24.6047
5	1.38097	23.2237
6	1.30346	21.9202
7	1.2303	20.6899
8	1.16125	19.5287
9	1.09607	18.4326
10	1.03455	17.3981
11	0.976487	16.4216
12	0.921681	15.4999
13	0.86995	14.63
14	0.821123	13.8088
15	0.775037	13.0338
16	0.731537	12.3023
17	0.690479	11.6118
18	0.651725	10.9601
19	0.615146	10.3449
20	0.58062	9.76429

SCALE LENGTH = 31.25

Fret	Fret Interval	Remaining Scale Length
1	1.75394	29.4961
2	1.6555	27.8406
3	1.56258	26.278
4	1.47488	24.8031
5	1.3921	23.411
6	1.31397	22.097
7	1.24022	20.8568
8	1.17061	19.6862
9	1.10491	18.5813
10	1.0429	17.5384
11	0.984362	16.554
12	0.929114	15.6249
13	0.876966	14.7479
14	0.827745	13.9202
15	0.781287	13.1389
16	0.737436	12.4015
17	0.696047	11.7054
18	0.656981	11.0484
19	0.620107	10.4283
20	0.585303	9.84303

SCALE LENGTH = 31.5

Fret	Fret Interval	Remaining Scale Length
1	1.76797	29.732
2	1.66874	28.0633
3	1.57508	26.4882
4	1.48668	25.0015
5	1.40324	23.5983
6	1.32448	22.2738
7	1.25014	21.0237
8	1.17998	19.8437
9	1.11375	18.7299
10	1.05124	17.6787
11	0.992237	16.6864
12	0.936547	15.7499
13	0.883982	14.8659
14	0.834367	14.0316
15	0.787537	13.244
16	0.743336	12.5007
17	0.701615	11.7991
18	0.662236	11.1368
19	0.625068	10.5118
20	0.589985	9.92178

SCALE LENGTH = 31.75

Fret	Fret Interval	Remaining Scale Length
1	1.78201	29.968
2	1.68199	28.286
3	1.58759	26.6984
4	1.49848	25.1999
5	1.41438	23.7856
6	1.33499	22.4506
7	1.26006	21.1905
8	1.18934	20.0012
9	1.12259	18.8786
10	1.05958	17.819
11	1.00011	16.8189
12	0.943979	15.8749
13	0.890997	14.9839
14	0.840989	14.1429
15	0.793788	13.3491
16	0.749235	12.5999
17	0.707184	11.8927
18	0.667492	11.2252
19	0.630028	10.5952
20	0.594667	10.0005

SCALE LENGTH = 32

Fret	Fret Interval	Remaining Scale Length
1	1.79604	30.204
2	1.69523	28.5087
3	1.60009	26.9086
4	1.51028	25.3984
5	142551	23.9729
6	1.3455	22.6273
7	1.26999	21.3574
8	1.19871	20.1587
9	1.13143	19.0272
10	1.06793	17.9593
11	1.00799	16.9513
12	0.951412	15.9999
13	0.898013	15.1019
14	0.847611	14.2543
15	0.800038	13.4542
16	0.755135	12.6991
17	0.712752	11.9864
18	0.672748	11.3136
19	0.634989	10.6786
20	0.59935	10.0793

SCALE LENGTH = 32.25

Fret	Fret Interval	Remaining Scale Length
1	1.81007	30.4399
2	1.70848	28.7315
3	1.61259	27.1189
4	1.52208	25.5968
5	1.43665	24.1601
6	1.35602	22.8041
7	1.27991	21.5242
8	1.20807	21.3161
9	1.14027	19.1759
10	1.07627	18.0996
11	1.01586	17.0837
12	0.958845	16.1249
13	0.905029	15.2199
14	0.854233	14.3656
15	0.806288	13.5594
16	0.761034	12.7983
17	0.71832	12.08
18	0.678004	11.402
19	0.63995	10.762
20	0.604032	10.158

SCALE LENGTH = 32.5

Fret	Fret Interval	Remaining Scale Length
1	1.8241	30.6759
2	1.72172	28.9542
3	1.62509	27.3291
4	1.53388	25.7952
5	1.44779	24.3474
6	1.36653	22.9809
7	1.28983	21.6911
8	1.21744	20.4736
9	1.14911	19.3245
10	1.08461	18.2399
11	1.02374	17.2162
12	0.966278	16.2499
13	0.912045	15.3379
14	0.860855	14.477
15	0.812539	13.6645
16	0.766934	12.8975
17	0.723889	12.1736
18	0.68326	11.4904
19	0.644911	10.8455
20	0.608715	10.2368

SCALE LENGTH = 32.75

Fret	Fret Interval	Remaining Scale Length
1	1.83813	30.9119
2	1.73496	29.1769
3	1.63759	27.5393
4	1.54568	25.9936
5	1.45892	24.5347
6	1.37704	23.1577
7	1.29975	21.8579
8	1.2268	20.6311
9	1.15795	19.4732
10	1.09295	18.3802
11	1.03161	17.3486
12	0.973711	16.3749
13	0.91906	15.4558
14	0.867477	14.5884
15	0.818789	13.7696
16	0.772833	12.9967
17	0.729457	12.2673
18	0.688516	11.5788
19	0.649872	10.9289
20	0.613397	10.3155

SCALE LENGTH = 33

Fret	Fret Interval	Remaining Scale Length
1	1.85216	31.1478
2	1.74821	29.3996
3	1.65009	27.7495
4	1.55748	26.1921
5	1.47006	24.722
6	1.38755	23.3345
7	1.30967	22.0248
8	1.23617	20.7886
9	1.16679	19.6218
10	1.1013	18.5205
11	1.03949	17.481
12	0.981144	16.4999
13	0.926076	15.5738
14	0.874099	14.6997
15	0.825039	13.8747
16	0.778733	13.096
17	0.735026	12.3609
18	0.693771	11.6672
19	0.654833	11.0123
20	0.618079	10.3942

SCALE LENGTH = 33.25

Fret	Fret Interval	Remaining Scale Length
1	1.8662	31.3838
2	1.76145	29.6224
3	1.66259	27.9598
4	1.56927	26.3905
5	1.4812	24.9093
6	1.39806	23.5112
7	1.3196	22.1916
8	1.24553	20.9461
9	1.17562	19.7705
10	1.10964	18.6608
11	1.04736	17.6135
12	0.988577	16.6249
13	0.933092	15.6918
14	0.880721	14.8111
15	0.831289	13.9798
16	0.784632	13.1952
17	0.740594	12.4546
18	0.699027	11.7555
19	0.659794	11.0957
20	0.622762	10.473

SCALE LENGTH = 33.5

Fret	Fret Interval	Remaining Scale Length
1	1.88023	31.6198
2	1.7747	29.8451
3	1.67509	28.17
4	1.58107	26.5889
5	1.49233	25.0966
6	1.40857	23.688
7	1.32952	22.3585
8	1.2549	21.1036
9	1.18446	19.9191
10	1.11798	18.8011
11	1.05524	17.7459
12	0.99601	16.7499
13	0.940108	15.8098
14	0.887343	14.9224
15	0.83574	14.0849
16	0.790532	13.2944
17	0.746162	12.5482
18	0.704283	11.8439
19	0.664754	11.1792
20	0.627444	10.5517

SCALE LENGTH = 33.75

Fret	Fret Interval	Remaining Scale Length
1	1.89426	31.8557
2	1.78794	30.0678
3	1.68759	28.3802
4	1.59287	26.7873
5	1.50347	25.2839
6	1.41909	23.8648
7	1.33944	22.5253
8	1.26426	21.2611
9	1.1933	20.0678
10	1.12633	18.9414
11	1.06311	17.8783
12	1.00344	16.8749
13	0.947123	15.9278
14	0.893965	15.0338
15	0.84379	14.19
16	0.796431	13.3936
17	0.751731	12.6419
18	0.709539	11.9323
19	1.669715	11.2626
20	0.632127	10.6305

SCALE LENGTH = 34

Fret	Fret Interval	Remaining Scale Length
1	1.90829	32.0917
2	1.80118	30.2905
3	1.70009	28.5904
4	1.60467	26.9858
5	1.51461	25.4712
6	1.4296	24.0416
7	1.34936	22.6922
8	1.27363	21.4168
9	1.20214	20.2164
10	1.13467	19.0818
11	1.07099	18.0108
12	1.01088	16.9999
13	0.954139	16.0458
14	0.900587	15.1452
15	0.85004	14.2951
16	0.802331	13.4928
17	0.757299	12.7355
18	0.714795	12.0207
19	0.674676	11.346
20	0.636809	10.7092

SCALE LENGTH = 34.25

Fret	Fret Interval	Remaining Scale Length
1	1.92232	32.3277
2	1.81443	30.5132
3	1.71259	28.8007
4	1.61647	27.1842
5	1.52574	25.6584
6	1.44011	24.2183
7	1.35928	22.8591
8	1.28299	21.5761
9	1.21098	20.3651
10	1.14301	19.2221
11	1.07886	18.1432
12	1.01831	17.1249
13	0.961155	16.1637
14	0.907209	15.2565
15	0.856291	14.4002
16	0.80823	13.592
17	0.762867	12.8291
18	0.720051	12.1091
19	0.679637	11.4295
20	0.641492	10.788

SCALE LENGTH = 34.5

Fret	Fret Interval	Remaining Scale Length
1	1.93635	32.5636
2	1.82767	30.736
3	1.72509	29.0109
4	1.62827	27.3826
5	1.53688	25.8457
6	1.45062	24.3951
7	1.3692	23.0259
8	1.29236	21.7335
9	1.21982	20.5137
10	1.15136	19.3624
11	1.08674	18.2756
12	1.02574	17.2499
13	0.968171	16.2817
14	0.913831	15.3679
15	0.862541	14.5054
16	0.81413	13.6912
17	0.768436	12.9228
18	0.725307	12.1975
19	0.684598	11.5129
20	0.646174	10.8667

The eighteen rule can be used for laying out the scale but, though the results will be generally satisfactory, it is best to use a more accurate figure than the rounded-off figure of 18. The scale length divided by 17.817 gives the distance from the nut to the first fret. The remaining distance divided by 17.817 gives the distance from the first fret to the second fret. Continuing in this fashion to the nineteenth or twentieth (or more) frets, the scale should then be checked before transferring the measurements to the fingerboard. The twelfth fret should lie at the midpoint of the scale and the fifth fret should lie midway between the nut and the twelfth fret.

You can construct a scale geometrically rather than by cranking out mind-numbing fractions with pencil and paper. On a heavy sheet of paper, or on a thin sheet of aluminum or brass if the scale is to be kept for future use, draw a straight line the exact length of the scale. Calculate the distance to the first fret and with a pair of dividers mark out this distance. Now swing the dividers around, pivoting around the nut (or zero fret) so that a quarter arc is described which intersects a perpendicular drawn up from the nut. From this intersection draw a straight line down to the other end of the scale (the saddle). A perpendicular drawn at the first fret will intersect the tangent line and will automatically give the distance between the first fret and the second. Adjust the dividers at the first fret to the distance between the tangent and base line and draw an arc to the base line; this will give the distance to the second fret. Continue in the same fashion for the remaining frets.

The fret slots, regardless of whether they are cut by machine or by hand, should be cut before gluing the board onto the neck and body, as they can be cut more quickly and more accurately this way than after the board is glued. Don't attempt to drive the frets until after the gluing, however, as the action of driving the frets will buckle the fingerboard and make it impossible to obtain level frets and good action.

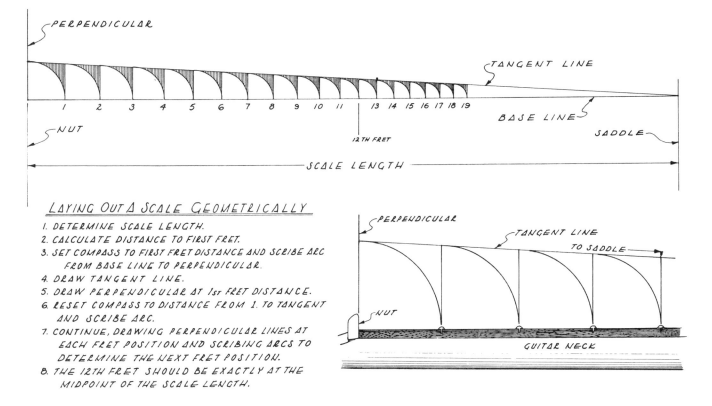

LAYING OUT A SCALE GEOMETRICALLY

1. DETERMINE SCALE LENGTH.
2. CALCULATE DISTANCE TO FIRST FRET.
3. SET COMPASS TO FIRST FRET DISTANCE AND SCRIBE ARC FROM BASE LINE TO PERPENDICULAR.
4. DRAW TANGENT LINE.
5. DRAW PERPENDICULAR AT 1st FRET DISTANCE.
6. RESET COMPASS TO DISTANCE FROM 1. TO TANGENT AND SCRIBE ARC.
7. CONTINUE, DRAWING PERPENDICULAR LINES AT EACH FRET POSITION AND SCRIBING ARCS TO DETERMINE THE NEXT FRET POSITION.
8. THE 12TH FRET SHOULD BE EXACTLY AT THE MIDPOINT OF THE SCALE LENGTH.

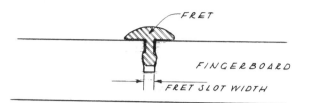

THE FRET SLOT SHOULD BE THE SAME
WIDTH AS THE TANG OF THE FRET. THE
DIMPLES IN THE TANG HOLD THE FRET DOWN.

The fingerboard and neck should now be warmed with the alcohol lamp and glued with hot fresh glue of medium consistency. Apply glue to both surfaces, rub both parts together to force out excess glue, and clamp, using a straight caul block on the top of the board to distribute clamp pressure evenly over its entire length. Particular care should be taken to see that the edges are glued down properly since the moisture in the glue tends to swell the wood and bend it away from the glue surfaces. Scoring the glue surfaces is a good idea since it helps prevent the parts from slipping as well as increasing the gluing area. With normal precautions, there is no need to align the fingerboard with either wood or metal pins between it and the neck, though this may be done if you feel so inclined.

A final scraping and sanding after the glue has dried will prepare the board for fretting. If relief is to be put into the neck, it can be done at this time by adjusting the thickness of the fingerboard so that maximum relief is obtained gradually at the fifth fret. The relief should be limited to the distance between the nut and the twelfth fret; there should be no relief beyond the twelfth fret.

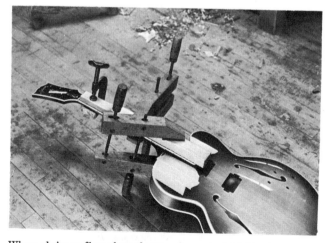

When gluing a fingerboard, use a long straight block on top to spread out the pressure of the clamps. Notice the notches in the block for the frets. (Gibson Repair Dept.)

Fretting

Fretwire should be purchased in long continuous lengths, avoiding, if at all possible, wire which has been cut into individual lengths. Apart from the extra cost and waste involved, the short lengths make the wire difficult to hold in proper alignment when driving it into the board. Nickel silver of the best quality available and of an appropriate size should be used; do not use brass wire. The softness of brass makes fretwire made of this material totally unsuitable for anything but the cheapest instruments. The majority of fretwire available today is manufactured with the serrations already built into the tang. If one is working with unserrated fretwire, the serrations will have to be put in by hand using a corner of a file or a small hammer with the head specially ground into a chisel tip.

The fret must be held in accurate alignment when driving it into the fingerboard and for this reason the fretwire should be cut into long lengths (a couple of feet or so) so that it can be held easily. Arch the fret slightly so that the outer ends of the fretwire touch the fingerboard first and with a small hammer start driving the fret by tapping down the outer ends. When the ends have been driven far enough to ensure good alignment, extend the hammer blows gradually across the entire fret and continue tapping until the entire fret has been seated. Particular care should be taken to see that the fret ends are firmly seated; heavy or careless blows with the hammer can destroy the alignment and pop the fret ends up. Once this occurs, the only solution is to remove the fret and reshape it or start with a fresh fret section. With the fret seated, cut off the end of the fret with a small three-corner (extraslim taper) file. The same specially prepared end nippers used for lifting old frets work nicely, too, and are recommended. A pair of diagonals can be used but the action of the tool will tend to lift up the fret end if cut too close to the fingerboard edge.

Glue can be used in the fret slot though it is not really necessary. The glue does tend to lubricate the fret as it is being driven and the amount squeezed out of the slot gives a useful indication of how well the fret has been driven. It is a serious mistake to use glue for the purpose of holding the fret down. Any repair, if it is to be called expert, must be done in accordance with sound and proven principles, so that the instrument will allow future adjustments and repairs to be carried out correctly and artistically. Fretting and refretting should be carried out with the thought in mind that at some future date the instrument will again require refretting. Frets glued in with, for example, epoxy cement are a poor joke to play on some unsuspecting future repairman who is expecting only a straightforward refretting job. If glue is used, use only white glue.

The portion of the fingerboard over the top of the guitar has enough give so that in most instruments the frets cannot be driven properly without additional support. All that is required is a heavy block of metal or wood held inside the guitar (beneath the fingerboard) to absorb the force of the hammer blows. A hardwood block weighted with lead will do about as well as a metal block.

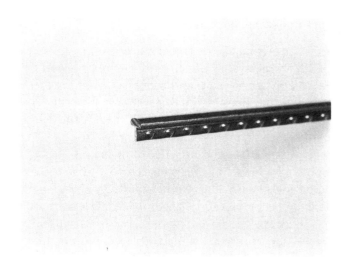

Closeup of a section of fretwire.

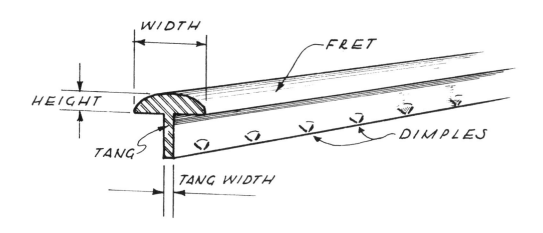

THE PRINCIPLE DIMENSIONS OF A FRET

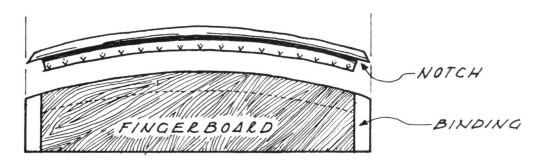

THE FRET ENDS MUST BE NOTCHED WHEN THEY ARE TO OVERLAP THE BINDING. WHEN REFRETTING IN THIS STYLE, LEAVE FRET ENDS EXTRA LONG, FILING OFF THE EXCESS AFTER ALL THE FRETS HAVE BEEN DRIVEN IN.

Final Adjusting and Leveling

After driving all the frets and rechecking to see that all are as level as possible, take a mill smooth file (ten or twelve inch) and file the ends of the frets flush with the sides of the fingerboards. The file should be run lengthwise along the edge of the board rather than up and down in order to keep from pulling a fret end up. Also with the mill smooth file, bevel the fret ends at a forty-five degree angle. With a large mill smooth twelve inch file which is known to be absolutely flat, level the frets, taking off only enough material from the top of each one to reveal a shiny filed area. With experience, the frets can be leveled while preserving the relief which was originally put into the neck.

The final steps are to reprofile the fret tops and to round off the fret ends. Reprofiling is necessary in order to restore the roundness to the fret tops after the leveling process. Although there are files especially made for the purpose, the experienced repairman will find that better all-around results are to be obtained with a small three-corner (extra-slim taper) file with a fine cut. The three-corner file will give greater control over widely differing sizes of fretwire while the special fret file is limited to one profile and one ideal fret size.

The fret ends must be finished off with the three-corner file (or an appropriate Swiss pattern file) by taking off the sharp corners left by the beveling. Since only a small amount of material is to be removed when rounding the corners, care should be taken neither to file excessively nor to gouge nicks in the fingerboard itself. Careful sanding with 320 and 600 grit sandpaper and a final rub with 0000 steel wool, together with an application of lemon oil to preserve the fingerboard, will complete the job.

It cannot be emphasized too strongly that careful preparation is the key to successful fretting or refretting. The actual technique of fretting and the little tricks which accompany it are gained only through experience. A new fingerboard or fretwork which has been artistically executed is a worthy achievement.

Refretting

Most fingerboards can be refretted several times before they are worn enough to require replacement. When fret wear is severe enough that leveling and reshaping the existing frets will not do, refretting the fingerboard is required. It should be noted that, in some instances, refretting is done for reasons other than fret wear.

When fret height is too low, it is sometimes difficult to produce a clear tone, especially in the lower positions. An excessive amount of pressure is required to hold the string down, and even then, because the low fret prevents the string from making hard contact with it, fret buzz can sometimes be produced with hard playing. This kind of buzz can be baffling to the inexperienced repairman when the usual adjustments, such as fret leveling, neck adjustment, and action adjustment, fail to cure the problem. In fact, the buzz gets worse with each attempt at fret leveling! Refretting with a higher fretwire (not necessarily wider) is the solution.

Some players like the feel of a particular size of fretwire and this is another reason for refretting.

Most classical guitarists prefer a medium size of fretwire. The medium size gives the best combination of speed, feel, and wear. For steel string acoustical and electric guitars, the choice is a toss-up between medium size and jumbo. The medium size produces a "faster" neck than the jumbo, while the jumbo wears longer. In terms of feel each has its adherents. Martin, for example, uses the medium size in all of its guitars, while Gibson, with a few exceptions, uses the jumbo wire. Fender and Guild use a variety of sizes. Interestingly enough, though the jumbo fret is better adapted to hard playing with medium or heavy gauge strings, the jumbo size is also preferred by many blues and rock players who use light or extra light rock strings and who play with a light touch.

Classical and flamenco guitars are invariably refretted with medium wire. Steel string and electrics, though, are frequently converted from medium to jumbo, which is an indication of present-day trends and techniques. Converting from jumbo to medium frets is rarely done. Electric basses should always be refretted with jumbo frets.

Below Left

These frets are badly worn and must be replaced. The majority of wear usually takes place under the first two strings.

Below Right

Badly worn frets are seen more often on steel string guitars than on nylon string instruments. The frets on this 000-18 are deeply grooved from the strings and must be replaced.

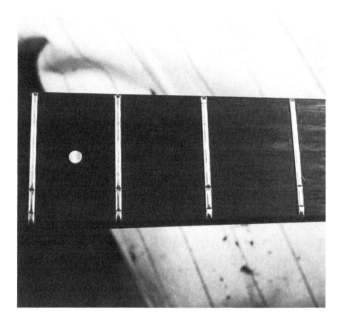

Below Left

A common fret problem is loose fret ends. Hammering the fret end down usually doesn't work because of the spring in the fret. To correct this problem, the fret must be pulled, reshaped, tang notched if necessary, and finally reset.

Below Right

Although frets usually loosen at the ends, it is possible for them to loosen and pop up in the middle, as well. The sixteenth and seventeenth frets on this Ovation must be reset.

The string "bending" techniques used by blues and rock guitarists is another reason for refretting with jumbo frets. To "bend" a string, the string is pushed sideways across the fret, raising the pitch a half step or more. In order to facilitate this technique, light gauge strings together with a plain third string, rather than a wound third, are employed. With low frets, however, it is all too easy for the fingers to slip off the string as it is bent, since most of the pressure of the fingers is spread out in contact with the fingerboard rather than with the string. In order to increase the pressure of the string against the fingers, the string must be raised higher off the fingerboard by the use of jumbo frets. As the rock guitarist would put it, this allows the fingers to "get under the strings." Additionally, the increased pressure, it is felt, also helps to increase the "sustain" of the fretted note. Some players also leave the treble string action a bit higher than absolutely necessary (with rock and roll strings this is no handicap) in order to further increase the pressure of the string against the fingers. As an example illustrating the use of jumbo frets, the Gibson Les Paul Custom guitar, favored by many rock guitarists, comes with very low "fretless wonder" frets. The large majority of these guitars are converted at one time or another (many while still new) to jumbo frets.

When pulling out old frets, two methods can be used. A pair of end cutting pliers which have been ground flat on the outside surface can be used. As an alternate, a pair of wood chisels inserted on each side of the fret can be used. Frets can be pulled from rosewood and maple fingerboards quite cleanly. Ebony fingerboards are more difficult, particularly old boards where the wood has become very brittle. Lifting an occasional chip is almost unavoidable with an ebony board and should be no cause for concern, though every effort should be made to minimize this occurrence and to reglue the chips.

After pulling the frets, the fingerboard should be examined and dressed with plane and sandpaper as necessary to eliminate irregularities and to restore the original contour. If the neck has an adjustable truss rod, be sure to readjust the rod for neck straightness before this operation.

Fretwire should be chosen so that the fret tang is a proper fit in the fret slot. A number of different sizes must be kept in stock, because tang size must be considered as well as fret height and width.

Below Left

Frets may be pulled with the use of a modified endcutter. The outer surface of the cutter which contacts the fingerboard must be ground smooth and flat so that lifting of chips from the fingerboard will be kept to an absolute minimum.

Below Right

When driving in new frets, the fretwire should be left in a long strip so that you can hold on to the free end while driving the fret in. Tap the ends in first, before gradually proceeding across the entire fret.

In refretting fingerboards with binding, two methods may be used. The first method, applicable in the majority of cases, is to remove the binding before refretting. After refretting, the binding is reglued and, if necessary, the finish between binding and neck touched up. Binding with multiple layers of black and white, such as on the Gibson L-5 and S-400, and binding which is difficult to remove are left on during refretting. This requires cutting the fretwire to correct size and notching the ends so that the tang will fit between the bound edges of the board. It is important to leave the fret slightly long during this process. The fret ends are automatically trimmed to correct length when the frets are beveled with the mill smooth file. All models of Martin guitars which have bound fingerboards, such as the D-35 and the 000-45, are refretted by the latter method. On these guitars, the fret ends extend to the outside edge of the binding rather than to the inside edge. Therefore, the fret ends must be notched regardless of whether the binding is removable.

From this point on, refretting continues as described in the section on fretting, p.92. A few additional refretting hints, though, may be helpful.

Guitars which have been refretted several times have fret slots which frequently are wider at the ends than in the middle. The fretwire can be additionally serrated at the ends with the technique described in the section on fretting.

Maple fingerboards such as those used on Fender electrics have a highly polished finish which should be protected when working on the frets. This is most easily done by placing masking tape between the frets. If the fingerboard must be refinished, several coats of a clear lacquer or epoxy finish can be sprayed on.

On Fenders and other guitars with detachable necks, you may find it easier to work on the neck by removing it from the body and holding the heel in a vise with padded jaws.

Fingerboards which are heavily worn on the edges (giving a scalloped effect) must be planed and sanded so that there is a distinct edge between the top surface of the board and the side. If the board is left rounded, it will be difficult to get the fret end to lie flat without sharp edges protruding.

Below Left
Cut off the excess with a triangle file after the fret has been driven in. An end nipper may also be used.

Below Right
File the ends flush. When binding is to be replaced as on this ES-175 do not bevel the ends till after the binding is on.

Below Left

With the binding on and the fret ends leveled, file the top surface of the frets to ensure all are level with each other. File only till a shiny line appears across the tops of each fret. Unless you are intentionally lowering the overall height of the frets, it is best to leave each fret as high as possible.

Below Right

Round off the fret ends. This is the last step before finishing off the frets with sandpaper and steel wool.

Below Left

When binding is reglued, string wrapped around the fingerboard does a good job. The fingerboard on the D'Angelico shrank, allowing the fret ends to protrude, pushing the binding away from the fingergoard edge. The binding was removed to allow filing the fret ends flush. The same system of clamping with string (or tape) can be used when gluing new bindings as well as old.

Below Right

Guitars with multiple fingerboard binding, as this S-400, present additional difficulties when refretting. Each fret must be trimmed individually before placement, since it is impractical to remove the binding before refretting.

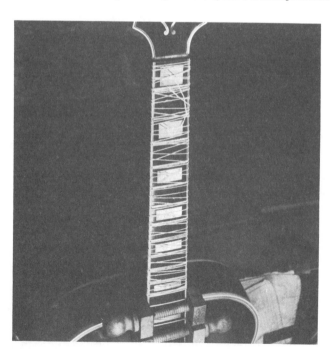 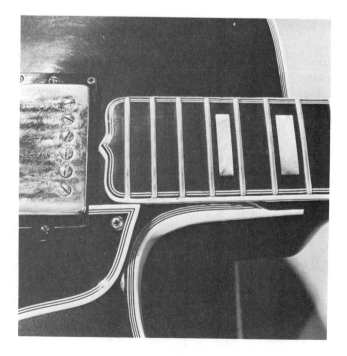

Truss Rod

The purpose of a truss rod is to provide additional stiffness in the neck and to compensate for the tension of the strings. In most classical or nylon string guitars, the truss rod is neither necessary nor desirable, provided the neck is constructed properly and with the proper choice of wood. On most steel string guitars (both six- and twelve-string), especially those strung with medium gauge or heavier strings, a truss rod is an absolute necessity. On guitars strung with very light rock and roll or "slinky" strings, an adjustable truss rod, though not necessary to compensate for the tension of the strings, is an aid in setting up the neck for proper relief and action.

There are two types of truss rods—the adjustable and the nonadjustable. Since principles of operation are different for the two types, it is important to understand the theory of operation before repairing or installing one in an actual guitar.

Nonadjustable Type

The principle of the nonadjustable truss rod is to provide maximum stiffness to the neck. In many of the older guitars, both nylon and steel string, this was provided by inlaying an ebony insert down the length of the neck below the fingerboard. Though rarely used on steel string guitars today, this method is still seen on some classical guitars. Since the tension of nylon strings is moderate, the addition of a stronger wood to a neck, though not absolutely necessary, provides an additional bit of insurance against warpage.

A rigid steel bar is used in the usual nonadjustable truss rod and adds substantially to the stiffness of a neck. Early steel string guitars employed a simple flat bar, about 3/8 by 3/32 inch wide and the length of the neck. This was set into the neck just below the fingerboard. Certain models of the Washburn had this bar extend through the end-block and through the top almost to the end of the fingerboard.

Another rod which proved satisfactory over a period of many years was the T-bar used on the Martin steel string line. This bar, which was about 3/8 inch in both height and width, combined light weight with excellent stiffness and was a substantial improvement over the simpler flat bar stock.

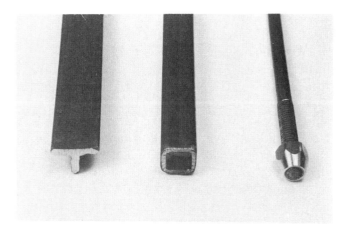

Truss rods. The two fixed rods on the left are used on Martin guitars. The adjustable rod on the right is used on Gibson guitars.

Martin currently uses a hollow bar 3/8 inch square and the results appear to be as good as with the old T-bar. The hollow square bar is easier to install than the T-bar; for most original installations, this style would be the best choice.

Of course a solid square bar can also be used, though, while satisfactory, it will add some unnecessary weight. Do not use a round tube or bar as this configuration will not give the maximum stiffness to the neck.

Installation

There is a good range of styles to choose from, and what you use will depend on what is available and the amount of stiffness required. Flat bar stock, T-bar, hollow and solid square bar, and U channel stock are all satisfactory. If the material you have is a replacement part for a guitar which is known to have a good neck, there is little to worry about. If your material is untested, it would be best to compare it with other bars to see if it has the necessary stiffness.

One of the main requirements in fitting a nonadjustable bar is to obtain a snug fit. A loose bar can rattle on some notes and in some cases be worse than having no rod at all! The best installations are with a stiff bar, snugly fitted and glued securely into place. You should remember that, even with the best bar, a small amount of flexing is unavoidable. For this reason, especially when medium or heavy gauge strings are to be used, you should set up your neck and fingerboard so that, with no tension, there will be a small amount of reverse bow in the neck. With the strings up to pitch, the reverse bow will disappear and the neck will have the proper amount of relief.

Adjustable Type

With the notable exception of Martin, most manufacturers of steel string guitars use an adjustable truss rod in the necks of their guitars. Rather than adding extra stiffness to the neck, the adjustable truss rod (with a couple of exceptions) operates by putting the neck under compression. One end of the rod, usually at the heel, is fastened so that it can't rotate. The other end is threaded so that, when tightened with a nut, the area of the neck between the two ends of the rod is put under compression. Because there is more wood above the truss rod—this includes the fingerboard as well as the upper half of the neck—than below, the neck will compress more below the truss rod. Because of this uneven compression effect, tightening of the truss rod will give a reverse bow, counteracting the tension of the strings. For successful operation, there are certain criteria which *must* be met; these should be kept in mind when repairing or installing a truss rod.

The wood in the neck above the truss rod—and this includes the fingerboard—must be stronger than the wood below. If the fingerboard is loosely glued, or if the frets are loose, this may adversely affect the operation of the rod. If during the course of repair the fingerboard must be replaced, be sure to use good ebony or rosewood and don't make the fingerboard any thinner than the original since a good portion of the strength of a neck lies in the fingerboard.

The truss rod must be set as deeply into the neck as possible. The closer the rod is to the back of the neck the better, since this location increases the difference in strength above the truss rod and below. A rod which has been set into the neck just below the fingerboard rarely works well and sometimes not at all since it is compressing just the fingerboard against all of the wood in the neck. Sometimes in this situation the neck warpage is increased when tightening the adjusting nut!

In addition to the truss rod described above, which is the most common type, there are a couple of others which may be of interest. The Harmony truss rod is composed of two rods, parallel to each other and fastened together at the heel end. At the peghead, the lower rod is threaded and carries the adjusting nut. In front of the adjusting nut is a collar large enough to contact the end of the upper

Below Left
Some guitars, notably those from Fender, have their truss rod adjustment at the upper end of the neck.

Below Right
This Rickenbacker guitar has two truss rods. Notice that each rod consists of a double bar which can be removed without taking the fingerboard off. Replacing a broken truss rod, in this instance, is a cinch! The style of operation is similar to the Harmony rod described in the text.

rod. When the nut is tightened, the upper rod is put under compression. Under compression, the upper steel rod is very rigid, and the net effect, as the adjusting nut is tightened, is to bend the neck in a reverse bow, the same as the conventional truss rod. An interesting point with the Harmony rod is that, since the rod is not fastened to the neck at all, a broken rod can usually be withdrawn and replaced by a new one without removing the fingerboard.

The older Epiphones used a bar which was adjustable with an allen wrench below the upper end of the fingerboard on their archtop models. This rod was threaded into a stationary nut near the heel of the guitar. The end of the rod nearest the peghead pressed against a stationary block. By turning the rod, the stationary block and the threaded nut were forced away from each other, creating a bend in the neck.

A last variation is one which can be adjusted for a bend in both directions. The rod is threaded near the ends with a left-hand thread on one side and a right-hand thread on the other. This rod, unlike the conventional one, is set into the neck just below the fingerboard and with the two nuts stationary. Turning the rod in one direction draws the nuts together, bowing the neck up. Turning the rod in the opposite direction forces the nuts apart, giving the neck a reverse bow. In most cases, the additional complexity of this system is not worth the bother since you will usually be adjusting to counteract the tension of the strings. However, if you have a reverse warp and are using rock and roll strings, in many cases the tension of the strings won't be enough to take out the warp. This particular situation is made to order for the two-way rod because with the conventional rod the only solution would be to heat bend the neck in order to straighten it.

Installation

Installation of a conventional truss rod should be quite straightforward since you now know what to do and what to avoid. You may purchase a factory rod from any number of guitar companies or you may make your own by threading a rod of about 3/32 inch diameter at one end. The blank end can be bent over at right angles (about half an inch will be enough) or a short bar can be fastened to the end to prevent the stationary end from rotating. The stationary end of the rod will be fastened to the neck directly over the heel. The threaded end will project into the peghead and past the nut by about half an inch. The neck will have to be slotted to take the rod. If the neck is separate from the body, this may be done on a table saw. If the neck is still attached to the body or if this is a repair or installation on a used guitar, you should use a router. Be sure to slot the neck deep enough so that the rod will be 1/4 to 3/8 inch below the upper surface of the neck. At the same time you may also hollow out the peghead area around the threaded end in order to allow clearance for a socket wrench or nut driver. Set the truss rod into the neck and glue a maple inlay piece snugly over the rod. Note that the proper position for the adjusting nut is *not* directly below the nut but in the peghead above it by about a quarter inch. This position allows use of a smaller truss rod cover and gives a generally neater appearance.

When installing your truss rod, plan ahead and put some relief in the neck with no string tension and with the truss rod nut loose. In this way, you will always have *some* tension in the rod regardless of the string gauge. A reverse warp is not affected by a conventional truss rod, so if you plan to use light gauge or rock and roll strings it is better to start with too much relief (which can be adjusted out) rather than with too little (which cannot).

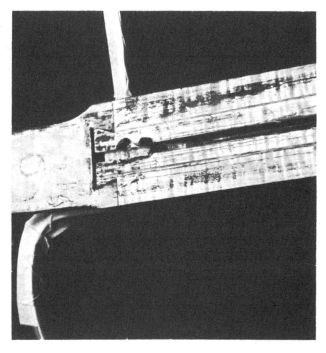

A broken truss rod, as on this Gibson, requires complete removal of the fingerboard. In this example, the truss rod broke at the extreme end (opposite the nut) and removal required cutting away the wood inlay over the truss rod for a distance of four or five inches.

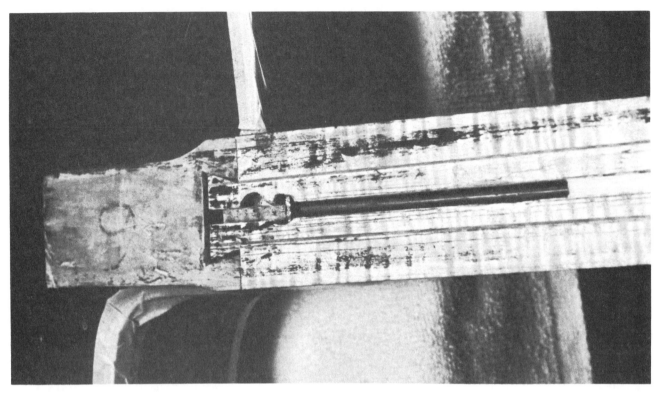

The truss rod has been replaced by pushing it through from the body toward the peghead.

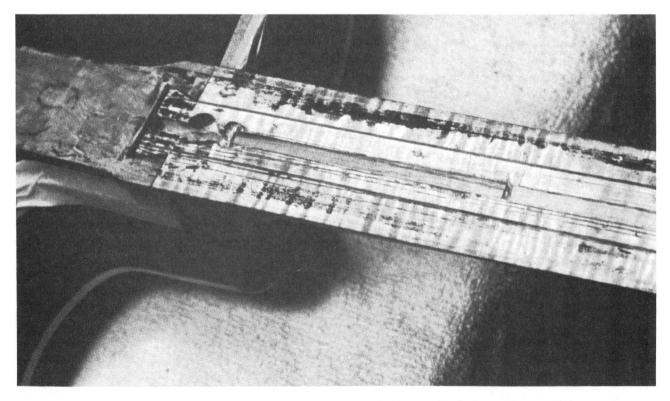

The wood inlay over the truss rod is replaced and the fingerboard is reglued, completing the repair.

The Bridge

Though the steps involved in regluing or replacing a bridge are simple and straightforward, attention to detail and a high degree of precision is required in order to ensure permanence and accuracy of scale.

Removal

There are four steps required in this repair, the first of which is removal. Guitars with bridges completely pulled off and new guitars with bridges to be glued on for the first time will, of course, not require this step. However, a broken bridge or one which has pulled partially loose must be removed, and for this operation one needs only a thin table knife.

If there are open spots, the knife is started there; if not, the best spot is at one of the corners of the bridge feet. One should work the knife slowly, around the edges at first and then toward the center, though this should be taken as a general guide only, since the problems of the particular job at hand may modify the procedure. If the knife feels as if it is encountering unusual resistance or is starting to dig into the top, it should be withdrawn and worked in from the other side. No moisture is used. Some repairmen report good results by using heat to soften the glue. This can be done with an alcohol lamp or an electric iron placed on top of the bridge. Keep in mind that this method is practical only on unlacquered bridges, however; for most classical guitars where the bridge is finished, no heat can be used.

Occasionally, machine or wood screws are used to help hold the bridge in place and these must be removed before bridge removal can be completed. Hardwood pins may also be found in some bridges to locate and position the bridge while gluing. This feature is to be found occasionally (though not exclusively) on Mexican guitars. All of this hardware inside the bridge is of no particular help in holding a bridge on and can only harm the tone of the instrument. A carefully glued bridge is *permanent* under any string tension or climatic condition normally encountered. Reliance on bolts or screws, particularly when none are present originally, is the mark of the amateur.

This bridge is about to pull off! Only the bridge pins are holding it on.

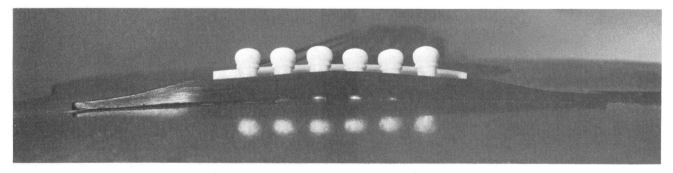

Things are not always what they seem; this bridge is not about to pull off. The bridge on this Gibson LG-0 is plastic and is held in place with three screws rather than with glue. Warpage of the plastic causes this condition and can only be cured by replacing with another plastic bridge or by gluing on a conventional wood bridge.

Below Left
When removing a bridge, it is usually easiest to start the palate knife at a corner. Pin bridges such as on this Guild are easier to remove than Spanish-style bridges.

Below Right
Working the table knife through at an angle produces the best results when pulling off a bridge.

 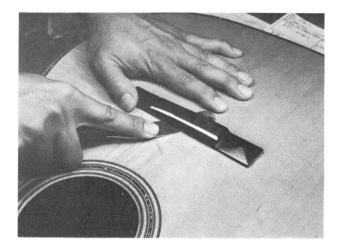

Cleaning

A thorough cleaning with scraper and sandpaper of the area to be glued is very important, particularly when the glue used previously was one that failed because of "creep." Rosewood bridges as well as all new bridges should be scraped to expose a fresh surface for gluing. Rosewood is not difficult to glue providing one works with clean, fresh surfaces. No solvent is required to clean the gluing surface.

Some bridges are arched to fit the arching to the top. In cleaning, therefore, you should be careful to retain the same contour. Bridges which have pulled loose only partially, however, frequently become badly warped from the tension of the strings. Such bridges, providing their condition and value warrants the effort, can be saved by straightening. The bridge should be heated gently with an alcohol lamp and then clamped at the appropriate spots to return it to its original contours. In some cases, the straightening can be done by hand since the heated wood becomes quite flexible.

When the top is refinished, the area for the bridge must be masked off to preserve a clean gluing surface. (Gibson Repair Dept.)

Placement

The positioning of the bridge must be done with care and with regard to the type of guitar and the style of music it is designed for. Most classical and flamenco guitars have bridges positioned so that there is more clearance from string to edge of fingerboard on the treble side than on the bass side. The greater clearance on the treble side facilitates execution of left-hand technique without danger of pulling the first string off the edge of the fingerboard. With steel string guitars, the greater tension of the strings lessens the danger of pulling a string off the edge of the board and it is permissible to have equal spacing on both treble and bass sides.

Proper placement of the bridge for correct intonation is critical and the first rule to remember is, don't trust the manufacturer to have the bridge in the correct position. I've seen too many new guitars which had bridges in the wrong place, not to mention older instruments which had bridges reglued incorrectly. Trust *no one*, and take your own measurement; only then will you know that the bridge is in the right place.

The actual placement of the bridge, measured from the front edge of the saddle to the front edge of the nut, is equal to the scale length plus compensation. The scale length is equal to twice the distance from the nut to the twelfth fret. For example, if the distance from the nut to the twelfth fret is 12 1/2 inches and the proper compensation is 1/16 inch, the scale length is 25 inches

The new bridge is carefully positioned before clamping. (Gibson Repair Dept.)

The clamps are placed through the soundhole and tightened. Note the use of the block above the bridge. This block serves the purpose of evening out the pressure of the clamps, allowing fewer clamps, and preventing damage to the bridge. (Gibson Repair Dept.)

and the distance from nut to saddle is 25 1/16 inches. For the proper amount of compensation the reader should refer to the section on string compensation.

Since scratches and pencil marks are too easily obscured when the actual gluing is done and do nothing to prevent accidental slippage while clamping, positioning of the bridge should be done with slips of veneer taped or clamped to the face of the guitar. A position guide in front of each foot and one guide at one end is sufficient.

Note the use of the blocks for positioning the bridge and the tape over the string holes to keep out glue.

Gluing

As a final step, the gluing surfaces should be roughened, not only to present a better gluing surface, but also to help prevent accidental slippage while clamping. Gluing of the bridge requires at least three (occasionally five or more when the top is thin and uneven) deep C clamps and a pot of fresh hot glue of moderate thickness. You may wish to use a block beneath the clamps, shaped to the upper surface of the bridge, to spread out the force of the clamps. In some cases, this method allows fewer clamps to be used. Apply glue to both surfaces and clamp the bridge, wiping away the surplus glue while it is still liquid. The position guides can be removed as soon as the clamps are set. With the Spanish or classical-type bridge, a strip of tape covering the string holes will keep glue from accidentally plugging the holes. Under favorable conditions the instrument can be strung up after twelve hours drying time, though it is better, especially for steel string guitars, to allow twenty-four hours or more before final cleanup, adjustment, and restringing.

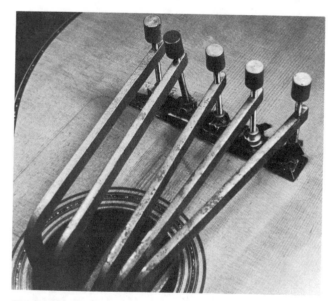

Tape, as in this repair, can be used to pad the clamp jaws. Glue and clamp evenly, using up to five or more clamps if necessary.

Gluing on a lute bridge sometimes requires a more elaborate setup than is needed for a guitar.

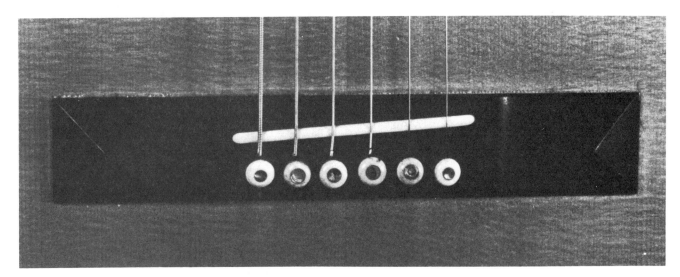

This replacement bridge was carved to duplicate the original (with the pyramid feet). The saddle has been compensated, rather than left straight as on the original, in order to improve intonation.

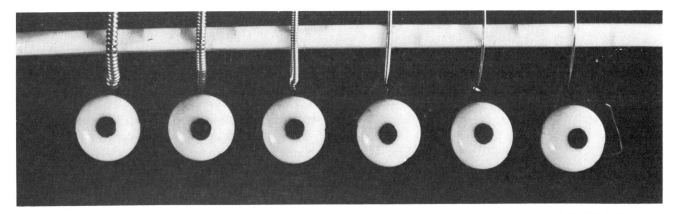

In addition to the usual compensation from bass side to treble side, the saddle can be compensated for each individual string. Note the increased compensation in the B string with respect to the E and G.

Repairing Cracks and Missing Sections

Due to the nature of guitar construction and the physical properties and dimensions of the woods used, cracks, when they do occur, can tax the skill of the most experienced repairman. The more extensive repairs may require precise lining up of cracked sections, replacement of missing parts with matching wood, addition of reinforcing studs or cleats where necessary, and final touchup and matching of the finish, all of which require an artistic eye as well as extensive experience and skill. The type and extent of the repair should only be enough to put the instrument in sound physical and tonal condition; particularly with older or more valuable instruments, the work of the maker should be respected by keeping the instrument in as original a condition as possible.

The seriousness of a crack is not necessarily related to its length since the nature of the crack and its location can have a considerable influence on the method and cost of repair. Compared to a violin, whose construction allows for fairly easy removal of the top, the construction of the usual guitar renders the removal of the top or back a complex and time consuming project. Because of the nature of the binding and purfling, which often is composed of intricate inlays and veneers, the removal of one of the plates (usually the back is most convenient) is reserved for major repairs or restorations which could not otherwise be done. In many cases, all inside work can be done through the soundhole which, fortunately, is usually large enough to allow the insertion of clamps, inspection lamps and mirrors, probes, and (most conveniently) hands. The arch top plectrum guitar with f holes presents more of a problem though there is less need for inside work because of the simplicity of the inside and the generally heavy construction. Binding and purfling on most plectrum guitars are usually simple so that back or top removal, when required, can be done with less difficulty.

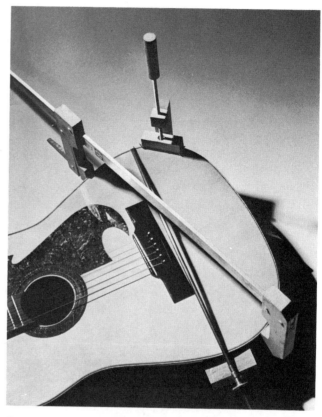

Sometimes a number of different types of clamps are required for a particular job. In this operation, a top crack and loose edge (upper part of photo) are being glued simultaneously.

Simple Cracks

Cracks with tight fitting edges, with edges which are or can be placed in perfect alignment, and with edges which are clean and free of dirt or old glue can be classed as *simple* and require a minimum of time and effort to repair. Length is not particularly important, though a crack that extends the entire length of the side or back is, obviously, going to take more time and effort than the usual short one. The matter of a tight fit with proper alignment is an important point to consider since, with cracks in this category as well as with cracks in general, the amount of time spent in actual gluing is small compared to the time spent in study, preparation, and touchup. Time spent in study and in trial alignment and clamping without glue can mean the difference between an invisible repair and disaster.

If the edges are already aligned, it is only a matter of working in glue and clamping. Edges out of line will require aligning with probes and hands, working either from the inside of the guitar through the soundhole or from the outside, or both, as the situation demands. The amount of effort used to align the edge can be slight to considerable, as when "popping out" a misaligned edge where, for example, the inside surface of one edge is resting against the outside surface of the adjacent edge. Apply pressure adjacent to the misaligned edge and apply the clamps. At this point, if the edges have aligned and stay in alignment easily, the repairman can proceed with the repair. If the crack refuses to align or stays in alignment only with difficulty, it is well to consider the use of temporary internal braces or a helper to aid in the gluing. The added difficulties put the repair out of the simple category and will probably require additional inside work with cleats as well. If, however, all has gone well to this point, the clamps can now be removed and the crack glued, using medium light to medium heavy glue. Very small and tight cracks require fairly light glue in order to ensure adequate penetration, while larger cracks, where glue can be more easily worked in, can take the medium thick glue.

The glue should be rubbed in from the outside while "working" (slightly opening and closing) the edge with the hand or probe. The slight movement of the edge, the moisture in the glue, and the rubbing combine to work the glue completely through the joint. When the glue has been worked completely through the crack, as evidenced by a thin bead of glue visible from the inside, align the edges as perfectly as possible, clamp, and wipe away the excess glue with a damp cloth. If the work has been skillfully done, the edges will be perfectly matched, will require no scraping or sanding, and will need only a slight touchup of the finish. Inasmuch as the top, sides, and back of the guitar are quite thin to start with, particular pains should be taken to line up the edges so that only the barest minimum of sanding, if any at all, will be required to match up the edge. It is not permissible to allow careless or hasty work with the thought of attempting correction by extensive scraping or sanding.

Below Left

A loose edge, as on this Martin classic, can occur for a number of reasons. In this example, the guitar was accidentally dropped on its side.

Below Right

In most cases, the entire edge can be reglued at one time. Use enough clamps so that the pressure can be placed evenly on the edge.

Loose Braces

Loose or cracked braces often make themselves known through loss of tone or through buzzes or rattles when certain notes are played. If not attended to promptly, the loss of strength can lead to other more serious damage such as cracks, splits, or warpage of various parts of the body. Braces can come loose because of unfavorable climatic conditions or from a sharp blow. A sharp blow or excessive pressure can also crack or split a brace, with the damage to the braces often occurring along with breaks in the adjacent areas of the top or back. The repairman must consider whether to glue the brace first, the damaged top (or back) first, or both simultaneously. The fact that the top of a guitar with its more numerous and more delicate bracing pattern is more difficult to work on than the back is compensated by the knowledge that the back, though simpler, requires work more often than the top. Top and back require slightly different techniques though the first step, determining the area of the looseness or break, is common to both.

The universal method of determining looseness of components, and of breaks or cracks in any part of the instrument, consists of tapping the instrument gently in the suspected area with the back of the knuckles. Sound areas will reveal themselves to the repairman by sounding out with a solid, dull thump. A crack, or area with a loose part, will report as a sharp, percussive "click." The two sounds are very distinctive and with brief practice one can quickly determine the area and extent of the damage. A further visual check together with moderate pressure in flexing the area under suspicion will also help determine the proper course of repair.

The usual inspection lamps and mirrors must be supplemented with special glue brushes and deep-throated C clamps. The glue brushes are simply small stiff-bristled brushes on the end of long wire handles. The C clamps which will probably have to be made in the shop should be of various sizes including lengths that will reach the lower bouts of the guitar.

Loose or cracked braces in the back can rarely be held in place with a clamp; this must be done with posts wedged between the brace and the top. The glue should be run in along the loosened or cracked area with the long-handled brush (bent to reach the desired area), viewing with the lamp and inspection mirror when necessary. Slight flexing or "working" of the affected area will draw the glue into the joint. Wipe away the excess glue and hold the brace down with the post, using only enough pressure to move the brace into its original position. In addition to cutting the post to the proper length, the top will have to be protected against excessive pressure. In some instances, the top of the post can be placed against a top brace; in others, a small platform will have to be fastened to the top of the post in order to spread the pressure

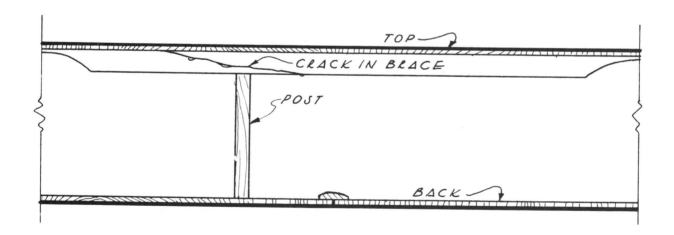

WHEN GLUEING A CRACKED OR LOOSE BRACE, A TEMPORARY POST MAY BE WEDGED BENEATH THE BRACE TIL THE GLUE DRIES.

over a wider area. When the glue is dry, remove the post and test again for looseness before placing the instrument in service. Be certain to remove the post because a forgotten "soundpost" will play havoc with the tone of the guitar!

Top braces may also be wedged into place, or a C clamp may be used instead. Gluings in the area of the bridge will almost certainly require the use of the inspection lamp and mirror. Working with a long-handled brush and a mirror through the limited confines of a soundhole is not the easiest task in the world, though it can be done neatly and without problems when the repair is preceded by careful study and preparation. As with many repair situations, the actual repair takes only a fraction of the time spent in study, trial fittings, and preparation.

A loose brace may occur together with a crack directly over the loosened area. Gluing the brace before the crack, however, may prevent proper alignment of the crack because of excess dried glue. If the nature of the damage allows sufficient gluing time, without rushing the job, it may be convenient to glue brace and crack in one operation.

Cracks with Missing Chips and Pieces

Cracks in this category can range from those which have small chips or splinters missing to those with extensive fractures, crushed wood, and large holes. The more complex repairs in this category can be quite a challenge to the talents and ingenuity of the repairman for they bring into use practically all the processes of the art of repairing. The selection and matching of wood for both tone and appearance, the fitting of new parts to the instrument, the addition of reinforcing members, the matching of finish—the repairman will have to be familiar with and skilled in all of these separate phases if he is to consistently produce work of high quality and craftsmanship.

The smaller breaks—those which are in the simple category, but with a missing chip or two—should first be repaired following the previous instructions. All excess glue must be thoroughly cleaned off, particularly around the area of the missing chip, before proceeding to replace or fill the section. You have a choice of filling the missing portion with wood, wood putty, wood dust mixed

Unfortunately, the person who worked on this guitar didn't take the time to reinlay the missing abalone and binding. The missing sections were filled with wood putty.

with glue, stick lacquer—the list can go on and on, depending on your ingenuity and imagination. Wood is unquestionably the best when the area of the missing portion is such that the color of the wood and the size and direction of the grain become noticeable. Wood putty, which requires drying time, shrinks and requires a fair amount of touchup since it is available only in limited colors. Wood dust mixed with glue retains the disadvantages of wood putty though it has the advantage of a good color match when care is taken in selecting wood.

The most versatile material—for small chips and splinters only—is stick lacquer or stick shellac. These materials, as the names suggest, come in stick form and are melted or "burned" into the depressions with a burn-in knife. They are available in a wide range of colors as well as transparencies which range from extra clear to semi-opaque and opaque. Since there is no drying time, and the material is dimensionally stable as well, the repair can be completed in minimum time. The material is brittle, though, which limits its use to the filling of very small areas.

Select a color and transparency which will most closely match the color of the surrounding wood or finish. If the exposed wood beneath the area to be filled differs greatly in color from the surrounding finish it is advisable to first stain the wood before using the stick lacquer. With a heated palate knife or special burn-in knife, melt a small amount of filler and apply it to the area to be filled. Fill, with smooth even strokes, keeping as much of it as possible off the surrounding finished surfaces. Pick up excess with the knife as the lacquer starts to cool. A gentle sanding with No. 320 sandpaper will level the surface and prepare the repair for final touchup.

Larger missing chips as well as holes in the body require more extensive repairs, including reinforcement as well as replacement of the missing portions with matching wood. A damaged area which is to be replaced with matching wood must be cut away only as much as necessary to obtain true edges. Since the replacement piece need not be square or rectangular, its shape should be determined by the shape of the damaged area and by the convenience in fitting. Straight sides are easier to fit than curved or irregular ones.

For the usual repair, the replacement of chips and missing parts is most easily attended to after the surrounding cracks have been glued. Trim the rough, ragged edges of the damaged area, keeping all edges as true as possible. It is well to prepare the reinforcement cleats at this time because, depending on the nature of the damage, it may be more convenient to glue in the reinforcements before putting in the repaired section rather than after. The main concern at this time, though, revolves around the selection and fitting of the new wood.

The shop must have not only the usual selection of woods used in guitar construction but also these same woods in varying degrees of color and grain characteristics. You should not, for example, replace a missing portion of a European spruce top with a piece of Sitka spruce since the characteristics are so different. Furthermore, a very old instrument is most easily matched with wood of similar age because the appearance of old wood is difficult to simulate when using relatively new wood. The important points to keep in mind when matching are color, variety of wood, and grain pattern and direction. If an exact color cannot be obtained, it is better to choose wood of a slightly lighter color since it is far easier to darken the new section than to lighten it. The new piece should be fitted as well as the skill of the repairman will allow, keeping in mind one small but important technique. When trimming the sides of the new piece, *bevel* them inward slightly so that, when fitted to the instrument, the piece can be wedged in snugly. This method of fitting replacement sections produces a very neat and inconspicuous glue joint.

Below Left

This 0-16NY Martin requires major rebuilding and this should only be attempted by skilled repairmen. The sides, including the lining, must be rebuilt. On this repair, the back was replaced, using the original braces.

Below Right

With the broken back off the 0-16NY, the sides can be rebuilt. This type of repair, where major sections are being replaced, requires knowledge of construction also.

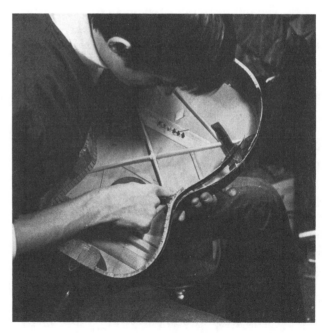

Below Left

Trimming the excess material from the new back. Since there is no binding on the back edge of this particular model, extra care must be taken to ensure a clean joint between the sides and back.

Below Right

After the new wood has been stained the finish is applied, allowed to dry thoroughly, and polished.

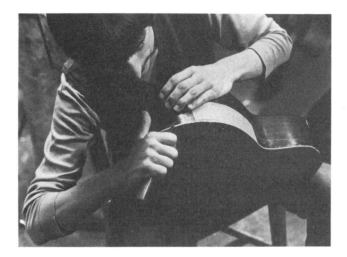 

Below Left

A badly splintered hole in the side of this guitar requires replacement with a new section.

Below Right

The new section must be matched for color and grain before bending and trimming to fit. A reinforcing strip has been added to the left edge. The three small screws to the right are temporary aids to positioning the new section.

The new section is glued in place, using clamps and blocks as necessary.

The repair is complete and ready for refinishing.

When repairing sides, the larger sections will have to be bent to conform to the contours of the sides. In any event, after the new piece has been glued and clamped into place and the excess wood on the surface removed with knife, scraper, and sandpaper, the repair can be concluded with the addition of reinforcing cleats (if not glued in earlier) and final touchup.

Open cracks, in which the edges of the crack have pulled away from each other leaving an open gap no matter how hard the parts are clamped, present another set of problems for the repairman. Such cracks may appear for a variety of reasons such as shrinkage of poorly seasoned wood, exposure to very dry climatic conditions, or long neglect of what was originally a small and tight fitting crack. Since it's difficult, in some cases, to determine whether or not the wood will continue to shrink, you should assume that the possibility of further shrinkage still exists, and repair accordingly.

Though it is possible, in some cases, to force the edges of an open crack or split together, this is poor practice since, in addition to placing the entire instrument under a strain (to the detriment of tone), the chances of the repair holding up over a long period of time are remote unless reinforced heavily. Even if successful there is an increased chance of another crack opening up alongside the original one. If, however, the instrument is known to have cracked due to prolonged exposure to excessively dry conditions, letting the guitar stand for a week or so at normal conditions may close

the crack completely, leaving little to do except repair as a simple crack. As an added precaution, reinforcement cleats should always be used behind the crack.

Filling an open crack with glue and sawdust is, except for the smallest openings, not a practice to be recommended. The best method, and the strongest as well, involves the inlaying of matching wood to take the place of the shrunken section. The edges of most open cracks are quite uneven so the first thing to be done is to gently run a very thin knife blade through the middle of the opening in order to more clearly define the edges; wood must not be removed. The inlay wood, which should match the surrounding material as closely as possible, can be prepared in several ways. The smallest openings can be fitted with an inlay taken from plane shavings while larger openings will require larger sections either cut by machine or stripped with a knife. Bevel the edges slightly so that the inlay can be wedged in snugly, leaving enough extra material on top to allow for later trimming. As a matter of fact, it is easier to fit an inlay when the height is half an inch or more because this adds extra stiffness while giving the fingers something to hold on to.

Aside from taking precautions to line up the opposite edges of the crack, no difficulties should be encountered. On cracks or splits of this nature, reinforcement cleats or studs should be used, the number and size varying, of course, depending on the location and extent of the crack.

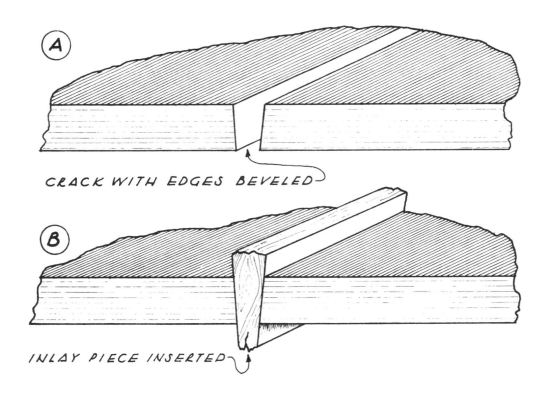

Ⓐ CRACK WITH EDGES BEVELED

Ⓑ INLAY PIECE INSERTED

Ⓐ WHEN A CRACK IS TO BE INLAID, THE FIRST STEP IS TO SMOOTH THE EDGES AND TO FORM A SLIGHT BEVEL.

Ⓑ THE INLAY PIECE IS SHAPED TO A MATCHING BEVEL, AND GLUED IN. THE EXCESS IS TRIMMED OFF _AFTER_ THE GLUE HAS DRIED.

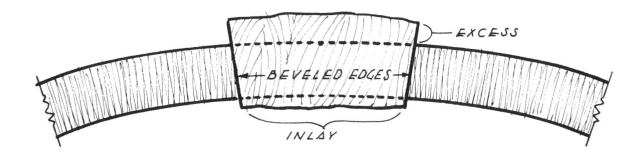

EXCESS

BEVELED EDGES

INLAY

WHENEVER A HOLE IS TO BE INLAID THE EDGES SHOULD BE BEVELED SO THAT THE INLAY PIECE CAN BE FITTED SNUGLY. THE EXCESS WOOD FROM THE INLAY PIECE IS TRIMMED AFTER THE INLAY HAS BEEN GLUED INTO PLACE.

Reinforcing Cracks

Cleats or studs used for reinforcing a crack are made from spruce for the top, while for the sides and back they can be spruce or a slightly harder wood, such as mahogany. Their dimensions can vary from small half inch squares to larger ones for reinforcing several parallel cracks at one time. Spacing can vary from one or two per inch to one per three inches, depending on the seriousness of the break. Thicknesses vary from 1/16 to 3/32 inch and the edges should be nicely beveled before inserting into the guitar unless the instrument has been previously opened. Very thin cleats are to be avoided as are very thick ones, since, in the first case, the moisture in the glue tends to warp the cleat away from the glue area and, in the second, the extra weight and size will hinder tone. Inside work on opened guitars can, of course, be more easily done since the edges of the cleat can be neatly tapered and finished *after* it has been glued in.

Tools necessary to insert cleats are very simple and consist of an inspection lamp, inspection mirror, and probes of varying lengths. Cleats near the soundhole can be inserted easily and require no further explanation. Cleats farther away require the use of a probe (made from a thin metal rod) the end of which has been sharpened into a chisel point. By sticking the cleat with the probe and by use of the mirror and inspection lamp, the cleat can be maneuvered to reinforce a crack in any part of the guitar. A drop of heavy glue on the cleat will stay put while the cleat is being inserted and at the same time will hold the cleat firmly while removing the probe.

Occasionally, where new pieces have to be used to replace a missing section, it will be found easier to glue in the reinforcing member before the new part. If the hole is big enough, C clamps can be inserted through it to hold the cleat in place while it is being glued.

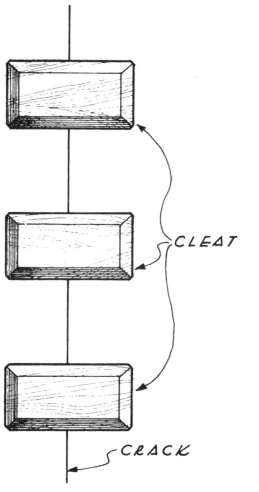

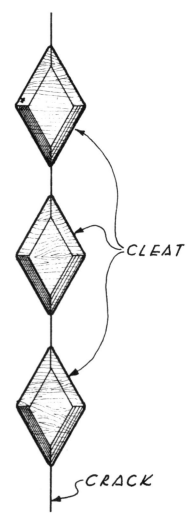

TWO STYLES OF CLEATS
THE GRAIN DIRECTION OF THE CLEATS GOES AT RIGHT ANGLES TO THE CRACK.

When placing cleats in hard-to-reach areas, stick the cleat in with a long probe. Apply glue to the cleat and guide into place, using mirror and inspection lamp if necessary.

hole, such as f hole plectrum guitars, a useful method of repair, when the usual methods fail, is to pull a cleat tight against a crack with string pulled right through the middle of the crack. The string is knotted at the end, threaded through the middle of the cleat, and finally pulled against the crack, taking care to align the cleat with its grain running across the section being glued. A small hole must be drilled through the crack, of course, but with suitable choice of string, the string and hole become nearly invisible after retouching the finish. By applying a cleat in this manner, the crack is lined up and reinforced at the same time. This method works best with dark-colored wood and should be avoided with the lighter woods such as spruce and maple.

Miscellaneous Techniques

All cleats and studs should be placed with the grain running across that of the glued section. The area must be clean and level, emphasizing the need for correct alignment. If the cleat is glued in after the original gluing has dried (cracks, inlays, new pieces) all excess glue which has appeared on the inside must be removed. An exception to the rule

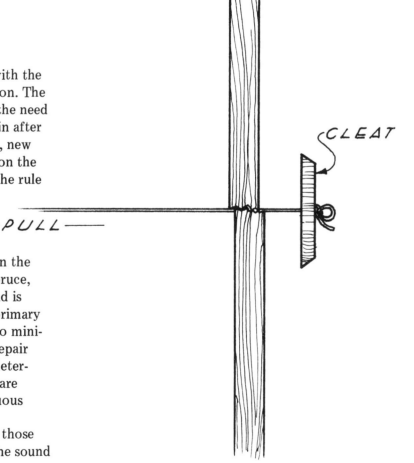

of always using hide glue can be made when the gluings involve very light woods, such as spruce, cypress, and maple. If the break is small and is located in an area where strength is not a primary concern, white glue may be used in order to minimize the staining effect of the glue. Each repair situation must be carefully considered to determine whether the properties of white glue are acceptable in exchange for its less conspicuous appearance.

On guitars with hard to align parts and those which are difficult to work with through the sound

IN SOME CASES, A CLEAT MAY BE PULLED TIGHT AGAINST A CRACK TO BRING TOGETHER A MISALIGNED EDGE.

Removing and Replacing Top or Back

In only the most extensive repairs or restorations is the removal of the top or back necessary or even desirable. Unlike the violin, where the style of construction and the thin glue used for gluing on the top make the opening operation relatively easy, the construction of the guitar with its elaborate purfling and binding makes the process of removal more complex and time consuming. Most inside work can be done through the soundhole. Repairs which cannot be done through the soundhole, or are most easily done from the inside, include restoration of warped parts, extensive repairs of cracked and missing sections, and regraduation of top and braces. Replacement of a top or back will also require removal of the corresponding old part, though here you hardly have the freedom of choice.

If the work does not specifically require the removal of the top, it is best to leave it alone and open the guitar from the back. There are a number of reasons for this departure from violin practice. For most guitars, removal of the top requires the prior removal of the fingerboard—the removal and replacement of which is a major operation in itself. The presence of purfling on the top (usually absent on the back) and the delicate nature of the purfling and binding, plus the fact that the top is made of soft spruce, are other reasons to avoid top removal. The removal of the back, with its simpler binding, is preferable in all cases other than situations requiring the actual replacement of the top.

The binding must first be removed (some of the cheaper guitars lack it) and for those instruments where this part is made of plastic the operation is simple since it can be easily peeled off and, in most cases, reused. In some cases, wood binding can be removed without damage, particularly when heat is applied to soften the glue. Generally, however, when fragile purfling accompanies the binding, it is simpler and quicker to replace the original with new binding and purfling. Some guitars which are heavily lacquered may be difficult to work with because the lacquer will chip and, at times, lift away slivers of wood from the back and sides as the binding is lifted away. By taking the precaution to score the lacquer around the edge of the binding the possibilities of chipping and lifting can be minimized.

With the glue joint between the lining and back exposed one can now proceed to the actual removal of the back. The only tool necessary is the thin table knife, this being inserted from the outside, first along one of the bouts or through an existing open edge. The knife should be worked slowly through the edge, being careful not to let it split or dig into the back. A little alcohol run into the glue joint in front of the knife blade will help the separating process. The separation of the endblocks is the most difficult part and is the last step in removing the back. A little more pressure must be applied at these two points because of the extended glue surface, and particular care must be taken not to let the knife dig into either the back or the endblock.

By working carefully, one can remove the back very cleanly. If the same back is to be replaced after the inside work has been completed, it is best not to attempt to clean up the gluing surface too much since the small irregularities created during removal serve to line up the parts in their original position during the regluing operation.

All necessary inside work can now be done. You should be thorough and attend to every detail since it is unlikely that the guitar will ever be opened again. In addition to the usual repair operations the guitar may also be regraduated and rebraced, though work of this sort should be done by experts only, especially when fine instruments are involved. Care should be exercised, when regraduation is performed, not to work the top and braces too thin since, in exchange for response and tone that is pleasing "under the ear," ultimate response and carrying power are sacrificed. A top that is already too thin may be veneered and regraduated though, again, this latter operation should also be reserved for experts.

By taking a few precautions, the regluing of the back should proceed with no problems. The endblocks should be glued first, taking special care to see that the neck angle is correct for proper string height and action. In the instance where the original neck angle has shifted and is incorrect, one can correct for this discrepancy at this time. After the endblocks have been glued and clamped, the remaining edges can be attended to, using the table knife and edge clamps. By dipping the knife blade in hot glue and running it in along the edge for distances of eight or nine inches at a time, one can work cleanly and without hurry. Working in stages, gluing and clamping a small section at a time, the

Plywood construction is extremely strong but when damage is extensive, as in this guitar top, repairs are much more difficult compared to an instrument with solid wood. This guitar had to have the top replaced.

Below Right

Extensive damage of this nature requires complete replacement of the top. No problem removing this top!

Below Left

A thin table knife or a palate knife is used to remove a top. An occasional drop of alcohol in the seam will help loosen the joint.

Below Right

Whenever the top or back is removed, repair on the sides becomes much easier to complete. Whenever this opportunity presents itself it is a good idea to cleat or reinforce all cracks, old as well as new.

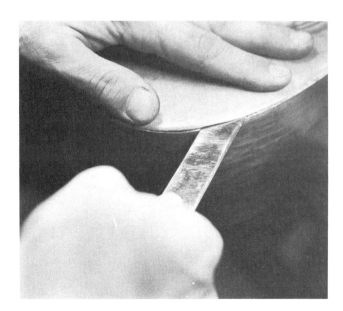 

entire back can be reglued without danger of the glue setting before the edge can be clamped. Attempting to reglue the entire back at one time will almost certainly lead to poor glue joints and untidy work as well.

After the glue has dried, the clamps may be removed and the excess glue washed away. The channel for the binding should be cleaned up, and when this has been taken care of, the last step—replacing the binding—may be attended to. If the old binding is reusable, it is only a matter of regluing it and touching up the finish. It should be noted that plastic binding occasionally shrinks upon removal. The binding may be stretched to its original length (after dipping it in boiling water) or a small section may be added to fill in the gap.

No such problems will be encountered when replacing with new binding, of course, though the repairman must contend with the additional step

of producing binding to match the original. Invariably, wood binding must be bent on the bending iron before it can be glued into place, and with both wood and plastic there is the additional step of trimming down the new parts before the finish can be retouched.

For wood binding, you may use either white glue or hide glue. Plastic binding can be glued with white glue if the gluing surface has first been roughed up with sandpaper; otherwise a cement such as Duco should be used. Whatever the glue, work in small lengths at a time, making especially sure that the binding at the waist is held in firmly.

You can hold the binding down with strips of tape or as an alternative you may wrap the body with string or large rubber bands. Use what you feel comfortable with as all three methods are commonly used.

Below Left

The excess material is trimmed from the soundhole inlay by first scraping and then sanding. The ends of the inlays are positioned at the soundhole so that they will be hidden by the fingerboard.

Below Right

A circle cutter with the bit narrowed and squared off is handy for cutting the recesses in the top for the soundhole inlays.

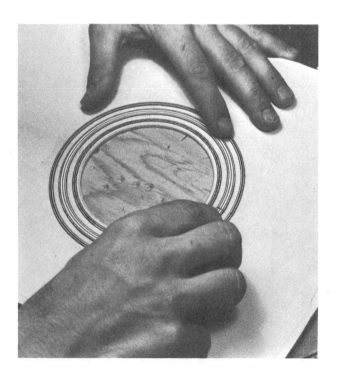

Below Left

After the soundhole has been cut and the rosette inlaid, the braces may be glued on. Note that the braces have been left square; gluing is much easier when the carving is left until later.

Below Right

Carving of the braces is nearly completed. The graduation of the braces can be seen clearly in this photo.

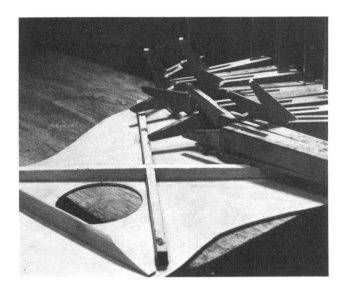 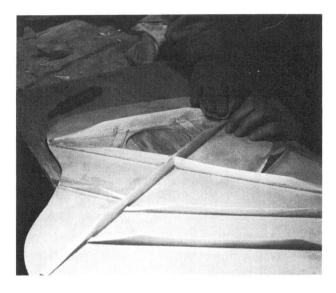

Below Left

Top glued and clamped. Although there are plenty of clamps, only gentle pressure is required for each clamp.

Below Right

Gluing a new top using spool clamps. (Gibson Repair Dept.)

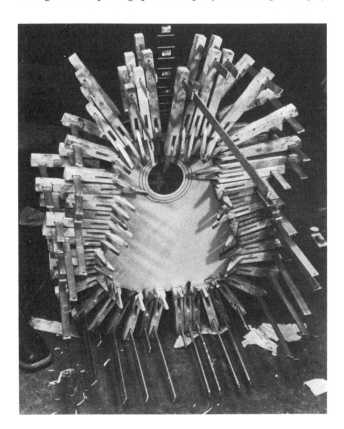 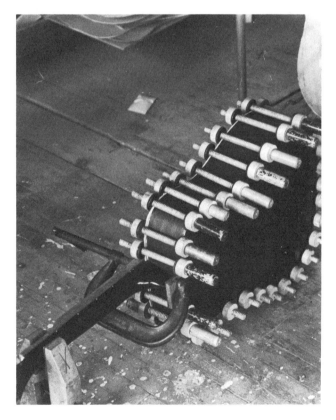

Below Left

A router is the best tool for cutting the recesses for the binding and purfling.

Below Right

The binding is held in place with tape while the glue dries. String wrapped around the body or large rubber bands may also be used.

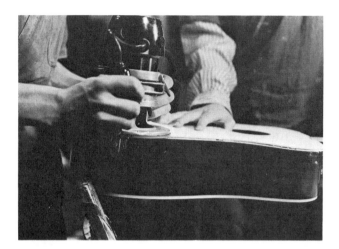

Below Left

These guitars have had the binding glued on and are hanging up to dry. Cloth tape (webbing) is used here though large rubber straps, tape, and string may also be used. (Gibson Repair Dept.)

Below Right

The guitar with the finished top. The original pickguard and bridge were used in this particular repair.

Below Left

A careless pickup installation can result in collapse of the top. The cutout for the front pickup went through the two bass bars, seriously weakening the top. Whenever the top is cut on a plectrum guitar, the bass bars (if cut) must be reinforced.

Below Right

This old Epiphone archtop is being converted to a cutaway style. The first step is to decide upon the outline of the cutaway.

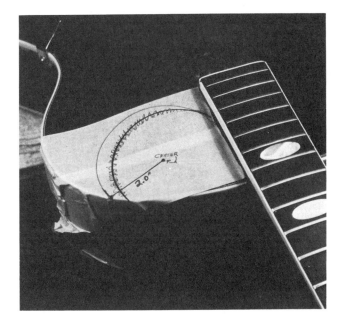

Below Left

The outline is cut with a band saw. There's no turning back at this point!

Below Right

It is interesting to note that, though this guitar dates from the forties, the back and sides are made of plywood. In this photo, in which the linings are being glued to the top and back, the three plies of the back can be clearly seen.

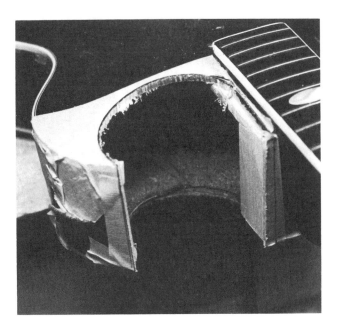

Below Left

After bending the new section on the bending iron, the excess is trimmed away before gluing the section to the body.

Below Right

Clamps can be difficult to apply in this area. A little ingenuity is called for in this situation.

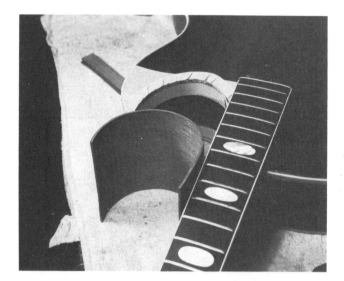 

Below Left

The new area is cut for the replacement binding.

Below Right

This photo shows the new binding in place. At this point the difficult work has been completed and only final cleanup and touchup remain.

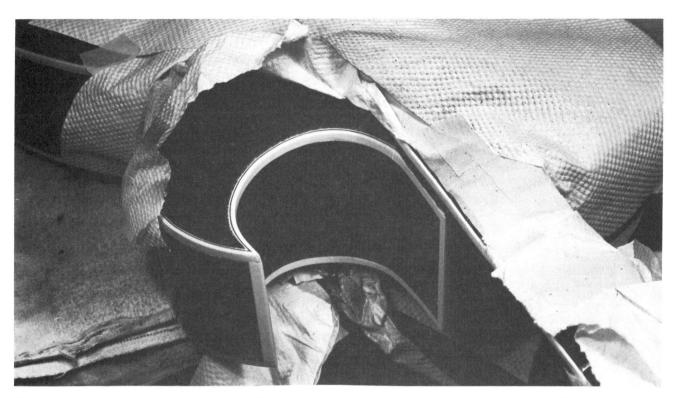

Where the new area is clearly defined and cut off by the binding, touchup is relatively easy and can be confined to a relatively small area. After the color coats have been sprayed, clear lacquer should be applied to protect the color while rubbing and polishing out.

The completed cutaway.

Touchup and Refinishing

Touchup Methods

Even the best repair can be made to look bad if care and attention is not paid to the final item—touching up the finish. There are many types of finishes used on guitars and a thorough knowledge of the characteristics of various types of stains, varnishes, lacquers, etc., is necessary. The whole area of touching up and matching finishes is quite interesting; too much time cannot be spent on mastering this important and, in many cases, difficult phase of repairing.

The method of touching up a finish will vary, depending on the nature of the damaged section. Two methods, brushing and French polishing, are basic and should be mastered by all repairmen. A third method, the use of the air brush, is relatively unknown in the string instrument repair field, though the tool itself is anything but new. Nevertheless, in many applications, the air brush is superior to any of the traditional methods, both in terms of finished appearance and in speed of application.

Brushing

For touchup work, a variety of brushes in different styles and sizes should be kept on hand. Most work of this sort will require brushes no larger than a quarter inch wide. The brush is well-suited for touching up small nicks and scratches or other areas where accurate placement of stain and finish is required. Compound surfaces which are difficult to reach by French polishing are especially suited for brush application. One problem with the brush is that it is not particularly suited for use with fast drying materials. *Fast drying finishes are a necessity for most repair work.* These finishes, however, make it difficult to do smooth work with a brush, especially when a good deal of color must be used in matching a finish. You must be careful not to rush the work by applying too much color and finish at one time, since under these conditions uniform color is difficult to obtain. There is also considerable danger of disturbing the previously applied coats. Though it is not necessarily best for all applications, one can use the brush for the smallest touchup as well as for complete refinishing.

When touching up areas which are dark or where the wood itself is dark, you may apply stain directly to the area, following with a clear finish to protect the color and to provide a base for rubbing and polishing. On areas which are light in color, it is preferable to first level and fill the surface with a clear sealer. This step is especially important when touching up a crack on woods such as spruce, cypress, or maple. If you were to apply stain directly to the crack on these light woods, the stain would immediately penetrate into the crack, as well as the softer fibers of the wood, accentuating the crack and making it *impossible* to blend the fresh area with the old. By applying the stain on top of the sealed surface, it is much easier to get a smooth distribution of color.

Brushes of the type used for fine lettering and artwork are suitable for touchup work and are available in very fine diameters and tips. You should be able to apply touchups in widths ranging down to 1/32 inch or less.

In most cases, the color must be applied with a fairly dry brush, the idea being to have each stroke dry as rapidly as possible so that succeeding strokes will not pick up the color or make it run. It is difficult to apply a lot of color evenly with a brush. A moderately tinted stain applied in many successive coats works much better than a few heavy coats.

The clear finish which is applied over all stains must be applied carefully so that the stain will not be disturbed by the brush. Avoid back and forth stroking; apply the first coat with smooth single strokes over each new area. On successive coats, less caution is necessary since the first clear coat will have sealed the stain.

Better results can sometimes be attained by tinting the clear topcoats in addition to the usual staining procedure. An example would be aged varnish or lacquer over a light-colored wood. If most of the color is distributed throughout the finish, then the touchup must be done the same way in order to retain the same visual effect from all angles.

French Polishing*

The problem of blending in the touchup area with the surrounding original surface is neatly solved by French polishing; since the process leaves a glossy surface, time is saved by not having to subsequently go over the area with rubbing and polishing compounds. When the occasion requires the use of stains and colors, the repairman has excellent control over the amount to be applied as well as the evenness of distribution.

Compared to the larger pads used in refinishing, the rubbing pads for touchup work are quite small and in many cases must be shaped to fit the area in question as in, for example, the area between fingerboard and top. The application of a clear finish is similar to the regular French polishing technique. The touchup area can be blended in with the surrounding areas in the latter stages by extending the area under the pad to include portions of the surrounding areas. Since the amount of finish applied at each stroke of the pad is quite small, there will be no hint of any discontinuity between the spot and the surrounding area.

Spots which require color need an additional step before the application of the clear finish. The blending stains or colors are rubbed on with thin French polish solution, with each coat building up the desired color until a match has been achieved. Of course the most obvious method of applying color is to mix it directly with the polishing solution. This system is suited primarily for large areas where uniformity of color is important. For smaller areas where more careful control over blending with adjacent areas is required, two alternate methods are more satisfactory.

In the first method, stains, available in dry form, are blended and applied directly to the touchup spot. After a preliminary French polishing has deposited a layer of finish on the spot, a fingertip is touched to the stain and then to the spot. A second very dry coat of polish is applied next. The process of alternately dusting the spot and polishing over it is continued until the desired color has been obtained. As an alternate, the stain can be carried in a separate bottle and applied directly to the rubbing

*See section on French polishing p. 130.

pad along with the usual polish. In either of the two methods the amount of color can be easily varied irrespective of the amount of French polish which acts principally as a solvent and as a vehicle for applying the color.

Using an Air Brush

The artist's air brush is a versatile tool and can be used to spray a variety of finishes. Because of the fine control possible over the area to be sprayed, little if any masking need be done and the touchup spot can be blended nicely with the adjacent areas. An important advantage of the air brush is that there is little danger of disturbing previous coats, even when large amounts of color are being applied. Colors, in this instance, must be mixed with the finish and in most cases should be on the thin side since a surprising amount of finish can be built up in a comparatively short time. In most cases a mist coat of thinner or reducer will help to blend all areas; in some cases no further rubbing or polishing will be required.

In any event, thin solutions are the rule since this is a necessity for proper atomization as well as for proper blending. Pressurized cans are available for use with the air brush, though for prolonged use a conventional air compressor is far more satisfactory since pressure remains constant. For anything but occasional use, the economics of the situation favor the compressor since pressure cans (or "bombs") are not cheap.

For proper operation, the air brush requires fairly high pressure (35 to 40 lb./sq. in.) for proper atomization of the finish. The volume of air required, though, is small and a diaphragm compressor of 1/4 to 1/3 horsepower is quite adequate. Be sure to keep the air brush clean at all times, since it is very sensitive and will not tolerate a buildup of old finish on the tip.

Finishes

Varnish

Before the widespread use of lacquer, varnishes, both oil and spirit, were universally used except for the small number of instruments—many of the best ones—which were and still are French-polished. Varnishes can vary so much in quality and characteristics that it is hard to make definite recommendations about them. A brief description of the main characteristics will help one decide whether to use them.

Spirit varnishes are simply resins or gums which have been dissolved in alcohol or another highly volatile solvent. By suitable choice of gums, one can vary the hardness to suit the application. Their main advantages are quick drying time and ease in polishing to a good gloss. Wearing qualities vary; certain types tend to powder and show white marks where bumped or scratched. Inexpensive Mexican and Spanish guitars often exhibit this characteristic. Though shellac is a spirit varnish, its use in the French polish technique eliminates many of the objections to the usual spirit varnish. Because of the fast drying time, spirit varnishes are somewhat difficult to apply in even coats. In order to eliminate brush marks, the finish must be built up a bit heavier than actually necessary to allow for rubbing and polishing without danger of cutting through it.

Oil varnishes possess excellent wearing qualities, are easy to apply with a brush because of their slow drying time, and polish fairly well. They are basically composed of resins and gums dissolved in oil, and the drying time is limited by the oxidizing properties of the oil. This slow drying time is a handicap to some refinishers and the relative softness of most oil varnishes prevents the attainment of the high gloss which can be gotten from other finishes.

The elastic nature of oil varnish tends to absorb or mute the higher frequencies produced by an instrument. For a violin this is permissible because the varnish can remove the scratchiness or edge from the tone and help to develop a richer, more full sound. By contrast, a spirit-varnished violin of the same quality produces a more brilliant, edgy tone.

A distinguishing feature of a really good guitar is that it possesses a clear, brilliant, and singing treble. In addition, the tone is one that sustains and carries. The acoustical requirements of finishes for guitars are almost in opposition to the requirements for violins. In a guitar everything should be done to preserve the treble range of the instrument. The guitar must also be responsive with a tone that sustains well at all frequencies, since the guitarist obviously does not have the use of a bow. The acoustical properties of the oil varnish favor the requirements of the violin. The requirements of a guitar are for a harder, thinner finish which will inhibit neither the treble response nor the sustaining qualities of the tone. The traditional favored finish for classical guitars is French polish. For most other types of guitars a lacquer finish is generally applied. If varnish is to be used at all, it should at least be one that has been specially formulated for use with musical instruments. For the reader who wishes to make his own varnish, reference to the violin literature will yeild abundant information on recipes as well as properties and techniques of application.

Lacquer

Lacquer possesses a number of features which make it particularly suitable as a guitar finish. Ease of application (when sprayed), excellent rubbing and polishing qualities, quick drying time, and durability are qualities which make lacquer a good choice for the refinisher as well as for the factory. Disregarding prejudice against finishes which are used by factories, however, we find that lacquer possesses fine acoustical qualities as well, providing it is applied in the thinnest possible coat commensurate with protection and appearance. It should be noted that an increasing number of fine handmade guitars utilize a lacquer finish. The trend is toward lacquer and other synthetic finishes (it is now used on some of the finest classical and flamenco instruments), displacing French polish which was once a criterion of a fine guitar.

Factories usually apply finishes which are too heavy for best possible tone. This is probably done out of necessity since a heavy coat can be rubbed down and polished without fear of cutting through the finish and at the same time can be expected to stand up better to abusive treatment.

Best results with lacquers are obtained by spraying. Although excellent work can also be done by brushing, the advantages of lacquer, such as ease of application and quick drying time, are lost because of the inevitable brush marks and because a retarding agent must be added to the lacquer in order to slow down drying time to a range suitable for use with a brush.

If only clear lacquer is to be applied it is a matter of applying just enough coats to allow for rubbing down and polishing. If, however, it is wished to add color to the finish, the finish schedule must be modified. A couple of coats of clear sealer should first be sprayed to seal the wood to prevent the color coats from bleeding unevenly into the softer parts of the wood. A sufficient number of color coats are then applied until the desired shade is obtained. On open grain woods, sanding sealer or wood filler is used to fill the grain. Clear coats are then applied to finish off. Usually only one or two sandings between coats are required, the number and amount necessary depending on the skill of the repairman. After the final sanding, the finish should show all pores filled with no orange peel (ripples on the finish, similar to the skin of an orange) or brush marks, and the surface should be dead level with a satin gloss. After the last coat and sanding, the instrument must be set aside for about a week in order to allow the finish to harden enough for polishing, particularly when a high gloss is desired.

Refinishing Materials

Stains

Stains are available in dry form as powders to be dissolved in alcohol or lacquer thinner or in liquid form which can be used by itself or added to a finish. The dry analine stains, soluble in alcohol, are available in a wide range of colors and can be used to tint shellac (and French polish) or sprayed directly onto the wood. They are very useful in touchup work.

For the majority of spray applications, better results can be obtained by using non-grain-raising stains which are compatible in either lacquer or shellac. These stains are sold in liquid form, in a wide range of colors, and can be sprayed directly onto the wood or mixed with the finish to give a tint. For lacquer, this is the best stain.

Wood Filler

Wood filler is used only on open grain woods such as rosewood and mahogany. The usual procedure is to use a color which is slightly darker than the finish/stain you plan to use. The filler is brushed on with the grain and then wiped off against the grain, filling the open pores in the process. Lacquer will not stick to the wood if the filler is not absolutely dry so allow plenty of time for this. If in doubt, apply a thin coat of shellac to seal the filler and provide a bonding surface for the lacquer.

Sanding Sealer

You may wish to use a sanding sealer in place of the wood filler. While sanding sealer builds much more slowly than wood filler, the end result is a more transparent deeper finish. You can, as the name implies, sand after each application, often waiting as little as a half hour. The sealer powders off nicely and doesn't load up the sandpaper. Application is the same as for lacquer; spray in overlapping strokes, thinning as necessary to obtain smooth application. Sanding sealer mixes easily with lacquer so there are no problems with the lacquer not sticking.

Lacquer

Two types of lacquer are suitable for finishing and refinishing guitars. Nitrocellulose lacquer has been the traditional finish on most factory-made guitars and is still used quite extensively. In terms of ease of application, drying time, gloss, and durability, the nitrocellulose lacquer scores well. Finish checks (cracks) can be a problem if you apply the lacquer too heavily or if the instrument is subjected to extremes of heat and cold. By choosing a high quality lacquer designed for wood finishes you will be starting off on the right track.

Acrylic lacquer is becoming more popular and is worth your consideration for a number of reasons. Acrylic is more durable and is more resistant to checking. The range of colors available is far greater than for nitrocellulose, so if the color you want is outside of the normal range of guitar colors—I'm thinking of "custom" finishes for solid body and thin body electrics in particular—you may have no choice but to use acrylic. A store that specializes in automotive finishes is the best place to look for acrylic rather than a furniture finishing store.

Thinner

The quality and type of thinner used for lacquer finishing is very important in attaining quality results. Be sure, as with the lacquer, to get the best available. Thinners are available to cover a range of temperature conditions and vary in their speed of evaporation. A thinner intended for use at low temperatures will evaporate quickly while a thinner intended for high temperature use will evaporate more slowly.

In general, a medium fast drying thinner is suitable for the widest range of spraying conditions. For small spray touchups and for small sections covered with a brush, a fast drying thinner will do well. You will have to be careful with the fast drying thinner as it is more susceptible to blushing. When blushing occurs, the finish will turn milky in color. In mild cases, the blushing will disappear when the finish dries. In severe cases, the blushing is permanent, and the finish will have to be stripped and redone. The slow drying thinner will give the best gloss. In some finishing situations a mist coat of slow drying thinner is sprayed on last to improve flow-out and gloss.

Varnish

Use only varnishes intended for use on musical instruments. I would recommend spirit varnishes as the most suitable for guitars. See also the section on varnish.

French Polish

French polish is basically orange shellac with other resins mixed in to promote additional hardness. The French polish finish is determined as much by the process of applying it as by the finish itself.

In French polishing, a rubbing pad is prepared by folding a number of layers of cloth beneath a smooth and lint-free outer cloth cover. The outer cover can vary from silk to an old well-washed T-shirt. Holding the pad tightly so there are no wrinkles, a small amount of polish is applied to the surface. After pressing the pad into the palm of the other hand to distribute the polish, the finish is applied to the instrument in long, even strokes. Start and finish each stroke off the instrument and keep the pad moving throughout the entire stroke so that it will not have a chance to stick to the surface.

A drop of raw linseed oil applied occasionally to the pad will help prevent it from sticking. When starting with bare wood, you can use a heavy polish solution first and apply coats frequently. As the finish begins to build, you will have to go to a thinner solution and polish less frequently in order to allow sufficient drying time. If roughness or ripples appear, these will have to be sanded with very fine sandpaper before continuing.

The final polishing operations are very important and must be done skillfully if a smooth high gloss is to be attained. Up to this point much of the effort has been to obtain sufficient thickness so that the instrument will be protected adequately. The last few coats of polish should be with a very thin solution and with a fairly dry pad. By polishing thoroughly with a very small amount of polish, you will obtain a high gloss which is free of streaks or ripples. At this point the finish must be dry and hard in order for the gloss to show evenly.

The last operation, spiriting off, is necessary in order to improve the gloss and to draw off the oil which has been rubbed in with the finish. This polishing operation is exactly the same as for normal polishing except that in this operation a few drops of pure alcohol are applied to the pad. With the conclusion of this final step, the guitar can be strung up and put back into service since no rubbing and polishing compounds are needed.

French polish is available in prepared form (in solution, usually with a built-in lubricant) under various trade names. While these preparations do not build as fast as shellac, they are excellent for building up the final gloss coats and for touchup work. Regardless of the polish used, the art of French polishing can only be mastered by long practice. Being able to detect differences in the "feel" of the pad as you polish is very important so that you will know how much polish or oil to add and when.

Other Finishes

With the exception of an epoxy-type finish for solid body guitars, only nitrocellulose and acrylic lacquer, French polish, and varnish are suitable for guitars. Do not brush on shellac and do not use finishes such as Varathane. Some people like the appearance of an oiled finish on solid body guitars but, while this is fine in terms of appearance, it creates big problems if a conventional finish is later applied. It is difficult to get a finish to stick to an oiled surface and the process of removing the oil can sometimes leave uneven areas where the oil has soaked in more than in others.

Abrasives

For refinishing work, a selection of sandpaper in the finer grades should be kept on hand. The range of grit should be from about 180 to 600. From 180 to 320, I would recommend aluminum oxide nonloading paper as this type will not clog with finish nearly as easily as the conventional papers. From 400 to 600, use wet or dry paper with a light oil such as lemon oil as a lubricant.

Steel wool is handy for use in place of sandpaper, especially on intricate, difficult-to-reach areas. The finest grade, 4-0, can be used for finish work as well as for polishing frets and fingerboards.

Rubbing and polishing compounds are available in a variety of grades of coarseness and are available for both hand and machine rubbing. For example, Dupont makes a series of rubbing compounds from 101 (coarse) to 606 (extrafine) for hand use. If the final sanding/spraying has been well done, only 606 is needed to give a high gloss.

Various polishes may be used to protect and maintain the gloss of an instrument, though here a distinction should be made between those polishes intended for use only to maintain a gloss and those polishes with a mild abrasive action to take out small scratches. In the latter category, Meguiar plastic cleaner (a heavy duty cleaner for polishing out minor scratches on plastic surfaces) is favored locally by a number of repairmen and builders.

Stripping and Preparation

Removal of the old finish on most guitars is accomplished most easily with the use of a paint remover. A paint remover intended for use on wood and which doesn't require neutralizing will save much time, leaving very little sanding to be done afterward. Be sure to stay away from any plastic parts such as pickguards and binding as the paint remover will attack and melt them just like the finish! Sanding with paper from 180 to 320 grit should be sparing but thorough, removing all of the old finish but as little of the wood as possible. Some finishes such as those applied by French polishing are often very thin and may be removed with sandpaper alone. All repairs should be done prior to the stripping operation, and small dents, scratchs, or missing chips should be taken care of by appropriate methods before the final

The old finish must be stripped and the body sanded before the new finish is applied.

A small hand sander may be used to reduce sanding time. (Gibson Repair Dept.)

sanding. Care should be exercised in the final sanding so that, as successively finer grades of sandpaper are used, all of the scratches left by the previous grade of paper are removed. Under the transparent finishes used on guitars the smallest scratches become very apparent after the final polishing.

Though all the color should be in the finish, occasionally the wood itself is stained to simulate the effect of age. Perhaps stain isn't the proper word since the effect desired is most realistically achieved by oxidizing the wood rather than by staining with dyes. A weak solution of potassium bichromate dissolved in water can be used. One should exercise good judgment when working with newer instruments. If oxidizing agents such as potassium bichromate are used at all, they should be used only to cut the whiteness from the new wood.

A technique used to bring out the grain of the wood is to "oil" it before application of the finish. Raw linseed oil, occasionally with a reddish-brown stain, is particularly effective when used on rosewood and mahogany. After the surfaces have been rubbed *dry*, the instrument is ready for French polishing. For lacquer or varnish, one must first seal the wood, and for this a coat of white shellac, brushed or sprayed on, is sufficient.

If it is desired to use a filler on the open-grained woods such as mahogany and rosewood, this should be applied after the first wash coat of shellac so that the stain in the filler will not discolor the white portions of the binding. Another wash coat is necessary after use of the filler.

Though it is customary to use filler on rosewood and mahogany (and other open-grained woods), its use is not particularly advantageous from the standpoint of either acoustics or appearance. The filler leaves the surface of the wood opaque and two dimensional. In some instances the surface takes on a cloudy appearance. Though use of a wood filler reduces overall finishing time, it leaves something to be desired in appearance when compared to a surface which has been filled by the finish itself.

Woods used in guitar construction—rosewood, maple, mahogany, to name a few—have a quality of depth as well as length and width. For a limited distance, it is possible to look into the pores of the wood as well as at the surface itself. This three dimensional quality is preserved if a clear filler such as sanding sealer is used rather than the usual type which renders the surface opaque. Instruments finished with a clear filler have an appearance of richness and depth; because the figure of the wood is emphasized, the better grades of instruments with the better woods benefit more from this finishing process than do the cheaper grades.

Spray Techniques

For the majority of refinishing and touchup work one of the smaller spray guns intended for light duty production and spot refinishing is a better choice over the larger guns. The smaller guns are adjustable down to a very fine pattern and have, at the same time, the capacity to do complete refinishings as well. These guns operate well on the diaphragm-type compressor, while the larger production guns, while covering a larger area, require a much larger volume of air which can only be supplied by the more costly piston-type compressor.

I've found the De Vilbiss P-EGA type gun to be very satisfactory for the needs of the repair shop and would suggest a gun of that size if one all-purpose gun is to be used. The extra cost of the larger gun and compressor would be justified only if refinishing was undertaken on a large volume basis.

A water trap should be used between the compressor and the gun to prevent water from getting through to the gun. This problem is more critical when the gun is stopped down for fine touchup. The air brush is also sensitive to water.

For some spraying situations it is necessary to cut down the air pressure to the gun; this is most conveniently done with an air valve inserted in the line just below the gun. On small touchups, for example, where you may wish to spray a wet coat, you will have to cut down air as well as the feed.

As a general rule, the larger the gun and the more air pressure and volume you have, the thicker the spraying material can be. Usually it is necessary to thin the finish a bit in order to produce a smooth pattern without flutter or spitting. Too much thinner will result in excess spraying and drying time as well as an increased possibility of runs and dribbles.

Provided you have enough air volume for the gun, 35 to 45 lb. pressure is satisfactory for most applications. Spraying distance can be anything from six to twelve inches depending on the appli-

A spray booth is desirable if any extensive spraying is to be done. (Gibson Repair Dept.)

cation and the gun, and the gun should always be held perpendicular to the work. Start each stroke before you get to the area to be sprayed and end the stroke after you pass the area, maintaining the same distance throughout. Overlap each stroke by fifty percent and, on alternate coats, spray crosswise and then lengthwise. This technique is especially useful when spraying stains and tinted lacquers as it helps to ensure an even color distribution.

Though lacquer dries quickly and many successive coats may be sprayed in a short time, trying to spray too much in one coat may cause small pinhole bubbles and blushing of the finish. Blushing is more apt to occur on humid or rainy days and, while it will usually disappear when the lacquer dries, it sometimes remains; don't take chances and don't rush things.

Sooner or later you will have to touch up or refinish a guitar which has been polished with a silicone polish. You will know it because the new finish will refuse to stick to the guitar whether it's bare wood or old finish. The new finish will bead up and pull away from spots here and there, giving

rise to what are known as "fisheyes." This is a serious problem and as far as I know the only cure is to mix some anti-fisheye solution in with the lacquer you are spraying. While this will cure the problem, the drying time is increased, so you should plan your refinishing schedule accordingly.

Another last tip which will prove helpful is to use a number of strong lights in your spray area and to position the guitar so that these lights will be reflected in the area you are spraying. In this way you will be able to see the newly sprayed area and the old, the evenness of the overlapping strokes, and the overall wetness of the coat as well as the color (if any) itself.

Lacquer Sunburst

Sunburst finishes which lend themselves particularly to spraying techniques, are limited mainly to plectrum and electric guitars; though popular at one time, they are only occasionally used on flattop guitars. A sunburst finish has no place on a classical guitar.

134

Below Left

When refinishing with a color or with a stain, it will be necessary to clean up the binding and purfling before spraying the clear coats. The binding edges are cleaned up with a scraper. This step is eliminated if only a clear finish is applied. (Gibson Repair Dept.)

Below Right

Position the guitar so that the lights will be reflected in the spray area. This will make it easier to judge the spray pattern.

Some striking effects can be obtained by experimenting with different color combinations though good taste limits the more radical combinations to use only on solid body or thin body semiacoustic guitars. The usual sunburst finish is used to simulate wear and age, and though the effect is somewhat exaggerated, it is in general similar to the shading of the varnish on a violin. When tastefully done, the effect is quite beautiful though, it must be emphasized, the technique is appropriate only on certain types of guitars. Even then, the sunburst guitar is "in" only for certain types of music!

The production of a sunburst finish begins with a coat or two of clear sanding sealer to seal the wood. All exposed parts which are to remain uncolored are then masked and the base coats, usually of a golden-brown tint, are applied in thin even coats. The actual shading is done with a brown-orange tint, though brown-black and black-red are also used occasionally. Each shading coat should be quite thin so that blending will be as smooth as possible. Areas generally left light are the centers of the top and back, the back of the neck, and the center sections of both upper and lower bouts. After removal of the masking tape, clear coats sprayed on top of the color layers will protect the shading and allow enough thickness for rubbing and polishing.

As far as spraying technique goes, the spray gun should be set for a "fan" pattern with the direction of the fan at right angles to the spraying direction. By testing on a scrap piece of wood you will note that the spray pattern is heavy in the middle, fading to light at the outer edges. When spraying the sunburst color you should hold the gun at a slight angle (rather than perpendicular which is the rule for conventional spraying), aiming toward the darker area. This method of shooting toward the darker areas accentuates the shading pattern of the gun and minimizes the chances of overspray landing on the light sections.

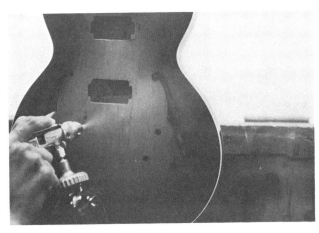

A sunburst finish requires a darker outside edge than the center. This is accomplished by aiming the gun toward the edge when spraying the dark stain.

Final Rub and Polish

If you have been really good with the spray gun, you may be able to eliminate sanding with the coarser grades of sandpaper, or even eliminate sanding completely. The rest of us will have to eliminate the occasional dust specks, dribble, and orange peel. This is done with sandpaper, backed up with cork pads on the larger, flatter surfaces.

Though many grades of sandpaper can be used, only three grades are necessary. The first sanding whould be with 320 nonloading paper. This paper should be used to completely level the surface, eliminating orange peel, brush marks, etc., until a completely satin gloss surface is achieved. Though the 320 paper is quite fine, it cuts quickly so that one should be careful not to sand through to the wood nor to cause scratches from excessive pressure. The second and third sanding steps are to sand with 400A and 600A wet or dry paper together with a light oil such as lemon oil as a lubricant. This last sanding step, with 600A paper, which will remove the scratches left by the previous sanding, should leave the surface with a dull gloss. If any deeper sandpaper marks are visible at this point, they should be removed by a further sanding with the 600A, rather than attempting to remove them by use of the rubbing compound. One may sand in any direction that is convenient; there is no need to sand with the grain as so many texts describe. Since it is the finish that is being prepared and not the wood, there is no need to be concerned with the direction of the wood grain.

There are many rubbing and polishing compounds, old as well as new, that can be used, though for our purposes we can limit our selection to two or three of varying fineness. The newer

Below Left

Use blocks whenever possible to spread out the pressure of the sandpaper. Sanding will be much more even and a more level surface will result. (Gibson Repair Dept.)

Below Right

Final sanding should be done with 600 wet or dry sandpaper with oil for lubricant

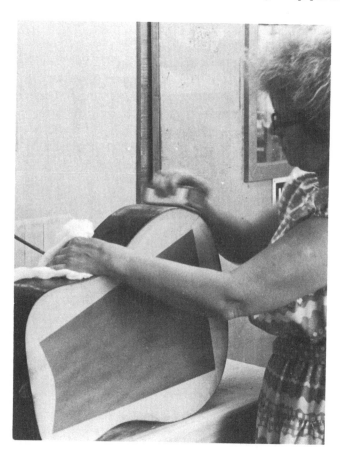

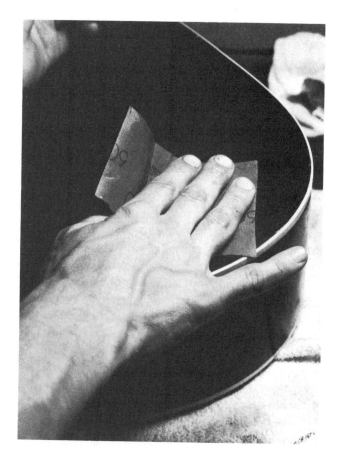

types of rubbing and polishing compounds are superior to the older types such as pumice and rottenstone. In many of the better types, compounded especially for hand rubbing, the grit tends to break down into finer and finer particles as rubbing progresses, so that in effect one grade of the new compound handles the range covered by several grades of the older style. For this reason, a medium grade of rubbing compound and an extra-fine grade of polishing compound are all that is necessary to bring up the surface to a high gloss.

Though instructions are given with the compounds, a certain amount of experience will be required to bring out the best gloss in the minimum amount of time. In general, the compound should be used sparingly and with fairly good pressure at first. The pressure should be eased off as the gloss develops and in the last polishing stages it is helpful to add a small amount of lemon oil to lubricate the rubbing pad and lessen the danger of scratching what is by now a highly polished surface.

A liquid polishing compound may be used to achieve the final bit of gloss and to take out traces of scratches left by the previous polishing compound. If instructions have been conscientiously followed to this point, taking particular care to remove all traces of scratches and dullness left by the previous sandpaper or compound at each stage of the schedule, one should end up with a mirror-like surface with *no* trace of scratches or dullness whatever. Highly polished finishes take time and effort (one must also gain experience with the properties of the rubbing and polishing compounds used) but the satisfaction and pride of completing a first-rate refinishing job is a reward that is hard to match.

Lacquer Finishing Schedules

Preparation

1. Strip old finish with paint remover (avoid all plastic binding and trim)
2. Sand with 220 and 320 paper.
3. Fill all chips and dents.
4. Sand with 320 paper, direction of wood grain only.
5. Mask all parts not to be finished; seal off soundhole.
6. Mask binding if stain or color coats are to be used.

Finish, Clear

1. Spray sanding sealer, sand; repeat until pores are filled. (Alternate: paste wood filler.)
2. Spray clear lacquer; lacquer may be tinted if appearance of age is required. Repeat this step until desired depth and color is obtained.
3. Spray clear gloss topcoats if tint has been used.

Finish, Color

1. Spray sanding sealer, sand; repeat until pores are filled. (Alternate: paste wood filler.)
2. Spray color coats.
3. Remove masking from binding and spray clear topcoats, adding tint if desired.
4. Spray final clear gloss topcoats.

Finish, Sunburst

1. Spray sanding sealer, sand; repeat until pores are filled. (Alternate: paste wood filler.)
2. Spray base tint over entire guitar (this color is usually yellow or gold-brown.) Tint should be mixed in thin lacquer solution.
3. Spray sunburst (usually various shades of reds and browns). Stain is mixed in a thin lacquer solution and is sprayed, aiming toward the edges and away from the light center sections.
4. Darken the sunburst stain and continue spraying thin coats (progressively toward the edges) till the desired shade is obtained.
5. Remove masking from binding and spray clear topcoats, adding tint if desired.
6. Spray final clear gloss topcoats.

Rubbing and Polishing

1. Allow sufficient time for drying (usually one week or longer) before final polishing.
2. Sand with 320 nonloading sandpaper till surface is leveled.
3. Sand with 600 paper (with lemon oil lubricant) till all previous sandpaper scratches are removed.
4. Rub with medium and fine grades of rubbing compound.
5. Hand polish with usual guitar polish.

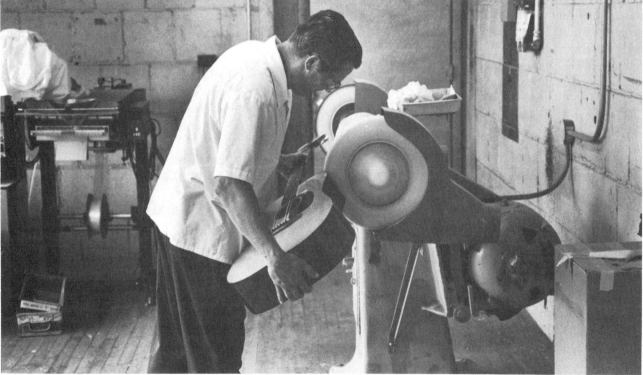

Final polishing may be done by hand or, as in these two photos, by machine. Machine polishing, though a great time saver, requires a great deal of skill and experience. Unless you will be specializing in refinishing, a small hand polisher (or hand polishing) will be adequate for most polishing situations. (Gibson Repair Dept.)

138

Electric Guitar Pickups and Controls

Pickup systems on guitars may be classified as electromagnetic or contact. Most steel string guitars use electromagnetic pickups. Thin hollow body and solid body guitars which are designed for amplified playing always use the magnetic pickup. On acoustical steel string instruments, such as flattop and plectrum guitars, best tone quality is attained with the magnetic pickup when such instruments are to be adapted for amplified playing.

All guitars which do not use steel strings must rely on (in one form or another) a contact pickup. Contact pickups are usually constructed so that they may be clipped onto various portions of the guitar face; in some cases, they may be incorporated into a special bridge. Vibrations transmitted from the guitar top to the pickup element (crystal or ceramic) are converted directly to an alternating voltage of corresponding frequency which can be fed to the input of the amplifier. Although tone and volume controls may be used, most pickups either feed directly in to the amplifier or, at most, have a volume control built into the pickup housing.

Advantages of the contact pickup include adaptability to a wide variety of instruments such as violin, ukulele, and banjo as well as the various types of guitar. Because the contact pickup does not require steel strings, as the electromagnetic pickup does, all types of guitars may be amplified, though in most cases the tone at best is mediocre compared to the original unamplified tone. Simplicity and low cost are prime factors in favor of the contact.

The disadvantage of poor tone quality, characterized by a lack of clarity and brilliance, largely nullifies the advantages, however. A few expensive pickups with the element built into the bridge are capable of fairly good tone quality but the cost (in the fifty-dollar range) should make one consider other alternatives. As a final consideration, the pickup will detect all vibrations transmitted to it, including miscellaneous noises from fingering and from handling the instrument; care must be taken to play cleanly.

Recently, a number of contact-type pickups have come to light which possess superior tone qualities compared to the usual contact pickups.

As an example, the Barcus Berry and FRAP transducers produce a surprisingly true and clear tone. Since the pickup may be attached to different portions of the top, the tonal balance may be adjusted over a wide range. For the player who wants amplification which is as true as possible to the acoustical sound, transducers of the Barcus-Berry type, apart from the use of a conventional microphone, are the best choices at the present time.

If you prefer a more "electric" sound from your steel string acoustic, the electromagnetic pickup is the best choice. The magnetic pickup is capable of producing excellent tone quality, low distortion, and a wide variety of tone colors. In addition, the pickups are quite rugged and are relatively noise-free, since they are sensitive mainly to the vibrations produced by the strings themselves.

The electromagnetic pickup is constructed with a coil of very fine wire wrapped around a permanent magnet. When the string, made of steel or nickel alloys, vibrates, it disturbs the magnetic field generated by the magnet. An alternating voltage is generated in the coil and the voltage, after passing through volume and tone controls, is fed to the amplifier. The better pickups have provision for varying the distance between pickup and string. Individual adjustments are usually provided for each string by varying the height of a small machine screw tapped into the magnet beneath each string. Overall pickup height is adjusted by varying the height of the mounting ring or by varying the adjustment screws around the edge of the pickup.

Replacement and Repair

The pickup and control systems in most guitars are, for the most part, quite simple and straightforward. For most repairmen used to working only on acoustical instruments the additional technical knowledge and mechanical skills can be acquired in a reasonably short time. An overall knowledge of electronics is advantageous, of course, but in the long run will not make an appreciable difference in the ability to troubleshoot electric guitars. Most problems in repair (and in laying out new pickup systems) are purely mechanical in nature and relate mainly to defects in wiring and control mounting. In time, you will develop a feel for electric guitar problems and from that point on troubleshooting and repair of pickups and controls will become fast and efficient.

The basic tools and materials required for electric guitar repair in addition to the usual basic repair tools are:

1) Small assortment of small screwdrivers (phillips and straight slot);
2) Several pliers, including one long-nose;
3) Small pair of diagonal wire cutters;
4) Wire stripper—a simple one will be adequate;
5) Small assortment of wrenches and nutdrivers;
6) Soldering gun or soldering pencil;
7) Rosin core solder—acid core solder must not be used;
8) Small assortment of shielded wire and hookup wire;
9) Small assortment of heat shrink, or spaghetti tubing, for insulation.

Basic Wiring Techniques

In laying out new wiring as well as in repairing the existing wiring, care should be taken to allow adequate slack between parts. Since most guitars require the controls and pickups to be fished up out of one of the pickup openings in the guitar top, the slack allows the harness to be removed and replaced without danger of breaking or shorting leads.

All leads should be insulated where there is danger of the lead touching adjacent parts or wiring. If the lead isn't already insulated, spaghetti tubing may be slipped over it for protection. When connecting leads, the stripped end of the wire should be inserted into the terminal and crimped back on itself once so that the connection will not have to depend upon solder alone for mechanical strength.

Soldering should be done with a properly tinned gun or iron so that solder will flow quickly into the connection. Since the parts are small, there is a danger of overheating the components if the connection is heated excessively. When the parts to be soldered are clean, the solder will flow quite rapidly into the connection (usually a second or two). I have found that best results are obtained

Below Left

The electronic components on most solid body instruments, such as on this EB-3, are easily accessible. (Gibson Repair Dept.)

Below Right

After the components are mounted in place, soldering of the various leads and terminals is done through the access cover in the back. (Gibson Repair Dept.)

when the solder is fed directly to the soldering gun tip while the tip is being held against the work. There is no need to heat the work before the solder is applied. With shielded wire, it is common practice to ground the outside shield to the metal case of the potentiometer. Excess heat will melt the plastic insulation used in some types of shielded wire so care should be taken. In every case it is good practice to run a ground wire between all controls which do not have a grounded shield wire running between them.

To reduce excess hum and noise from body contact, the strings must be grounded to the ground side of the pickups. In all cases, this is taken care of by running a wire from the bridge or tailpiece to a suitable ground point in the pickup control harness. Be sure to leave plenty of slack so that the controls and pickups may be removed and replaced easily.

Components

Pickups

The two main considerations in repairing and replacing pickups are: 1) electrical characteristics and 2) physical size and mounting provisions. In most cases, the repair of a pickup, when one is found to be defective, is impractical and replacement is the best solution. Rewinding of a pickup coil is a tedious task at best and should be undertaken only when a suitable replacement is unavailable or where modification of the tonal characteristics is desired.

With regard to replacement, physical dimensions and mounting considerations will dictate, to a large extent, the choice of pickup. With an exact replacement, the main precaution is to be sure that proper polarity is observed when soldering leads (outside shield or ground lead to ground and hot or positive lead to hot side of volume control).

When a pickup is to be replaced with a better quality unit, you should measure carefully to determine whether or not the proposed pickup will fit in the existing space. With both solid body and hollow body guitars, the mounting space below the pickup is usually adequate. On many guitars, however, the spacing between the strings and the top of the guitar may not be suitable for the dimensions of the pickup. Insufficient clearance is the most serious problem, and if the pickup has either limited or no height adjustment, installation will usually require extensive modification of the instrument.

Volume and Tone Controls

Controls invariably consist of potentiometers with a value of 250,000 or 500,000 ohms. Shaft style must be chosen to fit the knob and in some cases the threaded mount must be checked to see that it is long enough to allow fastening to the top—the thickness of the tops of electric guitars is fairly substantial.

The taper indicates the rate at which the resistance changes as the shaft is rotated. The audio taper changes resistance at a faster rate at the extreme counterclockwise (soft) end of rotation than it does at the extreme clockwise (loud) end. The linear taper changes resistance at the same rate throughout the range of rotation. A third type is the reverse audio taper which changes resistance quickly at the clockwise end of rotation and slowly at the counterclockwise end.

Most controls for guitars have an audio taper and it is best in most cases to stick to the same style. A change in taper, however, could make the controls more suited to the individual player's particular requirements. If, for example, the control is customarily used over the full range of its travel, the linear taper will give a smoother change without abruptness at the full counterclockwise end of rotation. Players who usually leave the controls near the counterclockwise end may desire a more gradual change at that position; the reverse audio taper would be the most satisfactory in this situation.

Capacitors

Capacitors are used in the tone control circuits in conjunction with a 500,000 ohm potentiometer. The capacitor, the effect of which is varied by the tone control, serves to shunt (or short) to ground some of the alternating current generated by the vibrating string/pickup. Since high frequencies are affected more than lows, the net effect is that the overtone or treble response is varied while the bass response remains relatively constant.

The value almost universally used is 0.02 microfarad. Larger values, up to 0.05 microfarads, are used on electric bass guitars. Since the voltage generated by the pickup is quite small, the voltage rating of the capacitor is not critical. Because the higher voltage units are physically stronger, a voltage rating of between 200 and 400 volts dc is recommended. It should be noted that, as progressively larger capacitance values are used, the effective tone range is extended to the lower frequencies. If carried to an extreme, all frequencies will be affected and the net effect is that the tone control will act like a volume control.

Switches

Rotary wafer, toggle, and slide switches are all used in electric guitars. When of good quality, all give satisfactory service. In the usual two-pickup system, the toggle switch is widely used. When three pickups are used, or a wider variety of tone and pickup positions is desired, multiple slide switches or rotary switches are often used.

In order to avoid noise (hum, miscellaneous pops) when changing tone and pickup positions, it is important that the circuit always remain closed. Therefore, when ordering switches, you should specify that they be of the shorting or make-before-break variety.

Circuits

Single Pickup System

The single-pickup circuit is straightforward and relatively trouble-free. Many of the lower-priced models of a particular line of guitars use this arrangement. Though limited in variety of tone positions, this is no handicap when the music doesn't require a wide tone range. For many jazz styles, the forward pickup position (the forward position, against the fingerboard, is the usual position for the single pickup) is used by itself, even when the guitar has multiple pickups. Some guitars mount the pickup midway between the fingerboard and the bridge; the sound, as may be expected, gains in brilliance and loses in mellowness.

Single Pickup System

This circuit is commonly used on many single-pickup guitars. The tone depends on the placement of the pickup as well as on the tone control. All connecting leads should be shielded. In some variations, the tone control is eliminated.

Double Pickup System

The double-pickup system is the most widely used setup. It offers a wide range of tone positions with a minimum of parts and is adaptable to most musical requirements.

The usual arrangement incorporates a toggle switch which selects forward pickup only, rear pickup only, or both pickups. Tone variation ranges from mellow (forward pickup only) to brilliant (rear pickup only). When both pickups are used, the effectiveness of each pickup can be varied, giving an infinite variety of tones between mellow and brilliant.

It should be noted that when both pickups are used together the pickup circuits are placed in parallel and a certain amount of interaction between controls is to be expected. Turning one volume control to full off position, for example, will silence both pickups.The volume controls, therefore, will control the overall volume as well as the ratio between pickups. Occasionally you will find that, when both volume controls are full on, the result will be a slight decrease in volume. This is not necessarily a sign of a defective system and is normally no problem since both controls are rarely placed on full volume.

Several variations of the double-pickup system are also used when economy or simplicity is

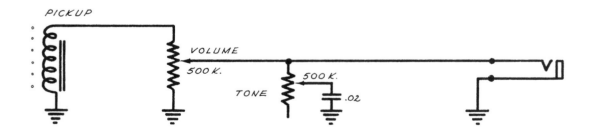

desired. One variation feeds both pickups into a common volume and tone control. Another variation retains individual volume controls but feeds the output into a common tone control. Because of limitations in tone and volume variations, these simplified circuits are presented for reference only.

Double Pickup System

Position 1 gives fingerboard pickup only and position 3 gives bridge pickup only. Position 2 ties in both pickups. In some systems, the tone control is tied in at the output side of the volume control, as in Variation I, rather than on the pickup side. The results are similar in either system. In position 2 the balance between pickups can be adjusted by varying the individual volume controls. Some guitars which use this popular system are: Gibson ES-175D, S400-CES, ES-335TDC. This system gives the maximum control over tone and volume on each pickup without going to more complex circuitry. On some systems, the tone control is connected as in Variation I.

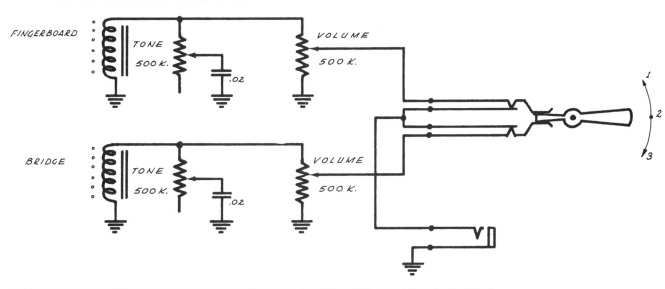

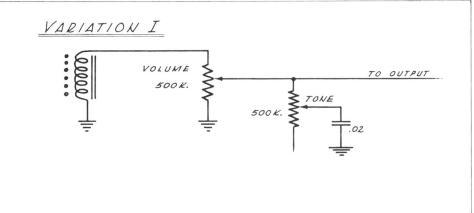

Two Volume Control, One Tone Control

In this variation on the double-pickup system, the single tone control is placed on the output side of the pickup switch and is always in the circuit regardless of the switch position. The Gibson flying V used this system.

Three-Pickup System
Gibson SG Custom

The combinations available with the SG Custom are: position 1, bridge pickup; position 2, fingerboard and middle pickup; position 3, fingerboard pickup. A tone control is functional in all switch positions and the outputs from both fingerboard and bridge pickups are fed through volume controls. The middle pickup, when in operation, is tied in with the fingerboard pickup. Since the fingerboard and bridge pickups are never switched together, there is no interaction between the two volume and tone controls. As with the Stratocaster, a wide variation in tone is possible, though the pickup combinations differ.

Fender Stratocaster

The pickups in the Stratocaster operate singly and never in pairs or in unison. Position 1 is for the bridge pickup. Position 2 is for the middle pickup and also switches in a tone control (2). Position 3 switches in the fingerboard pickup and tone control 3. The same volume control is used for all three pickups. Since the output of each pickup is kept separate and never mixed, the changes in tone are more abrupt when changing from one position to the next. Also, there is no tone control at all on position 1. The system is very compact and gives a wide variation in tone with a minimum of parts.

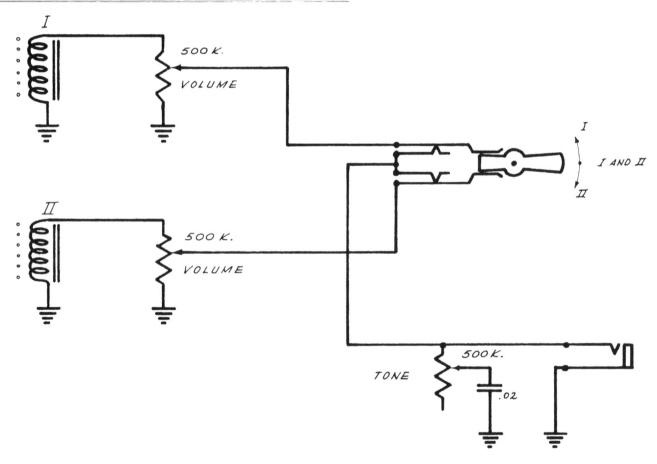

144

3-PICKUP SYSTEM
GIBSON S.G. CUSTOM

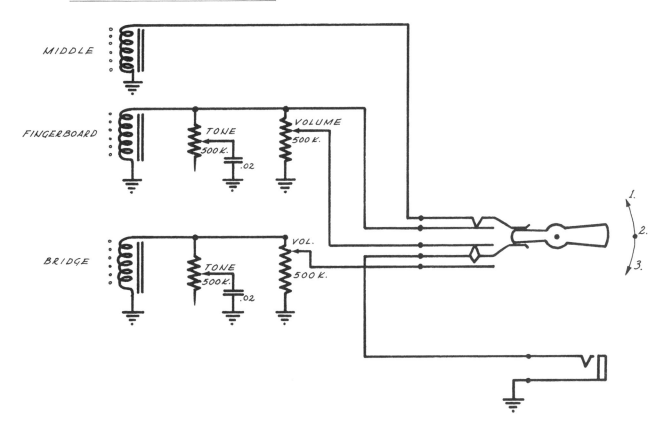

3-PICKUP SYSTEM
FENDER STRATOCASTER

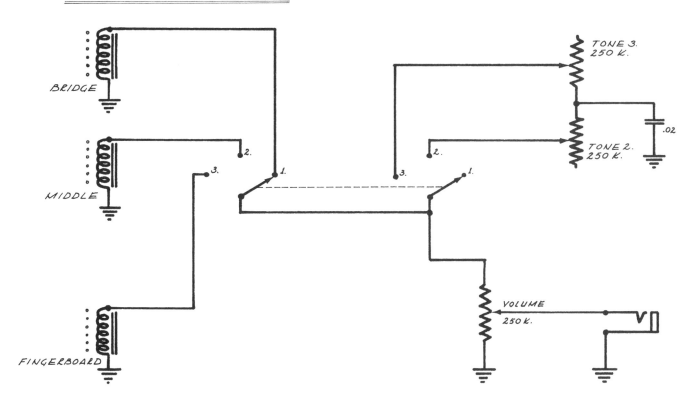

Master Volume Control

A master volume control is useful for setting the overall output of an electric guitar. Whenever the outputs of two or more pickups are mixed together, the volume controls must be juggled around to get both the proper tonal balance and the correct volume level. In addition, tone controls also affect the volume level. The master volume lets you adjust the overall volume independently of the tone and pickup combinations.

When adding this control to a guitar, the first step is to locate the hot lead to the output jack. In all monaural guitars, this is the lead that contacts the tip of the output plug. The master volume is inserted between this lead and the output jack.

Disconnect the lead at the jack and connect the lead to the right-hand terminal of the potentiometer (viewing the potentiometer from the back and with the terminals pointing up). The shield or ground lead is grounded to the case. The left-hand terminal is grounded to the case. The middle terminal is connected, through a shielded wire, to the original hot terminal of the output jack. The value of the control is not critical and any value from 500,000 ohm to 1 megohm audio or linear taper will work well.

Phase Reversal System
Fender Mustang

Additional tone coloring can be achieved by making use of phase reversal together with a double-pickup guitar. The Fender Mustang has a single set of volume and tone controls common to both pickups. Switches I and II offer pickup and tone combinations as follows:

Switch SW I	Position SW II	Output
1	off	P.U.I.
1	1	P.U.I and II
1	2	P.U.I., P.U.II reverse phase
2	off	P.U.I
2	1	P.U.I reverse phase, P.U.II
2	2	P.U.I and II
off	1	P.U.II
off	2	P.U.II
off	off	Standby

146

Basically, the combinations are: one pickup only (one switch off and the other in position 1 or 2); two pickups normal (switches I and II both in position 1 or both in position 2); two pickups with phase reversal (switch I in position 1 and switch II in position 2, or vice versa).

Phase reversal operates on the principle that both pickups in a two-pickup system must be in phase in order to produce maximum sound. If the pickups are 180 degrees out of phase, the positive cycle of one pickup will coincide with the negative cycle of the second pickup, giving reduced output. In actual practice, the tonal result is a thin, nasal sound with reduced bass response as well as a reduction in overall volume. Note that, though the Mustang has two phase reversal switches, only one is really needed. When switching, for example, switch I from position 2 to position 1, the pickup leads are reconnected with the leads reversed. The output phase of P.U.I is reversed with respect to the phase of P.U.II and the result is phase reversal. Reversing the phase of P.U.II with respect to the phase of P.U.I gives the same result.

Mixer Control, Phase Reversal
Gibson ES-340-TD

The ES-340-TD utilizes a mixer control to combine pickup output rather than a toggle switch and individual volume controls. The mixer control consists of two potentiometers concentric on the same shaft and wired so that when one potentiometer is at maximum the other is at minimum. When wired to their respective pickups, rotation to either extreme will give only P.U.I or P.U.II. Rotation to various intermediate positions will give infinitely variable combinations from both pickups; rotation to the midpoint will give equal output from both pickups.

Only one volume control is needed with this system (master volume) though there are individual tone controls—Tone I and II.

Parts A and B of the switch comprise a phase reversal switch for P.U.I. Position 1 is normal and position 2 is reversed phase. In position 3, the output lead to the master volume control is shorted to ground, silencing the system.

With this mixer control system it is possible to vary the amount of phase reversal effect in switch position 2 by varying the output from each pickup.

MASTER VOLUME CONTROL

I. OUTPUT BEFORE CONVERSION

II. OUTPUT WITH MASTER VOLUME CONTROL

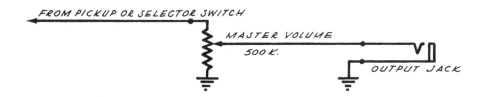

PHASE REVERSAL SYSTEM
FENDER MUSTANG

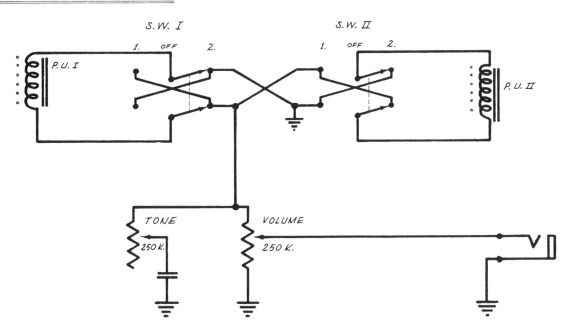

NOTE: S.W. I AND II ARE DPDT SLIDE SWITCHES
WITH CENTER OFF POSITION.

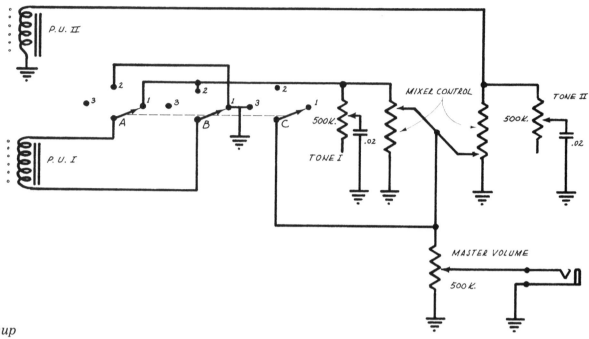

Bass Pickup
Fender Jazz Bass

The Fender Jazz Bass incorporates two pickups with individual volume controls working into a common tone control. Each pickup is wired to its volume control so that it can be turned up or down without affecting the other pickup. However, whenever the pickup volume is reduced, the effect is to gradually short the pickup to ground. Though theoretically the effect is to reduce the high frequency response, in the Fender Jazz Bass this effect is negligible and cannot be heard. There is no need for a pickup switch with this system, making it very compact.

FENDER JAZZ BASS

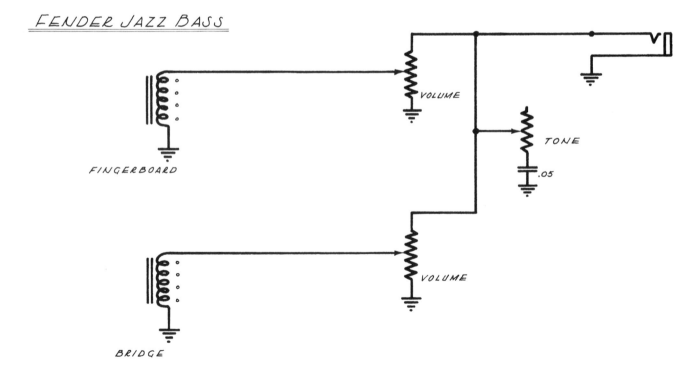

BASS PICKUP
GIBSON EB-3 (STEREO)

Gibson EB-3

The EB-3 pickup system uses two pickups together with additional tone control circuitry to increase the range of tone combinations. The pickups in the EB-3 are designed to give differing tone characteristics. The fingerboard pickup has an extended bass response while the bridge pickup emphasizes the treble range. Each pickup has an individual volume and tone control. The pickup selector switch, however, features four positions with functions as follows:

Position 1. Fingerboard pickup only.

Position 2. Bridge pickup only.

Position 3. Bridge pickup, fingerboard pickup. In this position, the fingerboard pickup operates through the additional components, a 0.02 microfarad capacitor and a small choke. The low end response is reduced and the net result is a thinner, more brilliant response.

Position 4. Fingerboard pickup only. Same configuration as in position 3.

With its additional circuit complexity, the EB-3 has a very wide tonal range. The configuration shown is for a stereo output; the bass is available in a monaural version as well.

Troubleshooting

Locating and repairing pickup system problems is best done by following a set procedure. Most problems may be diagnosed and repaired quite quickly since the symptoms will usually localize the source of trouble. In addition, you may expect certain components to give more trouble than others. With experience you will be able to predict trouble spots peculiar to individual makes and models.

Two troubleshooting checklists are shown. The first checklist details trouble areas based on the frequency in which they occur. The majority of problems fall within the first two categories. The second checklist pinpoints the source of troubles based on the symptoms given. When more than one component produces the same symptom, you will save time by consulting the first checklist to determine the most likely trouble area.

Checklist 1. Troubles Based on Frequency of Occurrence

1) *Output jack.* The most frequent single cause of problems is the output jack. If the retaining nut loosens, the resulting movement which can occur (through use or when carelessly tightening the nut) frequently breaks or shorts the wiring.

2) *Broken wiring or shorted wiring.* Broken or shorted wiring can occur in all parts of the pickup system. The usual problem points are the controls, switches, and output jack. The twisting motion produced by a loose control or switch will strain and break a wire in a very short time. It is also possible for a wire to short against an adjacent terminal or (less common) for a shielded wire to short internally.

A cold connection can produce symptoms similar to a broken wire. Where insufficient soldering heat was used, or where the connection was not clean when soldering, the resulting connection can open or develop a high resistance even though at a casual glance it appears to be good.

3) *Defective switches or potentiometers.* Mechanical failure—frequently through abuse— is the most frequent cause for failure of these parts. If these components are intermittent or noisy, contact and control cleaner can effect a cure. Unless the guitar is very old, or the component of low quality, it is unusual to have to replace a part because it is worn out. In this connection it should be noted that capacitors used with tone controls almost never fail electrically unless damaged by excess heat when soldering. Excess soldering heat can also damage potentiometers and switches; this is more of a problem with instruments which have been rewired using the original components.

4) *Pickups.* Pickups rarely develop problems unless subjected to excess heat when soldering leads or to physical abuse. An open winding is the usual problem, when troubles do occur, though intermittents occasionally occur also. One should be certain that the rest of the pickup system is not at fault before replacing the pickup since most pickups are quite expensive.

Checklist 2. Troubles Based on Systems

One component area—the wiring harness—can produce, depending on the defective section, every trouble symptom. You will do well to carefully inspect the wiring before going on to the components in the pickup system.

Most wiring problems are apparent from a visual inspection. Broken wiring, loose connections, shorts to adjacent terminals or wiring are all easily detected. Internal breaks (inside the shield), cold solder joints, intermittent connections may require testing with a continuity tester or with an ohm meter. The most important points to check are the various terminals on the controls, pickups, and switches for this is where most problems occur.

Open or shorted wiring in the hot side of the pickups will result in loss of sound, without background hum. An open ground or break in the shield will result in a loss of sound together with a loud background hum. If problems occur regardless of switch or control positions then attention should be directed to the wiring that is common to all the pickups. If the problem is in only one pickup position (and the other positions are all right) then attention should be focused on the wiring between the switch and the inoperative pickup section.

1) Loud hum—no sound
  A)   All positions
      a) Output jack
      b) Pickup switches
  B)   One Position
      a) Pickup switches
      b) Pickup
2) No sound, no hum
  A)   All positions
      a) Output jack
      b) Pickup switch
  B)   One position
      a) Pickup switch
      b) Pickup
      c) Volume control, tone control
3) Weak sound
  A)   All positions
      a) Pickup
      b) Pickup height adjustment
      c) Strings
      d) Poor connection in output jack

d) Poor connection in output jack
B)   One position
a) Pickup height adjustment
b) Pickup
c) Volume control, tone control
4) Tone control
A)   No change
a) Tone control potentiometer
b) Capacitor open
B)   Tone too mellow or too bright
a) Capacitor incorrect value
C)   Tone control acts like volume control
a) Capacitor incorrect value
b) Capacitor shorted
5) Intermittent operation
A)   All components can cause intermittent operation; check for continuity and short circuits in wiring.
6) Distortion
A)   Pickup
B)   Pickup height (too close to strings)
C)   Strings

Humbucking Pickup

The Gibson humbucking pickup is very popular for use in conversion of older Gibsons as well as other guitars. Apart from the tone quality which makes it popular with the guitarist, the pickup has a number of features which makes it adaptable to a wide variety of guitars—both hollow body and solid body. The instructions for mounting given here, although primarily intended for use in converting existing guitars with other pickups, can also be used when installing the pickups in new guitars. Some of the basic points of mounting the humbucking pickup can generally be applied to other pickup conversions; this section will be very useful to the repairman working with electric guitars.

The basic humbucking pickup is a high impedance unit with two coils inside a shielded housing. The adjustable pole piece screws protrude from the center of one coil and the entire pickup height is adjustable by means of a screw at each end of the case. The two adjusting screws go through a pickup mounting ring (which is itself available in different heights) allowing the pickup to "float" in suspension. Four small wood screws are used to mount the pickup ring to the top of the guitar. Since the pickup case is grounded to the shield of the shielded wire leading from the coils, all grounding is done automatically, and in addition there is no problem of mixing up polarity —something that could happen with, say, a Fender pickup.

Laying out the position of the pickup and routing out the opening for it is the first step in the installation. If you do more than an occasional conversion, you will want to make a template to speed up the layout process. With hollow body guitars, there is no problem of how deep to cut since you will only have to cut through the thickness of the top. There are two considerations, though, that might require some additional work.

If the guitar is an acoustical plectrum style of instrument, then there is the possibility that the two bass bars which run longitudinally across the top may be cut. If the bars are cut, be sure to reinforce the cut areas because the top, with the bars cut, is very weak and is easily collapsed. Most problems with bass bars occur on the front pickup next to the fingerboard.

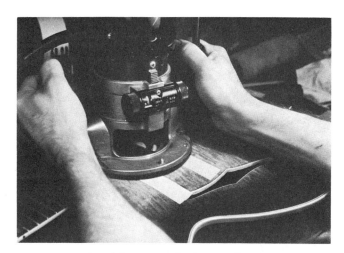

Cutting a top for pickups is easily done with a router. Where the same style of pickup is frequently used (the Gibson humbucking pickup is very popular) a template can be used.

If the hole for the old pickup will not be covered by the pickup ring of the new pickup you will have to inlay, and possibly touch up, the exposed area. The older style Gibson "Dog-Ear" pickup is just barely covered by the humbucking. The two mounting holes for the old pickup have to be plugged and touched up, though, complicating the job somewhat.

On solid body guitars, there is the question of how deep to rout as well as where to mount the pickup. In all cases, you should rout only deep enough to clear the pickup and to allow for the necessary range of adjustment. Note that the pickup height adjusting screws and the accompanying brackets extend below the pickup body. The body of the guitar will have to be cut deeper at these two points than for the main part of the pickup.

On many solid body guitars, the pickguard extends across the middle area of the top with the pickups mounted to the pickguard. On these guitars the pickup ring can be dispensed with entirely. You will have to be more exact in cutting the pickguard to fit the pickup, but the height adjusting screws will then mount directly into the pickguard. The front pickup on a Fender Telecaster can be done by this method, for example.

Keep in mind that the pole piece screws on the front pickup must be closest to the end of the fingerboard. The pole piece screws on the rear pickup are closest to the bridge. Also, the pickup rings, when used, are tapered (front to back) allowing you to position the pickups parallel to the strings.

Wiring is pretty straightforward, with the shield going to ground and the hot wire going to the volume control or switch, depending on wiring layout. The standard potentiometer value for all humbucking pickups is 500,000 ohms. Though most Fenders use a potentiometer value of 250,000 ohms, the humbucking pickups will work on Fender guitars very well with no control change.

Some rock and roll players, in order to get the last bit of volume from the pickup (increasing feedback), remove the pickup cover. This is done by unsoldering the two connections on the base of the pickup. The best way to do this is to heat the joint with a soldering gun and, when the solder is molten, slip a thin palate knife through the solder and between the cover and the base. Repeat with the other side and pull the cover off carefully. You don't get something for nothing, though, and the price you pay is an increase in noise and increased vulnerability to accidental damage. Only the conventional (large) humbucking pickups can have the covers removed. The small humbucking pickups, as used on the Johnny Smith and the current Les Paul Deluxe, rely on the covers to hold the coils in place.

Below Left

With most humbucking pickup conversions, the original pickup openings will require conversion to the shape shown in the photo.

Below Right

On this Gibson the rear pickup is being converted to the newer humbucking pickup. The plastic ring (to the right of the hole) is used in this example to match the appearance of the old front pickup which is being retained.

In concluding this manual, the following chapter, "How To Buy a Guitar," by Stu Goldberg, is informative for both dealer and customer alike. In selecting a guitar, you should be aware of those points which are *undesirable* as well as those which are *desirable.* Important points to consider, if the guitar of your choice does not play to your satisfaction, are whether it can be adjusted or easily repaired, or whether the problems are because of faulty or defective construction.

Obviously the customer and player should know enough about guitars to select one intelligently. It is just as important for the dealer to know his guitars in order to give the best possible service to his customers. And if a guitar is going to be rejected for defects or faulty workmanship, it might just as well be in the dealer's storeroom rather than after it has been sold.

Stu Goldberg, who has a guitar shop in San Francisco, is an importer of fine guitars as well, and writes with an authority based on many years experience. As an importer of many of the finest guitars from around the world, Stu has had personal contact with many of the finest guitar makers and factories both here and abroad. With his experience, Stu is eminently qualified to advise you on selecting a guitar—both from the standpoint of a dealer and from the standpoint of a guitar player.

Below Left

A Fender Telecaster conversion with two Gibson humbucking pickups and a Gibson Tune-O-Matic bridge. The new pickguard allows mounting of the pickups directly in the pickguard rather than in the customary mounting ring.

Below Right

A Fender Jazz Bass with a Gibson humbucking pickup (nearest the fingerboard) added to the original pickups. The extra volume control has been mounted in the pickguard directly to the right of the middle pickup.

Stu and Mike with their H.K. Special guitars. Stu Goldberg (right) and Mike King (left) playing guitars made for them by the author. Goldberg's guitar was constructed in 1967 and King's in 1969. Both guitars are steel string flattops with Brazilian rosewood back and sides, German spruce stops, Honduras mahogany necks, and bridge and fingerboard of ebony. Scale lengths 25-1/2 inches.

How To Buy a Guitar

By Stu Goldberg

There are so many types and sizes, makes and models of guitars, that my first word of advice is to visit every shop you can to try out instruments regardless of price or brand name. You should ask yourself: Where will I buy my guitar and why there? Is the selection of makes and models large enough for me to find something I'll like? What will I get for my money? Is a cheaper price all I want or am I offered services and any kind of guarantee at the time of purchase and even later on? What kind of reputation does the store have? Are the owners knowledgeable about their products or don't they seem to know them very well? How much time will they spend with me in comparing instruments and helping me get the most for my money?

Generally speaking, the customer has to put his complete faith and trust in the hands of the seller. Should any problems arise, it puts one at ease to know that his instrument is highly thought of by the person who sold it, who believes in it, and who has a vested interest in making it right. The seller should know his products—why they are good or in what ways they are weak, how they compare with other makes and models—and be able to constructively help in the selection of an instrument.

Note the differences in sound (volume, balance, tone), the quality of workmanship, the size, and the style of instrument. You will soon learn to discriminate and settle on a particular model or two. If you can't afford your first choice, find one in your price range which closely approximates it and will make you happy as an intermediate guitar.

Get some kind of commitment from the dealer. Ask him how much he will allow you in trade for this instrument when you return for the desired (first choice) guitar in six months or a year. Ask him to check out the guitar and make any necessary adjustments before you take it with you. Any buzzing or rattling of strings should be cleaned up and the action adjusted to your playing needs. The fact that these adjustments are usually necessary at the time of purchase is reason enough to be selective in choosing your instrument dealer.

Basically, that is—as they say—"where it's at." For it is the dealer alone to whom you can return if you have any problems or complaints.

And now, to the particulars—the scam what am! If you wish to become more personally involved, here is a list of points to carefully study and consider.

1) *Neck.* Almost the most important feature of a guitar, it should be: *a*) well-shaped and thin enough to get your hand around, not a "club"; *b*) reasonably straight; *c*) properly set into the body, not too steep or too far back.

To check points *b* and *c*, hold the guitar face up and body away from you and sight from the peghead down the upper edge of the fingerboard to see if it makes a reasonably straight line. Think of this upper fingerboard edge as a line extending from its end where the fingerboard sits on the box to where it would strike the bridge. This imaginary fingerboard edge extension should meet the bridge approximately an eighth of an inch above the guitar face. If this minimum criterion is met, it is assured that any action adjustment desired can be readily made.

Note: The questions of relief (what some people call a warp) and neck angle (steep or far back) require extensive explanation as there are differing schools of thought evidenced by the many models on the market.

2) *Fingerboard and Frets.* A classical or flamenco guitar should have a flat fingerboard and a steel string instrument should have a crowned or curved fingerboard. Frets should be cleanly set into the fingerboard, their upper edges crowned and smoothly finished. Fret ends should be tapered and should not protrude from the fingerboard edge.

3) *String Action at the Nut.* Press the string down against the fingerboard between the second and third frets and check the string clearance at the first fret. In this test the string should just barely clear the first fret for the optimum fingerstyle string action. Any greater distance will make for a more difficult fingering in the first position. If the action is high here, the nut should be adjusted.

4) *Action.* This is an extremely personal value which is as easily changed or "set up" as the length of one's trousers (assuming, of course, that the guitar is properly constructed). What

is proper playing action for the fingerpicker would only bring about much rattling and buzzing for the country-style flatpicker who "digs in." The main factors for consideration are the playing styles you use most (with or without any kind of picks), and the type and strength of the strings you prefer (light, medium, etc.). If you play hard, you will need to have a medium or high action in order to get a clean sound. As a finger-style player I personally prefer a "critical" action, where the strings are set up almost as close as possible to the fingerboard, allowing maximum playing ease, but buzzing and rattling if your touch is too heavy. The most important point to remember is the first line of this paragraph.

5) *Intonation.* No guitar will play in tune unless the strings have the proper amount of compensation. The scale length and proper fret intervals are determined by formula, and even the cheapest factory guitars generally have accurate fingerboards. In practice, however, the actual string length of the instrument is always slightly greater than the mathematical scale length; it is this small extra length (that must be added to the scale length) that is generally referred to as compensation. Check for correct compensation by comparing the harmonic produced at the twelfth fret with the note produced at the twelfth fret. If the fretted note is higher or lower than the harmonic, the string in question needs more, or less, compensation. Again, a problem of adjustment to be handled by the dealer.

6) *Bridge and Saddle.* The bridge height (or thickness, should allow for adjustments. It must not be so high that in order to lower the saddle (for string action) the wood itself has to be cut down and reshaped. It must not be so low that, when slightly raising the saddle, an excessive portion of the saddle would be sticking up. An overly tall saddle: *a*) requires that the bridge be thicker than usual; *b*) demands a deeper "bite" in the saddle slot; *c*) puts a greater strain on the bridge and face of the instrument; *d*) is generally a sign of an expedient (cheap) and incorrect adjustment for a badly set-in or reverse-bowed neck.

The strings should cross the saddle and "break" at an angle to go down into the string or pin holes. If they merely run straight

across the saddle or almost so, it is again a sign of other problems. The end result here is much rattling and buzzing. Further, I prefer a simple plastic, bone, or ivory saddle, and suggest against any screw-adjustable types.

7) *Neck Rod.* Steel string instruments usually have installed in the neck either a fixed or an adjustable rod. I wouldn't buy one without a rod. If yours has an adjustable type, ask the dealer to pull the plate and be sure it is under proper tension. The rods are sometimes left loose at the factory, especially in cheaper instruments.

8) *Bracing, Inlays, Finish.* Most classical guitars are fan-braced and most steel string guitars are X-braced under the soundhole except for really low-priced dime store brands. These sometimes have a tunnel bracing (two bars running under the face from the shoulders to the lower bouts, one on each side of the soundhole). Bracing of this type usually does not properly support the face, nor does it allow the face to move as it should.

Few instruments show high quality inlay work. This requires painstaking skill and patience, and more often than not you will find that shortcuts have been taken—like cutting out a large area, dropping in the fancy inlay, and seating it in with epoxy filler. Easy to see if you look carefully.

Most factory instruments are too heavily lacquer finished. This inhibits good tone quality but does protect the instrument from more abusive treatment.

9) *Types of Wood.* Many brands offer a terrific instrument for the price, using all laminated construction. But if you pay over $150, I believe that your guitar should have a solid wood top. The most costly instruments are generally made with rosewood or maple sides and back, spruce or cedar top, ebony bridge, and fingerboard, mahogany neck, 12 to 1 ratio heads. For less than $350 you will find either high quality laminated models (back and sides), or solid wood instruments of mahogany, walnut, and other less expensive woods.

10) *Sound*
(a) Volume and resonance. How loud is it when plucked or strummed? Do the strings ring out and sustain, or die quickly? Try single notes also, especially in the upper registers. Does it have

"presence"? Does the sound jump out at you, right now, or is it dull, restrained, or muted as though there should be more?

(b) Balance. Is sound evenly distributed, between bass and treble, or does one overshadow the other? Do you prefer a heavy bass, a stronger treble, or a more balanced instrument? You must decide which will best suit your playing style.

(c) Tone. Does the guitar have a clean, round sound? Is the treble bright, or merely harsh and strident? Does the bass come out full sounding and rich with a little snap to it, or is it muddy and undefined?

11) *Rattling, Buzzing.* Few instruments reach the dealer entirely free from small imperfections. Adjustments are often necessary to level frets, raise or lower actions, etc. Any reputable dealer will make or arrange for these corrections at time of purchase.

12) *Guarantee.* Instruments are usually "factory guaranteed" against defective materials or workmanship, but should return to the factory become necessary, the owner must pay the freight charges both ways, the cost of which is often prohibitive to the customer. And delays of up to six months are not uncommon, since factories are really not in the repair business. Also, the average adjustment is a minor one, so the dealer or a repair shop is the place to go. Find out in advance exactly where your dealer stands on this subject, and have him spell out his conditions to you. It was said before my time, "A thing that is bought or sold has no value unless it contains that which cannot be bought or sold. Look for the priceless ingredient. The priceless ingredient of every product in the marketplace is the honor and integrity of him who sells it. Consider his name before you buy."

Index